FROM TEXT TO TRADITION

A History of Second Temple and
Rabbinic Judaism

FROM TEXT TO TRADITION

A History of Second Temple and Rabbinic Judaism

by
LAWRENCE H. SCHIFFMAN

Ktav Publishing House, Inc.
Hoboken, New Jersey
1991

Library of Congress Cataloging-in-Publication Data

Schiffman, Lawrence H.
   From text to tradition : a history of Second Temple and Rabbinic
Judaism / by Lawrence H. Schiffman
      p.   cm.
   Includes bibliographical references and index.
   ISBN 0-88125-371-5. — ISBN 0-88125-372-3
   1. Judaism—History—Post-exilic period, 586 B.C.-A.D.
2. Judaism—History—Talmudic period, 10-425..   I. Title.
BM176.S35   1991
296'.09'014—dc20   91-709
                                          CIP

Manufactured in the United States of America

In Memory of my Father
Robert D. Schiffman

לזכר נשמת אבי מורי
ר׳ ראובן דוד בן ר׳ הרשל
תנצב״ה

Contents

Contents

List of Illustrations

List of Maps and Charts

Preface

The present volume owes its genesis to my good friend and publisher, Mr. Bernard Scharfstein, who saw the need for a one-volume study of the history of Second Temple and Rabbinic Judaism. His suggestion was extremely attractive to me because it presented the opportunity to draw together the results of some eighteen years of work on this subject, represented in my publications as well as in the classes and seminars I have taught my students at New York University.

In many ways this volume is a tribute to the atmosphere of learning and inquiry in Judaica in which I have worked over the years at New York University. For this I thank my colleagues and students in the Skirball Department of Hebrew and Judaic Studies, the Department of Near Eastern Languages and Literatures, and the Hagop Kevorkian Center for Near Eastern Studies. I must single out Professors Baruch A. Levine and Francis E. Peters, whose influence on my thinking on the issues dealt with in this book has been immeasurable.

Six readers have undertaken to critique this volume, and their helpful suggestions are greatly appreciated. Professors Daniel Schwartz of the Hebrew University and Daniel J. Lasker of Ben-Gurion University of the Negev have shared with me many hours of discussion of issues related to this volume. Professors Stuart S. Miller of the University of Connecticut, Michael D. Swartz of the University of Virginia, and Yaakov Elman of Yeshiva University are colleagues whose doctoral research I had the privilege to direct. Their work is a source of great pride to me, and I continue to learn much from them. Dr. Richard White of Ktav Publishing House contributed many illuminating comments. Dr. Philip E. Miller, Librarian of the Klau Library of the Hebrew Union College–Jewish Institute of Religion in New York, has been most gracious in his assistance. My wife, Marlene R. Schiffman, undertook to read the entire manuscript and to prepare the index, and her suggestions are evident on virtually every page. The title was suggested by Rabbi Geoffrey Goldberg of the Klau Library. Steven Fine and Hanan Eshel, both of the Hebrew University, were of great help to me in planning and gathering the illustrations. Sari Slater proofread the manuscript.

I have dedicated this volume to the memory of my father, Robert D. Schiffman, of blessed memory. His support and encouragement of my work and his sacrifices to make it possible for me to devote even more time to my research were unending. In many ways this book was written for him, for he always wanted me to write a book which was aimed at a wider circle of readers. Indeed, the book chronicles the tradition into which he was born and which shaped the lives of our entire family. יהא זכרו ברוך , May his memory be for a blessing!

FROM TEXT TO TRADITION

A History of Second Temple and
Rabbinic Judaism

1
Introduction

This book provides an outline of the history of Judaism during the all-important era of its postbiblical development, from the last years of the biblical period until the arrival of the consensus we know as Talmudic Judaism. By Judaism, we mean the collective religious, cultural, and legal tradition and civilization of the Jewish people as developed and passed down from biblical times until today. Judaism is not a monolithic phenomenon. Rather, it encompasses many different historical moments as well as many different approaches to the questions of God, man, and the world. All these "Judaisms" are tied together by the common thread of the continuity of tradition, and by the collective historical destiny of the Jewish People.

SIGNIFICANCE OF THE PERIOD

We shall concentrate here on an extremely significant stage in the development and history of Judaism, the period in which there took place the transition from the Judaism of the Hebrew Bible to what is known as Talmudic or Rabbinic Judaism. This in turn became the standard, called "normative" Judaism by a previous generation of scholars, for the medieval and modern developments that ensued. It represented a sustained and organized development and interpretation of the biblical traditions with which it began, and claimed a line of continuity from that tradition. This transition took place, primarily, during what are known in Jewish history as the Persian, Hellenistic, and Roman periods.

At the same time, another group, originally part of the Jewish people, laid claim to the Hebrew Scriptures. It was maintained by the early Christians that their interpretation was the authentic one, and that other Jews had diverged from the correct path. Both religions, then, claimed to be the legitimate successors to the Hebrew Bible. By the close of Late Antiquity, the classical Judaism of the rabbis and the Christianity of the church fathers had emerged as the primary "Western" religions.

For Judaism, we shall seek to trace the path by which this occurred. We will want to know by what complex events and developments the Judaism of the Bible became that of the Talmud. At the same time, we will want to understand how this Judaism, whether in Second Temple times or even later, serves as a backdrop and a background for an understanding of the rise of Christianity and the early church. Indeed, the relationship between Judaism and early Christianity lies behind and shapes much of the tragic history of the interplay of these two communities.

METHOD

The approach followed in this study is a historical one. We seek to trace the history of Judaism, the culture, religion, and civilization of the Jews. At the outset, this approach must be distinguished from what is usually termed "Jewish history." The latter is an attempt to deal with the social, political, and economic factors in which the Jews as a people play the primary role. In contrast, we do not seek to tell the story of people, but rather to tell the story of ideas. The ideas we speak of are those which make up the Jewish tradition and heritage. These ideas have gone through a definite historical process, and it is the purpose of this book to describe that process in detail. Jewish history, as we have defined it, will serve as a background against which to trace the history of ideas, a framework into which to place our data. The sections of this book dealing with the historical background, therefore, do not present a complete history of the Jews in Late Antiquity. They are intended only as a framework for our study of the development of the religious ideas of Judaism.

We shall have to be extremely mindful of the influence of political, social, and economic factors on the development of religious ideas. Nevertheless, we will not be able to deal in detail with much of the important history of the Jews in this period. We shall try, instead, to see how the basic ideas, beliefs, and practices of Judaism developed against this backdrop.

This study is based on the assumption that there is a history to these aspects of the Jewish tradition. It is axiomatic to our study that the historical development of the various beliefs and practices among the different groups and ideologies within Judaism can be observed, examined, and traced through the periods we are discussing. Behind the continuity so often asserted by the tradition there is a complex development that we seek to uncover. The existence of such a history should in no way be taken as a challenge to the affirmations of continuity made by the Jewish tradition. On the contrary, continuity can only be achieved in a tradition which adapts and develops. In the case of Judaism, stagnation would have led to an early epitaph.

Some remarks must be made about the periodization which serves as the basis for this volume. Modern historical scholarship has studied ancient Judaism as if a radical break occurred with the destruction of the Second Temple in 70 C.E. In Christian circles, this break was seen originally as the result of the Jews' rejection of Jesus, which itself was evidence that Judaism (as distinct from biblical "Israel") had gone astray from the correct path and, therefore, was an aberration. This same break has been posited more recently by both Jewish and Christian scholars, but it is now understood as having resulted from shifts in modes of piety and religious thought attendant on the destruction of the Temple.

The present study, however, sees the various transitions as having been much more gradual and complex. For this reason, its chronological limits are designed to monitor these complex and profound changes as they evolved in the Persian and Greco-Roman periods, eras also known in terms of the history of Judaism as the Second Temple and Rabbinic periods. Because we recognize the underlying continuity we see no reason to avoid the occasional use of the term "Judaism" to describe the religion of the Hebrew Bible, the earliest stage in the history of Judaism.

The method followed in this book will show that assumptions of a radical discontinuity between the various manifestations of Judaism in the Second Temple period and Rabbinic Judaism are highly overstated. In fact, Rabbinic Judaism represented the fruition of ideas already part of the earlier approaches, and provided an eventual rallying point around which a consensus emerged. Far from being something radically new and different, the Judaism of the rabbis of the Mishnah and Talmuds was deeply rooted in that of their predecessors.

ONE JUDAISM OR MANY?

Fundamental to any study of the history of Judaism in Late Antiquity is the question of how to understand the diversity of approaches and manifestations that existed at this time. The history of Judaism illustrates in detail both development over time, the historical factor, and variation even at the same time among different groups of Jews, each propounding its own answers to fundamental questions about God, man, and the world.

Two views of the subject immediately present themselves. The first sees each approach to Judaism as independent and self-contained, systematically presenting a fully developed set of answers to the questions at hand. This view effectively isolates each "Judaism" from the others, not only from those that existed at the same time, but also from those that came before and after. Alternatively, one can see the various approaches to Judaism as standing in a dynamic and interactive relationship to one another. In this case, each approach must be studied along-side those in the same period with which it competed, and also in relation to those which preceded and followed it. In this second method, one observes the constantly reciprocal influences between approaches, but also recognizes what each period and approach bequeathed to that which came after.

It is the second method that underlies this book. Accordingly, "Judaism" is understood here as a wide designation taking in a variety of ideologies and approaches that coexist with and influence one another. Rather than subdividing and compart-mentalizing the phenomenon we call Judaism, we prefer to understand the complex historical processes which led the whole, composite and dynamic as it was, to develop in the directions that it did.

The difficulty of finding adequate terminology for the various approaches to Judaism prevalent in Second Temple times has had some effect on our presentation. In religious studies, it is usual to distinguish a "sect" from the dominant or mainstream "church." Yet in the study of Judaism in the Second Temple period, the term "sect" is customarily used to describe all approaches to Judaism without implying that any of them was dominant. It is in this usage that "sect" appears in this work. Only after Judaism converged around the "mainstream" of tannaitic Judaism, a process which took centuries, can the term "sect" be used to describe those who diverged from its dominant or authoritative form.

SOURCES

The sources for the study of Judaism in the periods under scrutiny here are many and varied. Moreover, the sources present a variety of difficulties which must be considered when they are employed for historical research. The first problem is that in any study of Judaism in Late Antiquity, the sources themselves are a subject of the study. The history of Judaism is often revealed by the methods of composition and transmission of its texts and the attitude toward the texts of the emerging tradition. For example, the use of oral as opposed to written transmission, the attribution of specific statements to particular authorities, and other such techniques are indicative of the conceptual and theological universe of the authors or compilers. Therefore, the very sources which we use as evidence for our study are representative of specific stages in the history of Judaism. Thus, before any source can be used, it must be approached critically, and the extent of its reliability must be carefully evaluated.

Furthermore, many sources cannot be dated precisely. In some instances, it cannot be determined from which of the various groups of Jews in this period the text emerged. When the exact provenance of a source is not known, as is often the case, we cannot determine the extent to which the author's prejudices or beliefs may be represented in his work.

The final difficulty is that relating the history of Judaism was not the original purpose of any of the sources. The texts describe the beliefs and practices of insiders who adhered to one or another variety of Judaism and often polemicized against their opponents. As scholars and students, we must distill from these variegated sources material which answers our questions, and our questions are radically different from those which the authors of these texts asked and sought to answer.

The Hebrew Bible

If we want to know how the talmudic tradition in Judaism developed, we will have to be familiar with at least the fundamentals of biblical religion, culture, and civilization. This must be the starting point of our study just as it was the starting point of Judaism. Some of the later biblical compositions, the books of the prophets Haggai, Zechariah, and Malachi, and of Esther, Ezra and Nehemiah, deal explicitly with the Persian period, the first phase of the era to which this study is dedicated. The book of Daniel has been dated by modern scholars to Hellenistic times, although it is set in the last years of the Babylonian period and the opening years of the Persian. Moreover, the way in which the Bible was handed down and preserved provides us with important historical evidence, for one of the most important ways of distinguishing and characterizing approaches to Judaism is through their different attitudes to the Bible and its traditions.

Apocrypha and Pseudepigrapha

The Hellenistic and Roman periods saw the composition of a vast literature by Jews in and outside of Palestine. Many of these texts were eventually gathered into the apocrypha. This term denotes certain works similar to biblical writings in style and tone that were included in the corpus of biblical books of the Alexandrian Jews, the collection known as the Septuagint.

Other texts from the same period that are also similar to biblical writings but were not included in the Septuagint are usually termed pseudepigrapha. Strictly speaking, this term characterizes texts attributed to biblical figures, but it has become a general designation for this literature as a whole. Many of these books were preserved only by various Eastern Christian denominations.

Some of the apocrypha and pseudepigrapha were originally composed in Hebrew, some in Aramaic, and some in Greek. A number of them survive only in translations into Greek, Latin, Ethiopic, Slavonic, and other languages. Some are also preserved among the Dead Sea Scrolls.

Several of these apocryphal and pseudepigraphical texts are usually designated as apocalyptic literature. This is an elusive term and its usage varies; it is used here as a collective designation for texts which narrate how a supernatural figure reveals to a human being hidden truths about the secrets of the universe. These secrets usually include predictions of the eschatological (i.e., messianic) future. Such texts are found in the Bible and the Dead Sea Scrolls as well as in the apocrypha and pseudepigrapha.

The books of the apocrypha and pseudepigrapha provide evidence about the Judaism of the Hellenistic and Roman periods, especially about the many sectarian groups competing for the allegiance of the Jewish people during this time. They are primary sources for a period which, until the discovery of the Dead Sea Scrolls, was otherwise almost completely shrouded in mystery. By using these sources, we can begin to explain the background for the development of Rabbinic Judaism. They also contribute to our understanding of the environment in which early Christianity developed.

The Dead Sea Scrolls

Beginning in 1947 there came to light a hoard of manuscripts from caves along the shore of the Dead Sea. The bulk of these, from the caves of Qumran, are the documents of a group of Jews which inhabited the area from around 134 B.C.E. to 68 C.E. This group is usually termed the Dead Sea or Qumran sect and is often identified with the Essenes (discussed in chap. 6), although scholars are increasingly questioning this theory. Among the extensive collection of writings preserved at Qumran are numerous biblical manuscripts, greatly illuminating the history of the biblical text at this period, and various apocryphal and pseudepigraphal writings, some of which are the originals of texts otherwise preserved only in translation. Most importantly, the scrolls include the sect's own codes of law and conduct, messianic literature, and biblical commentaries. This literature gives us a window into the beliefs and practices of one of the many sects that dotted the landscape of Palestinian spiritual life at this time.

Recent research has begun to demonstrate the importance of the scrolls not only for the study of the Dead Sea sect, but also for an understanding of contemporaneous groups. As the remaining Dead Sea texts are published, we can expect to see the scrolls playing a greater and greater part in the reconstruction of the Judaism of Second Temple times.

Also found in the Dead Sea region were the scrolls from Masada, illuminating the biblical texts and other literature of the Jews who occupied this fortress in the last years of the Great Revolt (66–73 C.E.). A series of important documents and letters from the days of the Bar Kokhba Revolt (132–135 C.E.) has also been discovered. These include legal documents which provide historical data on the interrelationship of Jews, Nabatean Arabs, and Greeks in the Dead Sea region, as well as letters from Bar Kokhba to his commanders concerning military and governmental matters.

Philo and Josephus

The most substantial works produced by Greek-speaking Jewry are those of Philo Judaeus (ca. 20 B.C.E.–ca. 50 C.E.) and Josephus Flavius (ca. 38–ca. 100 C.E.). As a native of Alexandria in Egypt, Philo may be seen as representative of Diaspora Jewry, while Josephus may be taken as representing the Palestinian social and religious climate. Philo was fundamentally a philosopher, attempting to provide a synthesis of the Greek and the Judaic, of Platonism and Torah. Josephus was a historian seeking to explain to the Roman world why the Jews and the Romans had been unable to get along and how the Great Revolt of 66–73 C.E. had ensued. He relates the history of the Jews from earliest antiquity up to the end of the revolt. His *Antiquities* and *War* are the basic sources for most of Jewish history in

Hellenistic and Roman times, and our debt to him cannot be overstated.

However, both Philo and Josephus were personally involved in the historical events which they recount and must therefore be read with a critical eye. In both cases, too, their apologetic tendencies must not be forgotten, for both were interpreters of and apologists for Judaism to the Greco-Roman world.

Greek and Roman Sources

Numerous Greek and Latin sources, authored by non-Jews both in Palestine and elsewhere, provide interesting insights into the attitudes toward Jews of the gentiles who came in contact with them. Many of the most important authors of Classical Antiquity—Tacitus, Pliny, Juvenal, and Polybius, to name but a few—make reference to Jews or Judaism. Some of these accounts provide accurate historical information. Others, even if they do not accurately portray the Jewish communities and Jewish practices of the time, offer testimony as to how the Jews were perceived by their non-Jewish neighbors. Some material, in addition, illuminates governmental attitudes toward the Jews and their legal status in the Roman Empire. This enables us to understand the ways in which Gentile-Jewish relations in the Greco-Roman period prepared the way for subsequent anti-Semitism.

The New Testament

While the New Testament is primarily of historical value as a source for the history of earliest Christianity, much can also be gleaned from this collection of documents for the history of Judaism. The various allusions to the practices of the different Jewish groups, read with proper attention to the concerns of the authors, help to put what we know from other sources into proper perspective. Further, an understanding of the development of the religious ideas which led to the rise of Christianity sheds light on the Jewish background of this new faith. Nascent Christianity must be located within the matrix of the sectarian and apocalyptic groups which flourished in the preceding two centuries.

The New Testament materials do, however, present specific

critical problems. First, it is difficult to date the various books with precision. Second, the original language of parts of the corpus is not certain, so that theological and religious terminology cannot always be accurately understood. Taken together with the issue of the authors' concerns, these problems require that early Christian texts, like other religious texts, be used for historical research with caution.

Rabbinic Literature

The vast body of rabbinic literature, composed of the Mishnah, the Tosefta, the Palestinian and Babylonian Talmuds, and the Midrashim, is a virtual gold mine for the history of Judaism. At the same time, the manner in which these materials have been arranged and transmitted renders their use and analysis a complex and painstaking task. They contain numerous sayings, disputes, exegeses, and stories. While many of these are attributed to specific sages, much of the material is unattributed. Even for the attributed materials, questions about the dating of traditions make it difficult to draw historical conclusions.

The Mishnah is the basic document of Rabbinic Judaism. Compiled around 200 C.E., it is fundamentally a curriculum for the study of Jewish law, arranged topically. It contains material attributed to figures as early as the third century B.C.E. The vast bulk of the material is attributed to tannaim, sages from the latter years of the first century B.C.E. through the end of the second century C.E. The Tosefta was the earliest commentary on the Mishnah, and its compilation is therefore to be dated somewhat later. Yet many of the sayings preserved in the Tosefta are attributed to the same tannaim cited in the Mishnah. Again, the problem of dating is extremely important.

The two Talmuds are commentaries on the Mishnah by the amoraim, sages of the third to the sixth century. The Talmuds (Gemaras) are based on comparisons of the Mishnah with other tannaitic material (some of which overlaps that in the Tosefta) and include detailed discussions of the biblical sources of the various prescriptions. In addition, they include details on various Jewish laws and practices as understood by the amoraim in both Palestine and Babylonia. There are also numerous stories and legends, as well as accounts of historical events, theological discussions, and information on science, medicine, and a host of other topics. Before these materials can be used for historical research, they must be subjected to painstaking examination. First, the correct readings must be established, based on the manuscript tradition and citations in medieval sources. Second, the dating of the various collections and the material embedded in them must be established to the extent possible.

The midrashim constitute sustained interpretations of Scripture arranged according to the biblical sequence. The tannaitic midrashim preserve materials that emerged out of the discussions in the tannaitic academies but were redacted (collected and edited) in the amoraic period. The later amoraic expository midrashim have as their setting the synagogues of northern Palestine. The editing of some of these texts extended until the early Middle Ages. As with the Talmuds, these collections can be used for historical purposes only after the closest analysis of attributions and careful dating of materials, as well as detailed study of manuscript evidence and exegetical traditions.

Archaeological Evidence

The introduction of archaeological data into the study of the history of Judaism has been most obvious in the area of biblical studies, since archaeologists have concentrated on this period, but numerous finds from the Persian, Hellenistic, and Roman periods allow us to trace the interaction of cultures among the Jews in Palestine and to a lesser extent in the Diaspora. The interpretation of many obscure talmudic passages will undoubtedly become possible if and when future archaeological work uncovers the great centers in Palestine and Mesopotamia where tannaitic and amoraic Judaism, respectively, flourished and came to fruition. The rise of the Hellenistic movement in Palestine and the Diaspora has certainly come alive as a result of excavations throughout the Mediterranean basin. Specific finds have clarified problems of chronology and have aided in the reconstruction of political and economic history. The excavation of synagogues in the Galilee and the Golan has provided an entire chapter of Jewish history in the talmudic period.

DOMINANT TRENDS AND ISSUES

An inquiry into the history of Judaism in any particular age cannot consist merely of a recitation of facts regarding the period under discussion. Rather, it is essential to approach our topic with a specific thesis. Accordingly, this volume will demonstrate that certain dominant trends and issues shape and explain the development of postbiblical Judaism. Further, we will see that these factors, together with the received tradition of the Hebrew Scriptures, provide the fundamental unity which binds together the various approaches to Judaism that flourished in the period under study. Since we will observe these trends time and again throughout our study, we will briefly outline them here so that it will be possible to draw attention to them in the chapters that follow.

Role of Interpretation

Interpretation—more technically, exegesis—constitutes one of the basic patterns of development in the history of Judaism. The Bible itself shows evidence of internal interpretation, what scholars now call inner-biblical exegesis. For example, Deuteronomy may be seen, to a great extent, as a recapitulation and interpretation of the books which precede it. Other biblical books also often interpret earlier ones. Ezra and Nehemiah reveal pronounced tendencies toward exegesis of the type later called midrash.

In postbiblical times, issues pertaining to exegesis were what separated the various approaches to Judaism that we term sects for want of a better word. Not only did they differ on the specific interpretation of biblical passages, but they also disagreed on the methodology used for explaining Scripture and the theological and religious presumptions that lay beneath their interpretations. Trying to determine the exact meaning of the biblical text was a major activity among the sectaries of the Dead Sea Scrolls; and many of the apocryphal and pseudepigraphal texts, in attempting to "rewrite" the Bible, presented interpretations of it. Ultimately, the schism between Judaism and Christianity was expressed in terms of exegetical issues pertaining to the Hebrew Scriptures.

Rabbinic Judaism saw itself as based on an interpretative tradition which it called the oral law. According to the rabbis, the oral law accompanied the written Torah revealed by God to Moses at Sinai; it constituted a God-given interpretation of the written Torah. This notion is often referred to as the dual Torah concept. Yet for the rabbis the mechanism of interpretation was equally important regarding their own materials. The tannaim interpreted the words of earlier teachers, and the amoraim in the Talmuds (Gemaras) carried on a sustained effort to comment on the words of their predecessors in the Mishnah and other tannaitic collections. While it is beyond the chronological limits of this volume, we should note that much of the work of medieval Jewish scholars was devoted to the interpretation of talmudic literature, for in a very real sense, when the Babylonian Talmud achieved undisputed hegemony in the early Middle Ages, the rabbinic corpus joined the Bible as the canonized scripture of Judaism.

These interpretative approaches served a definite purpose for Judaism by making possible the historical development of the various manifestations of the Jewish tradition. It was through interpretation of the old that new ideas and approaches were created in each generation. Some of these interpretations were ultimately rejected by the historical processes that led to the eventual emergence of Rabbinic Judaism. Others left an indelible imprint. Without interpretation, and other techniques to be discussed here, the tradition would have stagnated at one stage or another. That which ultimately became timeless would have withered on the vine.

Internal and External Stimuli

Throughout its history, the development of Judaism has been the result of the subtle interplay of stimuli from within and from without. Together, the two have created a dynamic that has enabled change within the context of continuity. The external forces are the easiest to delineate. The Jews constantly found themselves at the mercy of the prevailing political powers. With political domination inevitably came cultural interaction, which often led the Jews to imbibe aspects of the dominant culture. As we will see, this was certainly the case with the Hellenizing movement. Even groups like the Pharisees which did not seek to adopt Greek cultural patterns were not left untouched by Hellenistic influences.

External economic and social factors also often brought about developments in Jewish law and practice and even theology. An example would be the destruction of the Temple in 70 C.E., which led to a complete readjustment in ritual and leadership patterns. More urgently, the destruction necessitated a theological response. While this may have been somewhat late in coming, it meant, when it did come, an extensive review of the questions of God's relationship to Israel and the place of national suffering in the theology of redemption.

More difficult to define are the internal stimuli, the inner dynamics that led Judaism to develop in certain ways. The need to interpret a body of sacred scriptures, discussed already, was one of these stimuli. Intimately connected was the tendency, especially evident in rabbinic circles, to study through questioning and discussion. The very nature of Judaism as a civilization, religion, culture, and nation led to the rise of new ideas and approaches. Judaism's intellectual emphases provided an avenue for its continued development through study and transmission of earlier traditions. Throughout Jewish history we hear the voices of those who credited divine inspiration, albeit indirect and refracted, with the march of Judaism from Sinai to its later forms.

Progressive Selection

The power of hindsight enables us to read the early history of Judaism as a series of choices made by a theoretical consensus influenced by the internal and external stimuli outlined above. As we will see in subsequent chapters, biblical Judaism, which itself comprised several trends and approaches, adjusted in this manner to the new circumstances of Hellenistic life and culture. This adjustment, however, left open a wide variety of options, represented by the sectarian tendencies of the Second Temple period and by the variety of Judaism developed in the Hellenistic Diaspora. From among these different possibilities, tannaitic Judaism, which saw itself as a continuation of the traditions of the Pharisees, eventually proved best able to preserve the Jewish people, together with their culture and civilization, in the face of the many vicissitudes confronting them. Thus the Judaism that emerged at the end of the talmudic era had been chosen by a kind of natural selection process in the spheres of history and religion.

Modernization and Synthesis

From its beginnings Jewish history has experienced a recurring pattern of meeting, or perhaps "confronting," some new, "modern" culture and coming to terms with it. This process has so far repeated itself four times. The first was when the Israelites invaded the promised land and came into contact with the superior culture of the Canaanites. The second took place in Late Antiquity when Judaism came into contact with Hellenistic culture. The third took place during the Middle Ages, when a major part of world Jewry found itself under Islamic domination. The most recent occurred in Europe in the eras of the Renaissance and the Enlightenment.

For the purposes of the present study, the second instance of this pattern—Judaism's meeting with Hellenism—is extremely important. Like the confrontations in biblical, medieval, and modern times, it was one in which Jews found themselves living in a radically changed world and formulated responses to it that were, in effect, a synthesis of Judaism with the dominant culture. Recognizing the significance of this pattern in Jewish history will help us to have a better understanding of the Jewish experience in the Hellenistic Diaspora and in conflict with Hellenizing forces in the Palestinian homeland.

SUMMARY

The rise of the rabbinic form of Judaism, with its detailed emphasis on Jewish law and ritual on the one hand, and its ability to adapt and develop on the other, was no accident. Judaism needed just such a combination of qualities to provide both constancy and responsiveness. The concept of the dual Torah, written and oral, gave Rabbinic Judaism that flexibility, defining the interpretations of the later rabbis as having Mosaic authority and standing in a continuous chain of tradition. At the same time, strict adherence to the principles of Jewish law meant that Talmudic Judaism could stand firm against the challenges posed by Christianity and then by Islam. For the rabbis of the Talmud, "Hear, O Israel, the Lord our God, the Lord is One" (Deut. 6:4) meant that no prophetic figure could rise above the status of mortal man. "And thou shalt love the Lord thy God with all thy heart, with all thy soul, and with all thy might" (Deut. 6:5) meant that life was to be lived according to the law of the Torah.

2

The Biblical Heritage

Judaism is fundamentally a revealed religion. It is based on the belief that God revealed Himself to the Jewish people through the agency of Moses. For this reason, its development, both in the biblical period and beyond, can be understood only in terms of a reshaping and reinterpretation of the biblical heritage. The traditions of the biblical world were axiomatic for later Judaism. Meaning and message were debated, but not authority. Biblical authority meant different things to the different groups of Jews in the Second Temple and rabbinic periods, but it was in the area of interpretation that they differed—all agreed on the basic principle that the biblical tradition was binding.

For this reason, we will begin with a historical sketch of the biblical period up to the rise of the Persian Empire, emphasizing those aspects of the biblical heritage that had the most profound cultural and religious influence on the subsequent history of Judaism.

HISTORICAL SKETCH

The history of Judaism began in the early second millennium B.C.E. in Mesopotamia, where, as a result of the destruction of the city Ur of the Chaldees and other external circumstances, a population movement was taking place. Among those migrating northward to Assyria was a family destined to come to the realization that there was but one God. This family, according to the biblical account, was led in successive generations by Abraham, Isaac, Jacob, and their wives. They later migrated to

17

Ancient Near East

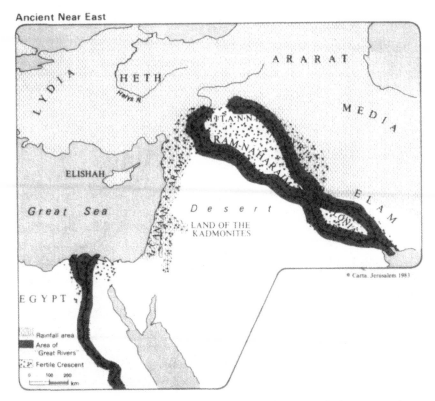

the land then called Canaan and there developed the monotheistic idea.

Some scholars have argued that the religion of the patriarchs was simply a form of monolatry, a religion in which only one God is worshipped although the existence of others is accepted, but the biblical evidence strongly supports the view that they were authentic monotheists. On the other hand, the later development of the biblical sacrificial system makes it evident that the early Israelites also believed in demonic powers, and God's divine retinue of angelic beings, as described in some of the psalms, is similar in some ways to the pantheons of polytheistic Mesopotamia and Ugarit (a town, on the site now known as Ras Shamra, in ancient Syria).

Sometime in the fourteenth century B.C.E., numerous West Semites, including some members of the patriarchal family, migrated to Egypt. The historical memory of the experience of slavery and redemption there was to set a definitive cast on the Jewish people and their religious faith. Leaving Egypt in approximately 1250 B.C.E. amidst cataclysmic events (the exodus), the children of Israel experienced, at Sinai, a religious and national awakening at which, according to biblical tradition, God revealed Himself to them. Under their leader and teacher Moses, they accepted the Torah as the law of God. It would be the guidepost for all subsequent Jewish history.

The historicity of the exodus has been denied by some modern scholars, who claim that the entire story was a later invention to provide a common history where none really existed, a history that was supposedly needed because the biblical Israelites were an amalgamation of diverse clans and peoples whose experiences and backgrounds were quite different. This, however, is a great oversimplification. While it is certainly true, as the biblical account testifies, that various groups joined themselves to the Israelites during the exodus and the period of wandering in the desert, as well as during the conquest of Canaan, it is also clear that the children of Israel, by this time, had a strong sense of peoplehood and had attained a high level of group identity and cohesiveness.

By the early twelfth century B.C.E. Israel had entered the land of Canaan, slowly conquering it and beginning to forge a new society. In the ideal, this society was to be based upon the traditions which the Israelites believed they had received at Sinai. In fact, the ideal was far from the reality. Canaanite influence was everywhere in evidence, and it was many years before the Israelites were able to purge their society of it.

The political and military challenge posed by the neighbors of the Israelites led to the setting up of a monarchy. During the period of the Judges (ca. 1200–ca. 1020 B.C.E.), the process of conquering and displacing the pre-Israelite natives, and of absorbing many of them, continued. Military threats were met by the rise of charismatic military figures (Hebrew *shofeṭim*, "judges,") who delivered the people from the enemy. Often, tribes would band together informally either to dislodge the previous inhabitants or to meet a challenge to their own occupation of the land. Yet no real central organization of the tribes of Israel existed. As the threat posed by the Philistines in-

THE BIBLICAL PERIOD
(all dates are B.C.E.)

early second millennium	Patriarchal period
14th cent.	Migration to Egypt
ca. 1280	Exodus from Egypt
ca. 1250–ca. 1200	Conquest of Canaan
ca. 1200–ca. 1020	Period of the judges
ca. 1020–ca. 1000	Saul
ca. 1000–961	David
961–922	Solomon
922	Division of monarchy
8th cent.	Amos and Hosea
740–700	Isaiah
727–698	Hezekiah
722	Destruction of Northern Kingdom
639–609	Josiah
627–ca. 585	Jeremiah
597	First Deportation from Judah
593–571	Ezekiel
586	Destruction of Kingdom of Judah and First Temple, mass deportations

creased, popular pressure for a centralized government eventually led to the rise of the monarchy.

The head of the new government was King Saul (ca. 1020–ca. 1000), in many ways one of the last of the judges, yet also the first of the kings. Like a judge, he had no organized bureaucracy, yet he had the legal and administrative powers of a monarch. King David (reigned ca. 1000–961 B.C.E.), coming to power as an immensely popular figure, conquered vast areas and established an empire, and his son King Solomon (961–922 B.C.E.) built the Jerusalem Temple.

The kingdom of Solomon split after his death into two small states, Judah in the south and Israel in the north. The Northern Kingdom was much more open to pagan influences. Throughout the period of the divided monarchy (from 922 B.C.E. on), the prophets struggled to prevent the Israelites from participating

The Kingdom of David and Solomon
(10th cent. B.C.E.)

The Divided Monarchy
(9th-8th cent. B.C.E.)

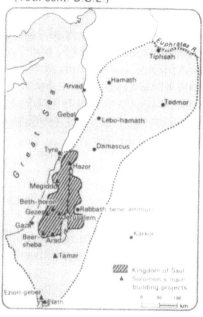

° Carta, Jerusalem 1983

in pagan worship. During this period two of the kings of Judah, Hezekiah (727–698 B.C.E.) and Josiah (639–609 B.C.E.), outlawed the various shrines throughout the country and centralized the sacrificial worship at the Holy Temple. In both Judah and Israel, syncretistic worship (the identification of the God of Israel and His worship with that of the pagan dieties) was widespread, even involving some of the kings, and the prophets castigated them for this transgression as well as for the many social ills that apparently plagued Israelite society in the period of the divided monarchy.

The fortunes of north and south were invariably linked in this period. Whenever the royal houses of the two kingdoms joined together to make common cause, their combined empire almost reached the extent of the earlier Solomonic empire. Whenever they bickered or fought with each other, they were reduced to the status of petty clients of Egypt or Mesopotamia. With time, however, both kingdoms were swallowed up by the surrounding empires. The north was destroyed by Assyria in 722 B.C.E., and the south, together with the Jerusalem Temple, by Babylonia in 586 B.C.E.

These developments were momentous for the history of Judaism. On the one hand, the Temple had to be replaced, even if temporarily. Although we have no evidence, some kind of non-Temple worship must have developed in the exile. Also, for the first time, there was now a sizable Jewish population outside of the Land of Israel. The Diaspora had been born, and Judaism had taken the first steps to becoming a world religion.

A HISTORIOGRAPHY OF CIVILIZATION

The foundation for the subsequent development of Judaism lies in the Torah, also referred to as the Five Books of Moses or the Pentateuch. The Torah is a combination of narrative and prescriptive legal material. Its early narratives in the Book of Genesis and the beginning of the Book of Exodus set out a variety of theological concepts and views of man's relationship to God and the world which serve as the basis of later Judaism. It tells the story of creation and the development of civilization, detailing the earliest stages of world history. It then focuses particularly on the fate of one nation, the Israelites, as they are enslaved in Egypt and then liberated to take possession of their own land.

The theory of creation presented in the Book of Genesis considers God the Creator of all, and later books of the Bible allude to and demythologize more mythical accounts which are today familiar to us from ancient Near Eastern sources. Genesis also relates the story of civilization, beginning with a description of developments that took place even before what anthropologists have termed the Neolithic revolution. This description emphasizes the evolution of civilization from the hunter-gatherer stage (the Garden of Eden) up to the rise of agriculture and herding, and the development of various arts and crafts. It then tells the flood story, emphasizing the dangers inherent in the decline of a society's moral standards. Here again the Torah demythologized a myth that was familiar in the ancient world, placing the emphasis on the morality of God and His concern for the morality of His creatures. Immediately thereafter, the

Torah sets out the table of nations, explaining how the peoples of the world descended from one another and how they were related. It then describes the dangers of urbanization by relating the story of the Tower of Babel.

Genesis also details the history of the patriarchal family. Much of this history concerns its place in the progressive religious selection which eventually led to Israel's role as recipient of the revelation of the Torah. Through the lives of Abraham, Isaac, Jacob, and their descendants, we follow the development of the monotheistic ideas of early Israelite religion. In each new generation, an unsuitable son—Ishmael, Esau—finds himself excluded from the line which eventually becomes Israel. Finally, with the sons of Jacob, the entire family is worthy of the mantle which the patriarch seeks to bestow.

The patriarchs worship God through private sacrifices carried out as part of momentous religious experiences during which they are said to commune directly with God. Here already is enshrined the covenant concept. God is portrayed as having entered into agreements with the forefathers to give Israel the land and make it a great and numerous people. Slavery and the exodus from Egypt are foretold to them, emphasizing early on that the history of Israel is to be seen as part of a divinely guided plan. The concept of God as a close family deity, worshipped within the familial context, is stressed over and over. All of these ideas became major pillars of subsequent Jewish tradition.

REVELATION AND LAW

Out of the experience at Sinai, and out of the Israelites' perception that they had been vouchsafed a revelation of God, emerged the Torah literature. The Torah is considered by Jewish tradition to be the result of direct divine revelation to Moses and, through him, to the Jewish people as a whole. Modern scholars have challenged this assertion, basing themselves on literary analyses of the Torah text. They have theorized that the Torah was redacted, or edited, from several documents, each the product of a different time and a different circle of authors. Until the modern era, however, such issues in no way affected the development of Judaism. For the talmudic rabbis and their medieval successors, as for contemporary Orthodox Judaism, the assumption of the sanctity and revealed character of the Torah was axiomatic. Since our purpose here is only to set the stage for a study of postbiblical Judaism, we need not go into the theories regarding the dating and authorship of the various parts of the Pentateuch. Our problem is rather to understand the nature of the text as it was written down and transmitted to later generations.

The Torah consists of a somewhat disparate group of materials, among which the legal, prescriptive codes play a prominent role. This is well illustrated by the Book of Exodus, which begins by relating the story of the slavery and redemption of Israel in its first part, but then takes up very different themes. First it presents a legal code, termed by scholars the Book of the Covenant, which concerns matters of civil and criminal law. This code shows many affinities with the laws of the ancient Near East and has often been compared to the Code of Hammurabi. Comparison shows repeatedly the tendency of biblical law to provide equality before the law to all citizens and to move away from excessive punishment, a pattern continued later in talmudic times. Immediately following this code is a festival calendar. Then come extensive prescriptive texts regarding the building of the Tabernacle, the portable tent sanctuary which would travel through the desert with the children of Israel. These are followed by a lengthy account of the building of the Tabernacle in accord with the instructions presented earlier.

Here we encounter the intricate biblical sacrificial system, which involved a detailed set of rituals for daily and festive occasions, as well as rites of expiation for the collective people of Israel and for individual transgressors. Closely related to sacrifice is the complex system of ritual purity and impurity. Those who came into contact with the dead or with certain creatures, or experienced certain bodily fluxes, were required to undergo purification rituals in order to enter the Tabernacle (the central shrine). All this is codified in the Book of Leviticus. The codes are descriptive, providing the circumstances of the offering and then listing the procedures for the specific sacrifices, including such matters as the times or occasions they are

PRIESTLY BLESSING. The priestly blessing (Numbers 6:22–27) played a major role in Jewish worship in the Temple and synagogue. Its text, inscribed in the ancient Hebrew script, was found on an amulet from the 7th–6th century B.C.E. at Ketef Hinnom in Jerusalem. This inscription is the earliest attestation of a text from the Torah. Some scholars have argued that this amulet proves that the blessing preexisted the book of Numbers. In our view, the use of this passage as an amulet indicates that it was already known in its present context. *Courtesy of the Israel Antiquities Authority.*

to be offered, the requisite animals, and associated offerings of grain, oil, and wine. In the case of the purity regulations, specific periods of impurity, rites of immersion or ablutions, and purificatory sacrifices are specified. Special emphasis is given to ethical and moral behavior as regards one's fellow man and to the laws of prohibited consanguineous marriages and the requirement of marital fidelity.

The Book of Numbers contains a detailed code of sacrifices for special occasions, presenting the appropriate daily and festival sacrifices. It is Numbers, not Leviticus, which spells these out in systematic detail. In addition, it describes the organization of the people and their camp in the desert period, as well as the religious and military challenges Israel faced during its wanderings.

The Book of Deuteronomy is essentially a self-contained code, recapitulating many laws already treated elsewhere in the Torah. In certain respects it is similar in form to the typical ancient Near Eastern treaty text. The narrative material at the beginning and end of the book parallels the prologue and epilogue in which the vassal signing a treaty with a ruler binds himself to observe its provisions. In between these two sections comes the body of the treaty; similarly, the code of Deuteronomy, between the book's introduction and conclusion, specifies the laws that Israel is bound to observe, dealing with such subjects as war, captives, purity, permitted and forbidden foods, festivals, marriage, divorce, rape, and various civil and criminal matters.

The organization of these codes within the Torah calls for some comment. Each code, in its present form, appears to be an independent composition with its own literary conventions and form. Further, the codes often overlap in content, and are written as if the other legal collections did not exist. No cross-references are made, at least not explicitly. This was one of the reasons why some scholars, beginning as early as the eighteenth century, theorized that the Torah had been put together by combining originally independent codes with various narrative traditions. This view of the Torah's composition, known as the documentary hypothesis, sees the pentateuchal narratives, the Book of the Covenant (the legal code at the end of Exodus), the

Priestly Code (Leviticus and parts of Numbers), the Holiness Code (Leviticus 17–26), and the Deuternomic Code as all being discrete, independent compositions.

The talmudic rabbis observed the very same textual overlaps and contradictions, but because of their different understanding of the Torah's origin used these details as the basis for their exegesis of the legal portions of the Pentateuch, what the tannaim called *midrash halakhah.* Later Judaism regarded all the peculiarities of the biblical text as grist for the mill of interpretation. Similar patterns of exegesis are observable even in the writings of the sects of the Second Commonwealth. Judaism in ancient times regarded the Torah as having been produced by divine revelation. Every aspect of its text and its diction, therefore, taught some lesson of divine law. Seen in this way and in this spirit, the Torah was able to serve as the basis for the ever-expanding interpretative traditions that constituted the manifold approaches to Judaism studied in this volume.

SACRIFICE AND PRIESTHOOD

Central to the biblical tradition is the notion that God is to be worshipped through the sacrificial system. The Bible describes this system as having operated in the desert period, the age of the Judges, and the First Temple era. The biblical codes specify in great detail the manner in which sacrifices and offerings were to be carried out and the occasions when they were required. The Torah also spells out the detailed laws of levitical purity with respect to causes of defilement and rites of purification as well as disqualification of the impure from participation in sacrificial worship.

Sacrifices were of various kinds. The most important categories were those meant to expiate sins and those regarded as meals shared, as it were, with the deity. The expiation offerings were designed to function almost exclusively in cases where the law had been transgressed accidentally. For such violations expiation could be gained through sacrifice. It is as if the animal were seen as suffering the fate the transgressor would have deserved had the offense been committed deliberately. The other type of sacrifice, the shared meal, involves God and man in an intimate relationship, a level of meeting possible only in the holy precincts of the central shrine. Here the burning of certain portions of the sacrificial animal as an offering to God and the eating of other portions by the celebrants created a bond of familial love between God and man. In this way the Israelite was supposed to enter into a close relationship with his God.

The sacrifices were to be conducted by priests descended from the first priest, Aaron, brother of Moses. Seen as specially selected to facilitate the close relationship between man and God, the members of the priesthood were able to bridge the gulf separating mortal from Creator. They were bidden to live lives of purity and holiness, and this entailed, among other things, both stricter marital laws, enumerated in the Bible, and taking special care to avoid ritual defilement. To ensure that the priests would give their full attention to their responsibilities, and not be distracted by the need to earn a livelihood, the Torah required that certain gifts be given to them and their levite assistants.

The Temple remained the center of Jewish piety until its destruction for a second time in 70 C.E. During most of the Second Temple period Aaronide priests provided leadership for the Jews of Palestine. When all hopes for an early restoration of sacrifice after 70 C.E. were dashed, the sacrificial system served as a model for the transposition of Temple-centered piety to synagogue, home, and family. Nonetheless, Jews continued to yearn for a restored Temple.

PROPHECY

The authority of the traditions of the Bible in Judaism is founded upon the concept of prophecy. The Bible describes various people as having received direct revelations from God. The revelation to Moses is seen by later tradition as prophecy *par excellence.*

In the accounts of the patriarchs, we encounter God in relation to man, communicating directly with him. This is not prophecy in the strict sense, however, since the phenomenon of prophecy, in the biblical view, involves the prophet's having

HORNED ALTAR FROM MEGIDDO. This altar, dating to the 10th century B.C.E., comes from the city of Megiddo, a regional and administrative center in Northern Israel. It displays the "horns", i.e. corners, described in the Bible. Similar exemplars were found at local cult sites and temples located throughout the Land of Israel. It was against this often syncretistic worship which the prophets railed and the Bible's requirement of the centralization of sacrificial worship was directed. *Courtesy of Israel Antiquities Authority.*

been charged with a message to communicate. It is only with
Moses, in the Book of Exodus, that we encounter a prophet who
is sent to the people to deliver the word of God. In other words,
prophecy has a social dimension. It is not simply a personal
religious experience. God sends Moses to deliver His word to
the people. Yet Moses' prophecy differed from that of the other
prophets. First, he is described by the Bible as communicating
directly with God, whereas the other prophets see God in a
dream or trance. Second, he combines in his person the roles of
priest, king, and lawgiver (if we may adopt the Hellenistic
characterization) alongside that of prophet.

The Bible allows us to trace the history of prophecy in ancient
Israel. Not counting Moses, the earliest prophets described in
the Bible were seers, charismatic figures who prophesied in a
trance, usually induced by the use of music and dance. Often
they banded together in guilds and were called "the sons of the
prophets." The guilds were based on the master-disciple relationship and were intended to pass on a tradition of prophecy.
There is no definite evidence that prophets of this kind were in
any way involved in the moral and religious ferment of the
times. They may have been foretellers of the future.

By the time of the first monarchs, Saul, David, and Solomon,
the role of the prophet had begun to change. It seems to have
taken on some of the charismatic qualities associated with the
judges in the period immediately after the conquest, and simul-
taneously the kings inherited the political and military aspects
of the judge's role. In the early days of the monarchy, the
prophet appears as a religious model in the king's entourage,
deeply involved in the life of the royal court but able, at the
same time, to castigate the ruler by means of pointed parables.
Other prophets, of lesser importance, may have been attached
to the major cultic sites, according to some scholars. By the
time of Elijah and Elisha, prophets were found in both the
northern and southern kingdoms and were often in conflict with
the kings. They had clearly taken on their well-known role as
critics of the Israelite society of the day, but had not yet
developed into literary figures.

By the ninth century B.C.E., in both Judah and Israel, the
minor prophets (so-called because of the size of their literary

output) were delivering scathing attacks on the two major transgressions of the time, syncretistic worship and the social ills besetting the country. These two issues would occupy the prophets for years to come. They demanded the extirpation of even minimal participation in idolatrous worship, and called for the amelioration of the injustices being perpetrated against the poor, unlanded classes, insisting, loudly and clearly, that the discharge of cultic duties was of no significance if it was not accompanied by a life of true moral and ethical principles. The earliest of the twelve minor prophets, whose number included such men as Amos and Hosea (eighth century B.C.E.), were the first to leave us written documents of prophetic discourse. They delivered their words in public and apparently recorded them in writing either for their own use or to circulate them more widely.

As the end of the monarchy drew near, and a complex admixture of political and religious issues presented itself, new horizons loomed for the prophets. Isaiah (ca. 740–ca. 700 B.C.E.), Jeremiah (ca. 627–ca. 585), and Ezekiel (593–571) confronted the new political realities as well as the growing Mesopotamian influence on Israelite worship. The prophecies of these men are infused with the history of the time in which they lived, for all three of them were intimately involved in the affairs of the day and determined to bring to the people of Israel the messages they believed they had received directly from the God of Israel.

Isaiah, Jeremiah, and Ezekiel brought to culmination the literary development of prophecy. These three great prophets composed poetry and prose that rank among the most beautiful achievements of Hebrew literature. The profundity, beauty, and length of the prophecies attributed to them rendered these men major figures in the eyes of later tradition.

As Judaism developed, the books of the prophets shaped many other aspects of the tradition, most especially the concept of the messianic era, which was rooted in the world of the prophets. Later on, Jewish mysticism took its cue from the prophetic visions of Isaiah and Ezekiel. Prophetic morality and its intimate connections with the ritual life of Judaism also had an enduring effect.

WISDOM LITERATURE

The corpus of biblical literature includes a group of texts termed "wisdom literature." This genre was based on a common ancient Near Eastern tradition of secular wisdom that by and large was not connected with any specific religion, for wisdom teachings cut across linguistic and cultural differences and were extremely important in both Mesopotamia and Egypt.

Wisdom texts, of whatever provenance, generally provided advice on ethical issues and on how to conduct one's life and family relationships. The wisdom writings in the Bible include several of the psalms, the Book of Proverbs, Job, and Ecclesiastes. Job deals primarily with the problem of evil, and Ecclesiastes with the seeming futility of human activity. As compared to the other books of the Bible, the wisdom texts make little mention of Israel's theological principles and historical experiences. The issues they present and the advice they proffer might well be described as pan–Near Eastern secular wisdom with a Jewish perspective.

Wisdom was apparently taught in schools specializing in this discipline, and the Book of Proverbs regularly refers to the master-disciple relationship. The wisdom tradition continued in several books of the Second Temple period and had a profound influence on the later development of Judaism.

SUMMARY

The biblical heritage laid the groundwork for the many developments we will survey in the following chapters. The Israelite religious and cultural tradition in biblical times was rich, and provided a set of scriptures for interpretation. The various groups and approaches to Judaism that came afterwards differed fundamentally in their interpretations of the biblical material which they inherited. They agreed, however, on one thing, the sanctity and the authority of the biblical heritage. Biblical law and theology would shape Judaism indelibly in future centuries.

3
Judaism in the Persian Period

The later years of the biblical era are termed the Persian period because Palestine and the rest of the Near East were under the domination of the Persian Empire at this time. The Persian period was crucial for the development of postbiblical Judaism, for it served as a transitional era in which certain biblical approaches were giving way to the new approaches of the later age. Yet in many ways, this period represents a direct continuation of the biblical heritage and of First Temple religious ideas and concepts.

HISTORICAL AND ARCHAEOLOGICAL BACKGROUND

In the fall of 539 B.C.E., Cyrus (II) the Great, already king of Persia and Medea, vanquished the Babylonian army and gained control of the entire area of Mesopotamia. He immediately adopted a policy which was to be characteristic of his reign: he encouraged the repatriation of exiles and the rebuilding of shrines, motivated by a benevolence which seemed to sit well both with his temperament and with the need to govern a large and farflung empire.

In 538 B.C.E., Cyrus decreed that the Temple of the Jews in Jerusalem was to be rebuilt and that all the exiles who wished might return to Judea, the Persian province of Yahud. This decree inaugurated the period of the Second Temple, also known as the Second Commonwealth. The rise of Cyrus and the fall of Babylon were viewed by the Jews as God's work. While then, as today, settling in the Land of Israel was an option exercised

Exile and Return to Zion
(6th-5th cent. B.C.E.)

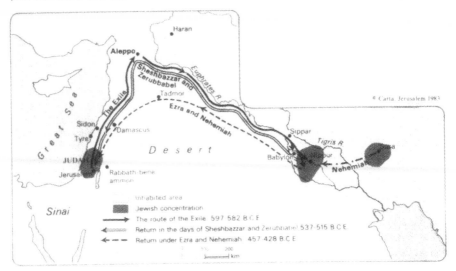

only by a devoted minority, the Jews of the Diaspora gave
financial and moral support to the newly reestablished community.

With the beginning of the Persian period, a new kind of
bureaucracy came into power. While at times the Judeans had
trouble with the government, Jews throughout the empire were
able to rise in the civil service and even formed military units
that were deployed on the frontiers of the Persian Empire.
Under Persian rule Jerusalem was rebuilt and its sacrificial ritual
reconstituted. In addition, and a most important development,
temporal (and not just religious) authority was granted to the
high priesthood.

Little is known about the period between the rebuilding of
Jerusalem under Ezra and Nehemiah in the sixth century B.C.E.
and the coming of Alexander the Great in the fourth, but the
incomplete biblical picture of this era is supplemented by archaeological evidence. Sites in northern Palestine, especially
along the coastal plain, show evidence of strong Phoenician
influence, especially evident in the building techniques. At the
same time, more southern sites show strong Aegean influence.
In fact, such influence was constantly on the increase in the
centuries leading up to the Persian period. Imported pottery

from the Hellenic world is found extensively. Most significant is the almost total dependence on Attic (Athenian) standards of coinage. Thus, it is evident that Hellenistic influence was already being felt throughout the country.

Other evidence indicates that Judea at the beginning of this era was an independent province. Samaria in the north remained a separate unit, however. A complex administrative bureaucracy collected and distributed taxes in kind. The discovery in Egypt of correspondence between the Jewish garrison of Elephantine (modern Assuan on the Nile) and the rulers of Jerusalem and Samaria has led to the realization that religious syncretism was still very much alive in this period. At the same time, many areas of Jewish law were moving toward standardization at this early date.

POLITICAL AFFAIRS

Shortly after 538 B.C.E. the Davidic scion Sheshbazzar set out from Babylon at the head of a group of returning Judeans and

THE PERSIAN PERIOD
(all dates are B.C.E.)

539	Cyrus conquers Babylonia
538	Edict of Cyrus
after 538	Sheshbazzar governor
between 538 and 522	Arrival of Zerubbabel
522–486	Darius I
ca. 520	Haggai and Zechariah
520–515	Second Temple built
465/4–424	Artaxerxes I
ca. 458	Arrival of Ezra
445–after 433	Nehemiah
423–404	Darius II
410	Temple at Elephantine destroyed
403–359	Artaxerxes II
402	Elephantine temple rebuilt
332	Alexander the Great conquers Near East

soon arrived in the Land of Israel. He apparently had the title *peḥah*, governor, as did his successor, Zerubbabel. Sheshbazzar must have immediately taken steps to begin rebuilding the Temple, but the Bible credits Zerubbabel with its completion (Ezra 3:6–11). With the rebuilding of the Temple came the restoration of the sacrificial ritual.

The early years of the Second Commonwealth were difficult ones. Judea was actually no more than a small area around Jerusalem, and by 522 B.C.E. its population must have numbered less than twenty thousand. The holy city itself was in ruins and scarcely inhabited. The Samaritans to the north, a mixed people made up of remnants of the populace of the destroyed northern kingdom of Israel and various groups brought in by the Assyrians, were openly hostile. Many Judeans were so preoccupied with eking out a living that they took little interest in the rebuilding of the Temple. The situation deteriorated to the point that work on the Temple had to cease temporarily.

At about this time, Zerubbabel, the nephew of Sheshbazzar, succeeded to the governorship. Zerubbabel was the son of Shealtiel son of Jehoiachin, a scion of the royal family of Judah. Sometime between 538 and 522 B.C.E. Zerubbabel had arrived in Jerusalem at the head of a group of returning exiles. The high priesthood was reconstituted under the Zadokite high priest Joshua ben Jehozadak. Nevertheless, eighteen years after the start of construction, the Temple had still not been completed.

The political circumstances leading to the ascension of Darius I (522–486 B.C.E.) to the throne of the Persian Empire aroused messianic expectations among the Jews of Judea, as shown in the books of Haggai and Zechariah, both composed around 520 B.C.E. These two prophets agitated for the completion of the Temple and the restoration of the pure worship of the God of Israel to the exclusion of all syncretistic practices. The leaders of Judea understood the importance of the Temple, and within four years it was finished. The work of building the Temple was apparently carried on despite efforts by the Samaritans to depict it as a messianic ploy aimed at reestablishing Judean independence under a Davidic king.

In March of 515 B.C.E. the Temple was completed amidst great rejoicing. Sacrifices and prayers for the king of Persia were offered. Judea now had its national and religious center. The future of the Jewish people in its ancestral land was assured for the foreseeable future. God could be properly worshipped in accord with the ancient traditions. There is some reason for thinking that the messianic agitation surrounding the person of Zerubbabel led the Persian authorities either to remove him from office or to not reappoint him when his term ended. In any case, from now until the time of Nehemiah (mid-5th century B.C.E.) the high priests ruled. Judea seems for a time to have been only a small theocratically ruled political unit within the larger province of Samaria.

This state of affairs lasted for about seventy years after the completion of the Second Temple. In the early years of this period, the Persian Empire attained its high point under Darius I. The little we know of the situation in Judea indicates that only limited progress was made toward repopulating it. Most of the empire's Jews remained in the Diaspora. The sparse evidence tells us that Jews were settled, for example, in Babylonia itself, in Sardis (in Asia Minor), and in Lower (northern) Egypt.

At the same time, Jews flourished in Elephantine in Upper (southern) Egypt throughout the fifth century B.C.E. There they were established in a military colony entrusted by the Persian Empire with the defense of its interests. Many Aramaic documents have survived from Elephantine, and these provide us with a window into the colony's culture and religion. The Elephantine Jews, in a temple of their own, practiced a syncretistic form of worship not unlike that of First Temple times, mixing pagan elements with the religion of the God of Israel.

By the mid-fifth century B.C.E., the population of Judea had probably doubled, and additional groups of exiles had returned. Some Jews now lived in more northerly parts of the country, in the territory of the erstwhile Kingdom of Israel. While the high priests controlled internal affairs, other matters rested in the hands of the governors of the province of Samaria who, according to the biblical account, were not above accusing the Jews of sedition when it was advantageous to them. Because of difficulties with their neighbors, the security of Judea deteriorated, and sometime during the reign of Artaxerxes I (465/64–424 B.C.E.) the rebuilding of the fortifications of Jerusalem was begun. The aristocracy of Samaria, with the help of an order from the king, was able to stop this project temporarily.

Monotheistic worship was certainly the norm in Judea. The books of Malachi and Nehemiah, however, speak of such problems as violations of sacrificial law, neglect of the Sabbath, and nonpayment of tithes. There was a breakdown of morality and a rise in divorce. Cheating of employees and preying on the weak became commonplace, and many of the poor were reduced to servitude. Intermarriage with the surrounding nations threatened the continuity of the Jewish community.

It was at this crucial juncture that the great reformers Ezra and Nehemiah made their appearance. Fortuitously, this was also a period of great instability in the Persian Empire. In an effort to shore up his lines of communication with Egypt, Artaxerxes wanted to regularize the situation in Palestine, and this provided Ezra and Nehemiah with the opportunity to make substantial progress.

The chronological relationship of the careers of these two great leaders poses serious difficulties. Nehemiah's career extended from 445 until sometime after 433 B.C.E. Ezra's dating is more difficult. The plain sense of the biblical text suggests that he arrived in Judea in 458 B.C.E. (thirteen years before Nehemiah) and completed his work shortly after Nehemiah's arrival. Some scholars take the view that he arrived long after Nehemiah's work had ended. A final approach, following the Greek text of the apocryphal 1 Esdras, suggests that Ezra arrived shortly before the end of Nehemiah's career in about 428 B.C.E.

According to the biblical account, which we see no compelling reason to set aside, Ezra left Babylon in 458 B.C.E. at the head of a considerable company of returnees. After a four-month journey, unaccompanied by a military escort, the caravan arrived in Jerusalem. Ezra came armed with a copy of the Torah and a document from the king authorizing him to enforce it. He was to teach the law and to set up the necessary administrative apparatus to see that it was followed. He had also obtained permission to collect contributions from the Jews of Babylonia to support the Temple in Jerusalem.

Ezra is described by the Bible as "a scribe of the law of the

God of Heaven." He was of priestly lineage and was probably appointed at the request of influential Jews at the Persian court. Those who see Ezra as coming after Nehemiah maintain that Nehemiah was responsible for his appointment. While it might seem unlikely that the monarchs of Persia would be concerned with the religious observances of the Jews of Judea, Ezra's mission can be understood from the standpoint of purely Persian interests. Under Persian rule, each subject people was allowed to live by its ancestral laws, which were enforced by the imperial government. Violations of the laws of the group to which one belonged constituted an offense against the state precisely because they led to instability. The maintenance of order in Judea, for example, would ensure the security of the land bridge to Egypt, and therefore the king required, in his own interest, that Jewish law be observed.

Immediately preceding the feast of Sukkot (Tabernacles) soon after his arrival, Ezra read the Torah publicly to the entire people. Indeed, this was a covenant-renewal ceremony in the strict sense. To make the Torah understandable to them, he had it explained. By this time, Aramaic, a West Semitic language, had become the spoken language of much of the Persian Empire and was the vernacular of most Jews. The biblical account relates that the people were greatly saddened when they learned that they had been lax in following the law, and it was only with difficulty that Ezra was able to restore the joy of the festival season. Throughout the festival the law was read on each day.

Nonetheless, Ezra continued to face violations of the Torah's regulations. Mixed marriages were a substantial problem. Their increase must have resulted from the small size of the Judean population and the attendant difficulty in finding spouses. Ezra led the people to enter into a covenant by which they voluntarily expelled the 113 foreign wives in the community. Already in this period the law that Jewish identity is determined through the mother was operative. The biblical narrative singles out the families in which the mother was not Jewish, for such unions led to the birth of non-Jewish children. Despite Ezra's considerable efforts, however, we can be sure that intermarriage continued, although on a much smaller scale.

The high point of Ezra's career was certainly the covenant renewal and reformation of Jewish life recorded at the end of the Book of Nehemiah (chaps. 9 and 10). The covenant he instituted bound the people to abstain from mixed marriages, refrain from work on the Sabbath, observe the laws of the sabbatical year, pay taxes for the communal maintenance of the Temple, and provide wood offerings for the sacrificial altar, first fruits, and tithes. A careful examination of the covenant, and of Ezra's decision to expel foreign wives, shows strong influence of the midrashic method of biblical interpretation, a matter to which we will return below. Those who date Ezra's arrival to the second term of Nehemiah see the covenant as the culmination of the joint efforts of the two men, but the biblical sources do not place them together.

Ezra now fades from the scene. He is often credited with having created postbiblical Judaism, a view somewhat overstated. What this leader, teacher, and scholar did was to establish the *basis* for the future of Judaism: from here on, the canonized Torah, the Five Books of Moses, would be the constitution of Jewish life. By pointing postbiblical Judaism on the road of scriptural interpretation, Ezra had ensured the continuity of the biblical heritage.

In December of 445 B.C.E. Nehemiah, the cupbearer to King Artaxerxes, was informed by his brother Hanani, who had just arrived from Jerusalem, of the difficult situation in Judea. Nehemiah approached the king and succeeded in getting permission to rebuild the walls of Jerusalem, obtaining the governorship of Judea and having it established as a province separate from Samaria. By 444 B.C.E. he had established his control over the newly created province. In a fifty-two-day stretch he managed to rebuild the city walls, although it is possible that this was a temporary fortification and that the permanent walls took another two years to complete.

Throughout the period of rebuilding, Sanballat, the governor of Samaria, aided by Tobiah, the ruler of Ammon, and Gashmu, an Arab chieftain, constantly opposed Nehemiah. Nonetheless, Nehemiah persevered. In order to create a commercial center for the country, he brought people from the hinterland into Jerusalem. With the walls up and the new population base established, Jerusalem's role as the center of Jewish life in Palestine was guaranteed.

In Nehemiah's time the population of Judea may be estimated at some fifty thousand souls, concentrated on the mountain ridge stretching from Beth Zur north to Bethel. The province had already been divided into districts when he came into office, probably remnants of the administrative system set up by the neo-Babylonian rulers after the conquest and destruction of Judah in 586 B.C.E. He allied himself with those who wanted to restore pure monotheism while his aristocratic opponents continued the old syncretistic tendencies against which the prophets had constantly railed.

After twelve years, Nehemiah's term as governor came to an end. Soon after returning to the Persian court, he was reappointed to the post. Nehemiah returned to Judea to find that conditions had worsened. The syncretistic party had scored substantial gains, and he had to expel Tobiah the Ammonite from an office in the Temple. Indeed, a descendant of the high priest Eliashiv had married the daughter of the Samaritan Sanballat. Nehemiah began a vigorous religious reform, fighting against the rising tide of intermarriage, and insisting that levitical tithes be paid and that wood for the altar be properly furnished. He strengthened and encouraged the strict observance of the Sabbath.

Those who take the view that Ezra came after Nehemiah see him as arriving at this time, perhaps having been brought by Nehemiah to help restore the proper observance of the Torah. We do not know exactly when Nehemiah's second term ended. It may have been with the death of Artaxerxes I in 424 B.C.E. He was definitely out of office by 408 B.C.E., when a Persian named Bagoas was governor of Judea according to the Elephantine documents.

The end of the fifth century and most of the fourth are represented by only scanty historical material. An Elephantine papyrus speaks of a Hananiah who governed Judea in 419 B.C.E. He may have been the same person as Hanani, the brother of Nehemiah, who had informed him about the difficulties confronting the Judean community. Josephus relates that the high priest at this time, one Yoḥanan, had a quarrel with his brother Joshua, who was plotting against him, and murdered him in the Temple. As a result, the shocked and dismayed Bagoas imposed severe restrictions on the Jews.

Considerably more information is available about the Jews of Elephantine during this period. We know that the syncretistic Jews of this colony attempted to celebrate Passover in accord with the law. In 410 B.C.E. the Jewish temple at Elephantine was destroyed in a riot incited by the priests of the local god Khnum with the help of the Persian commander. The Jews had trouble getting their temple rebuilt, perhaps because of the native Egyptian distaste for animal sacrifice. Attempts to enlist the help of Yoḥanan, the high priest mentioned in the preceding paragraph, failed because the laws in Deuteronomy make it clear that there was to be no sacrifice outside of God's chosen place, taken to be Jerusalem. In 408 B.C.E. the colonists of Elephantine wrote for help to Bagoas, the governor of Judea, and to Delaiah and Shelemiah, the sons of Sanballat, the governor of Samaria. Following the advice of Delaiah and Bagoas, they then petitioned the Persian satrap (provincial governor), who allowed them to rebuild the temple around 402 B.C.E. after they had voluntarily discontinued animal sacrifices and the attendant offerings.

The first two-thirds of the fourth century were a period of persistent decline in the Persian Empire at large. Of the Jewish communities, whether in Palestine or outside, virtually nothing is known. In all probability the building of the Samaritan temple on Mount Gerizim commenced in the last years of the Persian period. Silver coins of the Attic drachma type were minted by the semi-autonomous commonwealth of Judea (Yahud). Seal impressions on jar handles indicate that the vessels were used for the collection of taxes in kind. The inscriptions specify the name of the official to whom the tax was paid. Some evidence suggests that the high priest was the chief administrator of the country.

As the Persian period drew to a close, the signs of Greek influence on the material culture of Palestine steadily increased. Greek mercenaries, traders, and scholars were visiting the country in ever larger numbers, making a distinctive mark on its character. Thus the dawning of the Hellenistic period, which

ELEPHANTINE PAPYRUS. In the 6th–5th centuries B.C.E. the Persian Empire employed Jewish soldiers, settled in a military colony, as part of their garrison in Egypt. At Elephantine (an island near present-day Aswan) on the Nile, these settlers built their colony which included a temple at which the God of Israel occupied the center of the pantheon. They left numerous Aramaic letters and business documents known as the Elephantine Papyri which have allowed the reconstruction of the history and nature of this community and have contributed as well to the history of the Jews in the Land of Israel at this time. *Courtesy of the Institute for Archaeology of the Hebrew University.*

we will discuss in chapter 4, came as the completion of a cultural process long under way.

THE SECOND TEMPLE

From the point of view of Judaism as a religion, there can be no doubt of the historical importance of the restoration of the sacrificial ritual in approximately 520 B.C.E. Written soon after the destruction of the First Temple, the Book of Ezekiel held up the dream of a rebuilt Temple in Jerusalem, including an enlarged Temple complex, in which sacrifice would be offered according to an even higher standard of priestly sanctity and ritual purity than that required in the levitical codes of the Torah. The restoration allowed Israel to continue its ancestral worship of God in the ways prescribed by its ancient literature. More importantly, it established the biblical sacrificial system as the dominant pattern of worship for the entire Second Temple period. Some groups, like the sect of the Dead Sea Scrolls, withdrew from participation in sacrifices, but the ritual of the Temple was seen by the majority of the Jewish people as the most efficacious manner by which to reach God and secure His favor.

The original structure of the Second Temple, before it was refurbished by the Hasmoneans, and later, more extensively, by Herod, was built, as already mentioned, at the decree of Cyrus. Indeed, vessels from the First Temple, recovered by the Persians from the Babylonians whom they had conquered, were returned to the Jews to facilitate and encourage the rebuilding of the Temple. Many Jews living outside the Land of Israel contributed financially to the project. A start was made in the time of Sheshbazzar, but the disturbances made continuation of the work impossible. Zerubbabel completed the project. He began by erecting a temporary altar on which to offer sacrifices. Since this act seemingly contradicted the requirements of pentateuchal law, the rabbis later termed it an emergency measure.

Opposition to the rebuilding of the Temple came especially from the nobles who had taken control of Judea after the exile. They were probably closely related to the aristocracy of Samaria. Among those who encouraged the project were the prophets Haggai and Zechariah. The rebuilding was resumed in the second year of the reign of Darius (521 B.C.E.). Despite continued harassment by their neighbors, the Judeans persevered in the work.

While there is no complete description of the Temple built by Zerubbabel, considerable detail can be gleaned from various sources. It had two courtyards. One report suggests dimensions of 500 by 100 cubits (about 750 by 150 feet) for the inner courtyard. There were at least four gates in the wall of the outer courtyard, and at least one of them faced a street. There were at least two gates to the inner courtyard. Various chambers surrounded the Temple in both courtyards. Most of these were in the outer courtyard, and were used for the storage of tithes, equipment, and vessels. Certain high officials apparently merited private chambers within the Temple precincts.

The returnees constructed their altar on the site of the altar of the First Temple. The Temple building was of hewn stone, with wooden beams reinforcing the walls from within. The Temple itself was 60 cubits (approximately 90 feet) high. The Holy of Holies was empty, as there was no ark and no cherubim.

The construction was completed in 515 B.C.E., and the rededication was celebrated amidst great pomp and ceremony. After twenty years of effort, sacrificial worship could now take place in accordance with the rules laid down by the codes of the Torah. The Temple would stand as rebuilt by Zerubbabel until the Hasmonean period. While substantial refurbishing was undertaken by Simon ben Yohanan (Simon the Just) ca. 200 B.C.E., he did not modify the basic structure. (Herod the Great would substantially refurbish the Temple starting in 20/19 B.C.E.) The returnees to Zion had fulfilled their dream; God's house had been rebuilt and He would continue to dwell in their midst.

THE SAMARITAN SCHISM

Throughout the Second Commonwealth Judeans and Samaritans were engaged in intermittent conflict. Many scholars, on the basis of studies of the Samaritan Pentateuch and the Samaritan script, have concluded that the schism should be dated to the building of the Samaritan Temple on Mount Gerizim late in the Persian period and its destruction by the Hasmonean king John Hyrcanus in 128 B.C.E. These scholars maintain that the officials of Samaria who opposed the rebuilding of Jerusalem cannot be identified with the later Samaritan sect. This distinction seems to be overdrawn. Granted that the schism was the result of a long process, its earliest stages are to be observed already in the early years of the Persian period.

The Samaritans were a mixed people, made up of Israelites who had not been exiled when the Northern Kingdom was destroyed in 722 B.C.E. and people of various foreign nationalities whom the Assyrians had resettled in the area in an attempt to ensure that Israel's national aspirations could not again come to the fore. This mixed group had adopted a syncretistic form of Judaism that combined old northern traditions with those of the resettled nations. When work began on the Temple, the Samaritans approached the Jews to join in the project. The Judeans rejected the Samaritans because of their questionable descent.

In First Temple times it was possible for foreigners to join the Jewish people in an informal way by moving physically and socially into the land and adhering to its religion and laws. During the exile, Judaism had been transformed from a nationality which depended on a connection to the land and culture to a religious and ethnic community which depended upon descent. How else could Judaism have ensured its continuity when deprived of its homeland? The returning Jews from Babylonia could not accept the questionable genealogy of the Samaritans. On the other hand, there was not yet a system for religious conversion like that developed somewhat later on in the Second Temple period. Hence, there was no choice but to reject the Samaritans, even had they agreed to abandon their syncretistic practices. In response to their rejection, the Samaritans attempted, although with limited success, to influence the Persian authorities to halt the rebuilding of the Temple and to limit the powers of the priestly and temporal government of the Jews.

The Samaritan issue was no doubt complicated by another long-smoldering problem. As far back as the earliest days of the monarchy there had been a division between north and south. It was this sectionalism which eventually led to the division of the kingdom after Solomon's death. We cannot doubt that the northerners had opposed the centralization of sacrificial worship at Jerusalem during Solomon's reign. The north rejected all efforts to centralize worship at the Jerusalem Temple. Accordingly, after the kingdom was divided, the northerners set up sanctuaries at Bethel and Dan. The very same opposition to the centralization of worship in Jerusalem must have helped to motivate the leaders of Samaria in their attempts to hinder the reconstruction of the Temple by the returning Judeans.

To a great extent, then, the Samaritan issue in the early Second Temple period was a continuation of the north-south schism of the First Temple period. Like their northern predecessors, the Samaritans insisted on their right to sacrifice outside Jerusalem. In the Persian period, the Judeans rejected the Samaritans due to their syncretistic worship and the presence of non-Israelite elements among their population. Obeying the laws in the Book of Deuteronomy and heeding the injunctions of the prophets, they could not accept the Samaritans.

MIDRASH AND THE FOUNDATIONS OF JEWISH LAW

During the exile, a feeling of patriotism and the desire to preserve the Israelite literary heritage in the wake of the destruction of the ancestral homeland were probably responsible for a new emphasis on the study of Israel's scriptures. When Ezra returned to Judea, he devoted himself to making the Torah the center of the religious life of his people. But the Torah had one deficiency as a legal text. There were apparent contradictions and inconsistencies between the legal rulings in its various sections. Now something new was called for. How were the contradictions between laws on the same subject to be handled? How were the multiple presentations of the same material to be understood?

The duplications in the Torah begged to be interpreted. Thus was born the method which later Hebrew termed *midrash*. Essentially, the exegetical (interpretative) technique of midrash can be defined as the explanation of one biblical passage in the light of another. In its earliest forms midrash dealt with matters of Jewish law, what the rabbis later called *halakhah*. In the early Second Temple period, the new dependence on the written law stimulated the development of the method of legal midrash. Its earliest record is in the books of Ezra and Nehemiah.

An example of the use of this technique in our period is the decision attributed to Ezra to expel foreign wives. Returning exiles had married non-Israelite women of "the people of the land" and children had been born to them. Ezra 9:1 presents a list of the nations with which Israel had intermarried. The list is itself evidence of a midrashic interpretation. Included are some nations with which the Torah had prohibited marriage unconditionally and other nations that could marry Israelites only after a specific number of generations according to other biblical sources. The technique of analogical midrash led to the conclusion, based on Deut. 7:3 and 23:8–9, that the nations were all to be treated alike; marriage with any of them was to be eternally proscribed. The expulsion of the foreign wives was based on this exegetical conclusion.

Another example relates to the proper observance of Sukkot (Tabernacles). Leviticus 23 commands the building of the sukkah, and dwelling in it during the seven-day festival. There is no mention of pilgrimage to the sanctuary. Deuteronomy 16 does not mention the obligation of dwelling in sukkot but describes the festival as a pilgrimage. Legal midrash led to the decision that the entire people was to assemble in Jerusalem and build sukkot there. Thus it was possible to fulfill the commands of both codes and in this way resolve the inconsistency.

Other decisions based on this technique are recorded in the covenant of Nehemiah 10. These show beyond any doubt that the use of the midrashic method for the determination of Jewish law in cases where the Pentateuch was either unclear or apparently contradictory became the norm in the Persian period. It remained in use for the derivation of new conclusions until well into the Middle Ages, and at the same time, as we will see, often served as a means of justifying legal rulings already practiced on the basis of ancient tradition.

To avoid confusion one point should be made very clear: the term midrash designates both an exegetical method and a collection of literary materials based on midrashic exegesis. Later on we will have occasion to discuss various midrashim of the latter sort. It would be incorrect to conclude from the early dating of the *technique* of legal midrash that the *contents* of the collections to be examined later are of similar antiquity.

THE LITERATURE OF THE PERIOD

The literature of the Persian period is primarily a continuation of the genres and traditions of First Temple times. Chronicles continues the historiographical method established in the books of the Former Prophets, and adapts much material from them. Haggai, Zechariah, and Malachi embody the classical forms of the literary prophets; only the issues are different. In Ezra and Nehemiah we meet a strange mix of the historiographic spirit of the First Temple period with a tendency, not previously seen in biblical writings, to copy documents from royal correspondence and quote them as such. The inclusion of documents and edicts was typical of Hellenistic historiographical methods and is also found in the books of the Maccabees discussed in chapter 7.

Ezra, Nehemiah, and Chronicles

Foremost among the historical compositions of this period are the books of Ezra, Nehemiah, and Chronicles. Many scholars see these books as a single work, redacted by the "Chronicler." However, despite some similarities in language and ideology, Chronicles is so radically different in structure and emphasis from Ezra and Nehemiah that it is difficult to accept this theory. In any case, all three books represent a continuation of the biblical historiographic tradition. We shall first consider Ezra and Nehemiah, which were known to the translators of the Septuagint and to the rabbis as one book, Ezra.

The Book of Ezra tells about the two groups of exiles who returned to Judea from Babylonia in the early days of the Second Commonwealth and the events connected with them, as well as the arrival of Zerubbabel and, later, of Ezra. The book describes the building of the altar, the celebration of the rebuilding of the Temple, and the expulsion of the foreign wives. From a close study of the text it appears that the author utilized the memoirs of Ezra or some other collection of documents concerning him as a basis for this composition.

PERSIAN PERIOD STATUETTES. A cache of fertility statuettes from a 5th–4th centuries B.C.E. Phoenician cult-place at Dor in the Persian period yielded numerous exemplars from which the above are drawn. These figurines were part of fertility worship and are indicative of the extent to which such cults were practiced in the Persian period in Palestine. In this period, Dor and other cities on the northern coast continued to be dominated by the Phoenicians. *Courtesy of Professor Ephraim Stern and the Institute for Archaeology of the Hebrew University.*

The Book of Nehemiah discusses the appointment and arrival of Nehemiah, the rebuilding of the walls of Jerusalem and the northern opposition to the project, the repopulation of the city, the covenant renewal and public reading of the Torah, and the various efforts of Nehemiah to reinforce and preserve Jewish observance in the Judean community. The book is based on Nehemiah's own account, written in the first person. An editor or author has, however, reworked the material at many points and added the account of the covenant renewal and material from other sources.

The Book of Nehemiah must have reached its final form after the Book of Ezra, since it can be shown that it was not utilized by the author of Ezra. Since the last high priest that the author of Ezra knows of is mentioned in an Elephantine document from 408 B.C.E., Nehemiah must have been finished during the reign of Darius II (423–404 B.C.E.) or shortly thereafter. Ezra must be dated slightly later and would have been completed in the reign of Artaxerxes II (403–359 B.C.E.).

The Book of Chronicles (Hebrew *Divre Ha-Yamim*), known in our Bibles as I and II Chronicles, is actually one book. I Chronicles begins with a genealogical survey of the generations from Adam up to the time of the monarchy and then deals with the history of King David. II Chronicles takes up the career of Solomon and the building of the Temple in Jerusalem. It then recounts the history of the kings of Judah up to the exile and concludes with the decree of Cyrus in a version only slightly different from that with which Ezra opens. In essence, Chronicles is a review of the history of Israel as described in the Pentateuch and the Former Prophets, with distinct emphasis on the Davidic period and the Davidic dynasty.

The genealogical lists at the beginning of the book are in some cases based on the Pentateuch, and in other cases on sources which are no longer extant. The lists are much more detailed for the tribes of Judah, Benjamin, and Simeon than for the other tribes, showing the book's bias in favor of the Davidic house and the Kingdom of Judah. The lists also provide important information about settlement patterns in ancient Israel and the absorption of the pre-Israelite inhabitants of the land. Extensive information regarding the priestly and levitical clans and their settlements is given as well. It has been suggested that one of the aims of the author was to substantiate the Judean territorial claims of the returnees from exile.

In order to emphasize King David's contribution, the author provides detailed information on the organization and administration of the Davidic Empire. Chronicles adds greatly to the account in the books of Samuel, even attributing to David the organization of the sacrificial worship at Jerusalem and the priestly and levitical courses (twenty-four groups of priests that ministered at the sanctuary in one-week rotations). The centrality of the Zadokite priesthood, descended from Zadok, who served as high priest during the reign of David, is also stressed throughout the book.

The author often adapts the narratives in Samuel and Kings to bring them into accord with his understanding of religious law. In this respect, he constitutes an early example of the "rewritten Bible," a literary genre that we will encounter again in the Hellenistic period. On the other hand, he adds many details that must have been taken from extrabiblical sources. His description of Solomon's reign focuses on the building and dedication of the Temple in Jerusalem. In describing the divided monarchy he emphasizes the religious reformations of Hezekiah and Josiah.

Chronicles is, in our view, to be seen as an independent work which was not written by the author of Ezra and Nehemiah. It should be dated to shortly after the time of Ezra, composed by the first half of the fourth century B.C.E., probably by the beginning of the century. Chronicles shows how the ancient past of Israel remained at the center of Judean consciousness as the Persian era drew to a close.

The Last of the Prophets

Against the background of the last years of the biblical period, as the returning exiles were struggling to reestablish Jewish sovereignty over their ancestral homeland, three prophets delivered their messages. These three men were the last of the prophets of Israel, for as the Talmud would later state, prophecy came to an end with Haggai, Zechariah, and Malachi. The reason for this is not hard to discern. The phenomenon of prophecy was part of Judaism's Near Eastern heritage. It depended on the feeling of the immediacy of God and His presence that is so much in evidence in the religion of the Hebrew Bible. As Greek and other foreign cultures came to exercise greater influence on Jews, such ideas began to seem odd. With the coming of Alexander the Great and the sweeping changes that followed in his wake, prophecy ceased altogether.

Haggai

The prophet Haggai prophesied in Jerusalem in 520 B.C.E. The book is written in clear and simple language and testifies to the prophet's having seen the Temple before its destruction in 586 B.C.E. It is therefore possible that advanced age accounts for the short duration of Haggai's prophetic career, at least to the extent that it is documented in the book as preserved for us. Evidence points to Haggai's having been an influential prophet, and it is therefore possible that other prophecies of his were delivered earlier but were not preserved.

Haggai's basic message was for the people to complete the building of the Temple, which had been started years before. The new Temple was destined to outshine the glory of its predecessor. He directed his message to Zerubbabel son of Shealtiel, the governor, himself of Davidic descent, and to Joshua son of Jehozadak, the high priest, and only then to the people at large. If the Temple was not completed, he warned, poverty, famine and, drought would continue to afflict the nation. Haggai's prophecies make clear the importance of priestly purity laws in the life of the people at this time. Apparently convinced that the weakening of the Persian Empire was an opportunity for the House of David to take up its old role in Jewish affairs, he prophesied that Zerubbabel would be the first of the restored Davidic monarchs. Idolatry would come to an end and the kingdom of Israel would be renewed.

Haggai's prophecies make use of the Torah and earlier prophets, often embodying interpretations of this literature. In this respect his book is a bridge to the new emphasis on exegesis in the literature of the Second Temple period. His prophecies were presumably edited by his students. The Talmudic sages attributed the editing to the Men of the Great Assembly, a group of

sages said by rabbinic tradition to have continued the work of
Ezra and Nehemiah.

Zechariah

Very little is known of the prophet Zechariah, one of at least
a dozen people so named in the Hebrew Bible. He began to
prophesy in 520 B.C.E., around the same time as Haggai, and
the last prophecy attributed to him is dated some two years
later. Evidence points to his having been a priest, and he was
apparently young when he began his career. Like Haggai, he
primarily taught the importance of rebuilding the Temple, and
Ezra testifies to his having helped, along with Haggai, Zerubbabel, and Joshua, to rebuild the sanctuary.

At the same time, Zechariah fought against the pessimism of
those Judeans who were impatient regarding the fulfillment of
earlier prophecies, promising them that ultimately all the visions would be fulfilled. Jerusalem would be greatly expanded
and God's presence would return to it. There the Jewish people
would be reunited. His prophecy likewise shows evidence of the
developing notion of dual leadership for the renewed Israel, with
the Davidic monarch and the Aaronide high priest assuming the
temporal and religious responsibilities respectively, a concept
that gained importance in the Hellenistic period, particularly in
the Dead Sea Scrolls.

Zechariah saw strange visions and related them to the people
along with his interpretations of these experiences. His visions
helped to shape the later apocalyptic texts of Judaism and
Christianity. Interesting is his allusion to the fast-days connected with the destruction of Jerusalem (8:19), which were
already being observed in his time. Ultimately, in Zechariah's
view, the fasts would become times of rejoicing when the nations
would join in recognizing and worshiping God.

Most scholars see chapters 9–14 as a later addition to the
prophecies of Zechariah, although some date them to First
Temple times. The extremely late Hellenistic dating must be
rejected, since the scanty evidence cited in its behalf can just as
easily support an earlier dating. In all likelihood, these prophecies were authored in the later years of the Persian period.

The second part of Zechariah deals with the same issues as

the first, but its literary form is different and there are certain inconsistencies of content. It prophesies the destruction of the neighboring nations and the coming of the messianic king. Israel will be gathered to its land, and God Himself will rule over His people. Jerusalem and Judea will be purified of all ritual defilement after their victory against the enemies of Israel.

The influence of these eschatological and apocalyptic prophecies on Jewish literature in the Second Temple period is marked. Indeed, seen from this vantage point, the Book of Zechariah is an important transition from the prophecies of the biblical period to the apocalyptic writings of the Second Temple era. In this respect it resembles the Book of Daniel, the dating of which is likewise under debate.

Malachi

The question of whether Malachi is a proper name or a Hebrew designation for a prophet, literally "messenger" (*mal'akh*, cf. *mal'akhi*, "my messenger," in Mal. 3:1), has always been a subject of controversy. In any case, Malachi is the name of the last book in the Prophets. It was written in the Persian period, after the completion of the Temple, but opinions are divided on whether it was written before or after the time of Ezra and Nehemiah. The prophet speaks of the destruction of Edom, in Transjordan, which is known to have been taken over by Arab tribes toward the end of the sixth century B.C.E.

Among the central topics treated in Malachi are God's love for Israel, the sacrificial ritual and the priests, intermarriage, the Day of the Lord, and the end of days. The book is written as a series of dialogues between the prophet and his audience, or between God and the nation. The priests are excoriated for offering sacrifices with blemishes, and the people for profaning God's name by presenting freewill offerings from blemished animals. Because the people do not offer the priestly gifts and tithes, various natural calamities befall their crops. The ideal priest is described. The emphasis on sacrifice and priesthood fits well the period of the early Second Temple. The prophet sees intermarriage as a profanation of God's name. He also opposes the divorcing of one's first wife to marry a younger woman.

The prophet asserts that a day is coming when justice will be done to evildoers, and God's angel will purify the sons of Levi (the priests). The book closes with a call to remember the Torah of Moses. Elijah will come to reunite fathers and sons so that the earth will not be destroyed on the Day of the Lord. Some see these verses as a later addition to Malachi, since they seem to constitute a fitting conclusion to the entire corpus of prophetic literature. In any case, the image of Elijah here was to have momentous influence on the subsequent history of Jewish messianism and folklore.

THE CANONIZATION OF THE HEBREW SCRIPTURES

The close of our discussion of the Persian period is an appropriate point to take up the question of the biblical canon, or corpus, and how and when it was defined. This problem will take us somewhat afield, since the process of canonization, defining the scope and contents of the Bible, spans several historical periods. Nonetheless, the implications of the process are crucial to the history of Judaism as it will be described in the following chapters.

The term "canon" refers to the closed corpus of biblical literature regarded as divinely inspired. The Hebrew biblical canon represents a long process of selection, as testified to by the Bible itself, which lists some twenty-two books that have been lost to us, no doubt, among other reasons, because they were not included in the canon. Books were only included if they were regarded as holy, that is, divinely inspired.

The Hebrew Bible is divided into three parts, Torah (Pentateuch), Prophets, and Writings. This division is not strictly one of content; it derives from the canonization process in that the three parts were closed at separate times. "The Torah of Moses" was already the name for the first part in the various postexilic books. We will not attempt here to deal with the complex questions regarding the history and authorship of the Torah. Suffice it to say that a unified, canonized Torah was available to Ezra for the public reading which took place in approximately 444 B.C.E. Further, the various legal interpretations (midrashim) found in the books of Ezra and Nehemiah are them-

THE HEBREW BIBLE

Torah (Pentateuch)

Genesis (Bereshit)
Exodus (Shemot)
Leviticus (Vayiqra)
Numbers (Bemidbar)
Deuteronomy (Devarim)

Nevi'im (Prophets)

Former Prophets
  Joshua
  Judges
  1 Samuel
  2 Samuel
  1 Kings
  2 Kings

Latter Prophets
  Isaiah
  Jeremiah
  Ezekiel
  Twelve Prophets
    Hosea
    Joel
    Amos

Latter Prophets (*Cont.*)
  Obadiah
  Jonah
  Micah
  Nahum
  Habakkuk
  Zephaniah
  Haggai
  Zechariah
  Malachi

Ketuvim (Writings)

Psalms (Tehillim)
Proverbs (Mishle)
Job
Five Scrolls
  Song of Songs (Shir Ha-Shirim)
  Ruth
  Lamentations (Ekhah)
  Ecclesiastes (Qohelet)
  Esther
Daniel
Ezra
Nehemiah
1 Chronicles
2 Chronicles

selves a result of the issues raised by a Torah in which there are apparent contradictions and repetitions. It can therefore be stated unquestionably that the canonization of the Torah was completed by the time of Ezra and Nehemiah.

Later rabbinic tradition asserts that prophecy ceased with the conquest of Alexander the Great in 332 B.C.E. In effect, this meant that books composed thereafter were not to be included in the prophetic canon, the second of the Hebrew Bible's three parts. This view can be substantiated by the absence of later debate about the canonicity of the prophets, the lack of Greek words in the prophetic books, and the inclusion of Daniel and

Chronicles in the Writings rather than in the Prophets. (The debate about Ezekiel recorded in talmudic sources concerned its place in the school curriculum, not in the Prophets.) It must be the case, therefore, that the Prophets were canonized late in the Persian period, probably by the start of the fourth century B.C.E.

The Writings are a diverse collection. Some of the books included in this corpus are earlier than the canonization of the Prophets and were placed in the Writings because of their literary form or because they were regarded as having a lesser degree of divine inspiration. Other books appear in this collection because they were authored after the canon of the Prophets was closed. As already mentioned, this was the case with Daniel and Chronicles. Song of Songs and Ecclesiastes are regarded by some scholars as of Hellenistic origin, but rabbinic tradition attributes them to Solomon. Daniel is widely regarded by modern scholars as having been written in the Hellenistic period. There is no evidence at all for the oft-repeated view that the Scriptures were formally canonized at Yavneh. While virtually all the Writings were regarded as canonical by the time of the destruction of the Temple in 70 C.E., arguments continued regarding the status of Proverbs, Song of Songs, Ecclesiastes, and Esther, and these disputes are attested in rabbinic literature. Second Temple literature indicates that a collection of Writings existed as early as the second century B.C.E. but was not yet regarded as formally closed. We shall have occasion later on to speak of the Hellenistic Jewish Bible, or Septuagint, which included in its canon several later books avowedly authored in the Hellenistic period.

The unfolding of the history of Judaism, and indeed of Christianity and Islam as well, takes place against the background of the interpretation of a revealed, authoritative body of literature. For Judaism this corpus is the text of the Hebrew Bible. The notion of a canon provides a fixed consensus on the contents of this body of sacred literature and, therefore, helps to give unity to the diverse interpretations proposed by the varieties of Judaism encountered throughout history. It was the decision of the Christians to reopen the canon for a moment, and to place the New Testament within it, that created one of the basic disagreements separating Judaism from Christianity. The Hebrew biblical canon drew the lines within which Judaism was to develop and provided grist for the mill of a long and varied history of exegesis. The concept of a canon, with the attendant notions of authority and sanctity, endowed the Hebrew Scriptures with their enduring place in the history of Judaism.

SUMMARY

The Persian period saw the establishment of the fundamental features of Second Temple Judaism. The interpretation of the Five Books of Moses was the dominant source of Jewish law. Temple worship was reestablished and until 70 C.E. remained the preferred avenue by which Jews approached their Creator. The priesthood came to control both secular and religious affairs. The Samaritans were excluded from the Jewish people, and Jewish identity was to be determined by descent through the mother. These developments brought to a close the biblical period in the history of Judaism. Upon this foundation future generations would construct the postbiblical Judaism to be investigated in the coming chapters.

4
The Hellenistic Age

The Hellenistic period begins formally with the arrival of Alexander the Great in the Near East in 334 B.C.E. However, this date should not be seen as the beginning of Greek influence in the region. The Near East as a whole and Palestine and its Jewish residents more particularly first came under Aegean influence in the fourteenth century B.C.E. As trade connections increased, this influence became much more extensive, and during the Persian period Greek coinage became the standard in the Land of Israel.

HELLENISM AS A CULTURAL PHENOMENON

The cultural phenomenon that we call Hellenism had a lasting impact on Judaism and the Jewish people. Hellenism was a synthesis of Greek (Hellenic) culture with the native cultures of the Near East. It was a dynamic phenomenon, with the ever-evolving Hellenistic ("Greek-like") culture continually becoming the raw material for new syntheses with other native cultures not yet under its sway. Indeed, it was not the Greeks themselves, but the Macedonians, whose civilization was derivative from that of the true Hellenes, who were mainly responsible for spreading Greek culture to the Near East. As Hellenism penetrated each new region, an amalgamation of the Hellenistic with the native took place, and this phenomenon resulted in the many different manifestations of Hellenistic culture observable in the Near East over many centuries.

It was Alexander's conquests that made possible the fateful

The Empire of Alexander the Great (4th cent. B.C.E.)

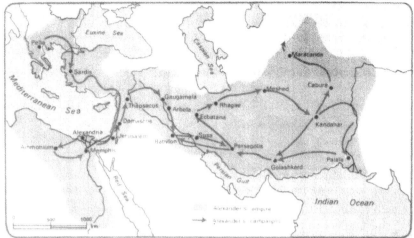

© Carta, Jerusalem 1983

union between East and West, but in fact there were deeper cultural reasons for the ease with which these two civilizations entered into a symbiotic relationship. Greek culture had by this time developed to its pinnacle. It had been liberated from the limitations of geography, and one could now be a Hellene by education and culture, not just by birth. Humanism had resulted from the primacy attributed to reason in Greek thought. Man now was at the center of the cosmos rather than merely of the polis (the Greek city) as he had been earlier. Concurrently, the native Near Eastern civilizations had run their course and were on the decline. Egypt and Mesopotamia apparently produced little of literary or intellectual import in this period, and the widespread interest in new religions observable in the sources indicates a hunger for new means of spiritual fulfillment. The time was ripe for a new cultural movement. Thus the peoples of the defeated Persian Empire could offer no more resistance to the Hellenic cultural onslaught than they had to the Macedonian army.

The Greek city, known as the polis, was the vehicle for the assimilation and Hellenization of the indigenous peoples of the Near East. Newly founded Greek cities, populated mostly by local people, were the cultural melting-pots of the East. The institutions of the Greek way of life were opened to all who wished to participate. The Greek language was rapidly adopted as a sign of Hellenization. People from the surrounding areas, streaming into the cities, quickly gained the legal and economic advantages afforded by citizenship in the polis—exemption from certain customs and duties and participation in the municipal government. In the Greek cities the upper classes of the Near East were acculturated through the schools and other institutions of the Hellenistic world.

Most interestingly, the native Near Easterners gravitated as well to the Hellenic arts and sciences and soon took the lead in such disciplines as literature and philosophy. The Greek emphasis on physical culture and on beauty also spread throughout the Near East. The religion of the Greeks was fused with that of the natives in many different forms and local cults. All of this was abetted by the polis and its official city cult, in which the Greek and the Near Eastern were in constant symbiosis.

Yet the indigenous peoples did not simply absorb the Hellenic and the Hellenistic; they redefined and reinterpreted their own traditional cultures in light of the "modern" civilization in which they now found themselves. The process of reinterpretation led to the several varieties of Hellenistic Judaism. Before taking these up, in particular as they relate to Palestinian Judaism, a brief survey of political developments during this period is in order, for they set the stage for the struggle over the extent of accommodation to Hellenism that would soon engulf the Jewish homeland.

UNDER PTOLEMIES AND SELEUCIDS

In the summer of 332 B.C.E., Palestine was conquered by Alexander the Great. The land and people of Israel were now part of the Hellenistic world. Alexander passed through Palestine first on his way to Gaza during his campaign to subjugate the Phoenician coast and then on his way from Egypt to Babylonia. He may have spent some time in Palestine dealing with a revolt in Samaria, and it is possible that he met then with Jewish leaders. By the time Alexander died at age thirty-three in 323 B.C.E., he had conquered the entire area from Macedonia to India. Palestine was part of this new empire.

JUDEA UNDER PTOLEMIES AND SELEUCIDS
(all dates are B.C.E.)

332	Alexander the Great conquers Palestine
323	Alexander's death and division of empire
301	Ptolemaic rule over Palestine established
242	Joseph ben Tobiah appointed tax collector
201	Seleucid conquest of Palestine
ca. 200	Simeon the Just
198	Seleucid control firmly established

THE PTOLEMAIC DYNASTY
(all dates are B.C.E.)

323–283	Ptolemy I Soter
283–246	Ptolemy II Philadelphus
246–221	Ptolemy III Euergetes
221–203	Ptolemy IV Philopator
203–181	Ptolemy V Epiphanes
181–146	Ptolemy VI Philometor
145–116	Ptolemy VII Physcon (Euergetes II)
116–108	Ptolemy VIII Lathyros (Soter II)
108–88	Ptolemy IX Alexander
88–80	Ptolemy VIII Lathyros (again)

After Alexander's death, his generals, known as the Diadochi ("successors"), were unable to maintain the unity of the empire and it soon fragmented. Individual generals were appointed, on the old Persian pattern, to rule as satraps over particular areas. In 323 B.C.E., Ptolemy took control of Egypt. This date is regarded as the beginning of the Ptolemaic Empire, although he was not officially crowned until 305 B.C.E. Seleucus became satrap of Babylon in 322 B.C.E. After some difficulties, he had established himself and his empire on a sound footing by 312 B.C.E., extending his authority to the entire eastern part of Alexander's domain. The rest went to Cassander in Macedonia and Lysimachus in Thrace. The Ptolemaic and Seleucid kingdoms were destined to play a profound role in the history of Hellenistic Palestine.

During the period of the Diadochi, Palestine changed hands between the Ptolemies and the Seleucids five times. The lack of

THE SELEUCID DYNASTY
(all dates are B.C.E.)

312–280	Seleucus I Nicator
280–261	Antiochus I Soter
261–246	Antiochus II Theos
246–226	Seleucus II Callinicus
226–223	Seleucus III Soter
223–187	Antiochus III the Great
187–175	Seleucus IV Philopator
175–164	Antiochus IV Epiphanes
164–163	Antiochus V Eupator
162–150	Demetrius I Soter
152–145	Alexander Balas
145–138	Demetrius II Nicator
145–138	Antiochus VI and Tryphon
138–129	Antiochus VII Sidetes
129–125	Demetrius II (again)
125–96	Antiochus VIII Grypus
125–95	Antiochus IX Cyzicenus
96–88	Demetrius III Eukairos
95–64	Seleucus VI

stability prevented Hellenism from making more than a modest beginning in the country in the early years of the Hellenistic period. The unstable situation must also have fostered some degree of local autonomy, enhancing the already significant role of the high priest in the affairs of Judea.

By 301 B.C.E., however, Ptolemy had finally established a firm hold on Palestine. Despite the damage caused by their ongoing conflict with the Seleucids, the Ptolemies were able to maintain at least de facto control over Palestine. Considerable information about this period comes from the Zenon papyri, a collection of administrative documents from the archives of an Egyptian finance minister, some of which were sent to him by his agent in the Land of Israel. These documents tell us of Palestine under the rule of Ptolemy II Philadelphus (283–246 B.C.E.). The country was often beset by Seleucid attacks and bedouin incursions. Ptolemaic military units were stationed throughout Palestine, and many Greek cities were established. Many of these were set up as cleruchies (military colonies) in which soldiers who married native women were given homes and fields, thus fostering the intermarriage which was so much a part of the Hellenistic world. In addition, an extensive Ptolemaic bureaucracy managed governmental affairs and taxation. Central to this officialdom was the goal of developing economic life and trade. Among the exports to Egypt from Palestine and southern Syria were grain, olive oil, smoked fish, cheese, meat, dried figs, honey, dates, and other products. Palestine also assumed importance as a crossroads for the spice trade.

In contrast with what we know about Ptolemaic affairs in Palestine, we have virtually no information about Jewish political developments. Judea continued to be governed by the high priest and the priestly aristocracy. One of the few incidents we know about is the quarrel about taxation between the high priest Onias II and Ptolemy III Euergetes (246–221 B.C.E.), who reportedly visited the Jerusalem Temple. The end result of the dispute was the appointment, in 242 B.C.E., of the young Joseph son of Tobiah, a nephew of the high priest, as tax collector for the entire country. The rivalry between the Tobiad family and the Oniad high priests eventually played a part in the attempted radical Hellenization of Judea later on in the second century B.C.E.

In 221 B.C.E. the Seleucid king Antiochus III invaded Palestine for the first time. When this attempt failed, he persisted in seeking an opportunity to gain control of this important land bridge. The death of King Ptolemy IV Philopator in 203 B.C.E. opened the way for him. In 201 B.C.E. he invaded the country again and quickly conquered it. By 198 B.C.E. the Seleucids were solidly in control, and would remain so up to the Maccabean Revolt (168–164 B.C.E.). By the time the Ptolemaic sway over Palestine came to an end, Greek cities had been established throughout the country, and Hellenism had sunk strong foundations, ultimately to tear the nation apart before Judea regained its independence.

In the years of conflict between the Ptolemies and Seleucids each of the rivals was supported by a Jewish party or faction. The Gerousia, or council of elders, mentioned for the first time in sources from this era, backed the Seleucids. Indeed, the high priest Simeon the Just (ca. 200 B.C.E.), who probably headed the Gerousia, is known to have supported the Seleucids. He must have regained the power over taxation which had been assigned to Joseph ben Tobiah and was now charged with refurbishing the Temple and the city. When Antiochus III (223–187 B.C.E) won control of Judea, he affirmed the right of the Jews to live according to their ancestral laws. Yet only some thirty years later the Jewish proponents of extreme Helleniza-tion would see his son, the Seleucid monarch Antiochus IV Epiphanes, as the agent who would carry out their plans to Hellenize Jerusalem and its people.

THE JERUSALEM TEMPLE AND PRIESTHOOD

We have already seen how difficult it had been to reestablish the Jerusalem Temple and how the Judean leaders struggled to make even a modest Temple building a reality. Over the years, various improvements were added to the Temple complex, so that by the eve of the Hellenistic reform, it had been expanded and refurbished, and had become a significant depository for the funds of both Palestinian and Diaspora Jews. Moreover, the Temple's position on a hill overlooking the city of Jerusalem gave it great strategic value. The entire hill, the Temple Mount, was occupied by the Temple precincts, although the mountain itself was no doubt somewhat smaller than the present-day structure, which was built by King Herod. Antiochus III confirmed the Jewish law that non-Jews could enter only the outermost area of the Temple Mount. People afflicted with ritual impurities were excluded from the Temple precincts.

The Temple structure was by now a complex of chambers devoted to specific purposes. Besides the courts of women, Israelites, and priests, and the Temple building itself, including the Holy of Holies, there were dressing rooms, storage areas, and other designated rooms. A stage was used for the priestly blessing and for the levitical songs which were part of the daily rituals. A large altar as well as special preparation areas made possible the sacrifice of animals in accord with pentateuchal legislation. The incense altar and the menorah were positioned in the priests' courtyard. Beautiful decorations adorned the Temple.

The officiants, both priests and Levites, were divided into twenty-four groups, called courses, each of which served for a week, rotating throughout the year. Each course was headed by one of its members and was, in turn, divided into subgroups. The priests sacrificed and offered the animals; the Levites assisted them and, in particular, sang psalms while the ritual took place. The laws of the Torah were strictly applied in order to guarantee the purity and sanctity of the priests, who were descendants of Aaron, the brother of Moses. The specialized vestments described in the Pentateuch were worn, and the ages of service were determined by the interpretation of the relevant biblical passages. Indeed, in most matters, the Torah and its exegesis were the authority on which decisions about sacrificial and priestly law were made.

Daily services were held in accord with the prescriptions of the Torah providing for morning and late afternoon sacrifices. The biblical psalms played a prominent role in the ritual, but it is difficult to determine to what extent other prayers were recited. It seems most likely that a detailed liturgy entered the Temple worship in the Hasmonean (Maccabean) period, as will be discussed more fully in chapter 12. Various musical instruments were played by the Levites to accompany the sacrifices and the psalms. Trumpets and shofars were sounded during various rites, as commanded by the Pentateuch. Special festival sacrifices and offerings, the bringing of tithes, other emoluments, voluntary sacrifices, and atonement offerings also were part of the Temple's regular ritual.

The Torah had commanded certain priestly and levitical portions and tithes as a means of ensuring that the Temple officials would be adequately supported. These offerings were collected and distributed by the Temple administration in the early years of the Second Temple. The high priest and his officials handled the collection and disbursement of other tax moneys as well for most of the Second Temple period. Later on, however, the central collection and distribution of tithes and offerings gave way to local handling of these portions, a pattern which had probably been in effect in First Temple times.

The Temple was much more than just a religious and cultic institution during the third and second centuries B.C.E. It served as the governmental center of the Jews to the extent to which the Jewish community operated as an autonomous unit within the Ptolemaic and Seleucid empires. The high priest and his assistants, over time, accumulated considerable temporal and financial power and controlled the internal affairs of the Judean populace. When, later on, Hellenizers attained the priesthood and attempted to turn the Temple into a Hellenistic cult center, they were therefore challenging not only the religious tradition, but also the very nature of the Jewish nation. When inexorable historical forces led, by the end of the first century C.E., to the destruction of the Temple and the abandonment of sacrifice as a primary religious activity, a new page would be turned in the history of Judaism.

THE GEROUSIA

Evidence of various kinds indicates that there was a Jewish representative body or council during the early Hellenistic period. The Talmud identifies those who were associated with Ezra and Nehemiah in the restoration period, and who continued their work after them, as having formed an early representative group, known as the "Men of the Great Assembly." Bodies of this type included members of the various leadership and aristocratic classes.

Although there is, in fact, no direct evidence in the Bible for the existence of a Jewish representative body, many biblical scholars, following Josephus, have pointed to the elders of the First Temple period as constituting a group of this type. Similar bodies of elders or aristocrats who were consulted by the ruler and whose approval he required functioned during the conquest of Canaan in the time of the judges. Talmudic literature assumed that the Men of the Great Assembly, in the era of the return, had handed down the traditions which ultimately made up Pharisaic-Rabbinic Judaism. Some modern scholars accept the existence of such a group, but see it as an ad hoc body, convened only on momentous occasions in the history of the nation.

No contemporary evidence can be cited for a representative group in the Persian period, but during the Hellenistic period the Gerousia (Greek for "council of elders") occupied this role.

HELLENISTIC HEAD FROM DOR. The city of Dor, located on the seacoast 20 km. south of present-day Haifa, was inhabited in the Canaanite, Israelite, Hellenistic, and Roman periods. In the Hellenistic era it was a polis, inhabited to a large extent by Jews, displaying thorough outward signs of Hellenization. This beautifully sculptured head from the Greco-Roman period indicates the extent of this cultural symbiosis. *Courtesy of Professor Ephraim Stern.*

There were also Jewish Gerousias in some parts of the Hellenistic Diaspora. The Gerousia may be seen as a forerunner of the
later Sanhedrin, known from the Herodian period, and also of
the Bet Din Ha-Gadol, the highest of the rabbinic courts.

In the edict he issued following his conquest of Jerusalem,
Antiochus III mentions that he was given a lavish reception by
the Gerousia, in consequence of which he exempted its members, together with the Temple officials, from certain taxes. He
says nothing of any separate welcoming ceremony conducted by
the high priest. Similarly, during the Maccabean period, we find
that Antiochus IV directed his official correspondence, not to
the high priest, but to the Gerousia, apparently seeing it as the
governing body of Judea. Jews outside the Land of Israel in the
same period also regarded the Gerousia as representing the
people as a whole. The membership of the Gerousia seems to
have included both priestly and lay leaders, the latter no doubt
coming from the aristocracy and connected closely with the
priesthood. This is consistent with the composition of the later
Sanhedrin, which was made up of both Pharisaic and Sadducean
(priestly) elements.

HELLENISTIC TRENDS IN PALESTINIAN JUDAISM

It was not long before the inexorable progress of Greek
cultural influence led to demands for a Hellenistic reformation
of Judaism (ca. 175 B.C.E.) and subsequently to the Maccabean
Revolt (168–164 B.C.E.). The two preceding centuries, as we
have seen, were years in which Hellenistic influence in Palestine
rapidly increased. A confrontation of cultures was fostered by
the founding of so many Greek cities, by the presence of
numerous foreigners in the country, and by the extensive commercial and cultural connections with the Hellenistic world. The
old way of Jewish life was severely challenged by the new
amalgamation of the Hellenic and the native. However, the
effects of the confrontation were not uniform in all parts of
Palestine and in all circles and classes. In fact, only a proper
understanding of the various trends and responses to the challenge will allow perspective on the subsequent events.

The Jewish group least affected by the process of Hellenization was the peasantry. The rural inhabitants of Judea at this time lived in small villages and tilled the soil, visiting the cities to sell their produce and occasionally making religious pilgrimages to Jerusalem. In the cities they came into contact with more Hellenized Jews and with non-Jews. They also came into contact with Greek-style pottery, tools, and equipment. These new objects brought with them their designations in Greek, which were quickly adopted into the native Hebrew dialects. Yet the language and culture of the rural peasantry remained Hebraic, and Hellenism tended to influence them only in the area of material culture. Thus they certainly had no intention of abandoning their ancestral way of life for the new cultural symbiosis.

The situation of the urban masses was very different. These people, mostly artisans and traders, lived in predominantly Jewish cities like Jerusalem, where they had greater and more frequent contacts with the Greek world and with their more Hellenized coreligionists than did the rural peasants. Such literary works as the Book of Ben Sira (Ecclesiasticus) show the moderate influence of Hellenistic culture on a traditional and pious Jew, probably a Jerusalemite, who lived in the early second century B.C.E. The urban population found it necessary to use Greek words and language to be understood; and increasingly, throughout the third and second centuries B.C.E., the effect of Hellenism on architecture and cultural life increased even among traditionally pious Jews. Certain aristocratic families, closely connected to the priesthood, were tending, perhaps as a result of greater contacts with the wider Hellenistic world, or for political and economic reasons, toward greater Hellenization. The Tobiad family, which had earlier controlled taxation on behalf of the Ptolemies, and other powerful families as well, sought to edge the nation toward participation in the new world which lay open to them within easy grasp.

Those Jews who were interested in a higher degree of Hellenization, however, gravitated to the Greek cities, mostly on the seacoast and in the area to the east known in Roman times as the Decapolis. In these areas Greek was the everyday language, and the dominant culture was Hellenistic. Such Jews had to compromise with the pagan cults, and they did this primarily by interpreting the city liturgies as extensions of their monotheistic Judaism; indeed, through a radical reinterpretation they held the Jewish Scriptures to be consistent with the mythology of the pagan cults. They attended the theater and sent their children to the Greek educational institutions, the gymnasium and the ephebion, where they in turn were inducted into greater extents of Hellenization and, ultimately, assimilation. The Hellenizers, as they were called, were willing to pay a price for the economic and cultural advantages of the polis. Abandoning their Jewish particularity for participation in the wider cosmos, they saw Judaism as becoming a part of the new world that Hellenistic culture was opening before them and sought to ease the transition from the antiquated life-style of the Near East to the new, cosmopolitan life of Hellenistic society.

These trends within Judean society coexisted for a time but eventually came into confrontation. Beginning in the late second century B.C.E., extreme Hellenizers of the type previously known only in the Greek cities gained control of the Jerusalem priesthood and attempted to transform Jerusalem into another Hellenistic polis. This event set the stage for the Maccabean revolt.

HELLENISTIC REFORM AND THE MACCABEAN REVOLT

The political background of the struggle over Hellenization must be sought in the years following the final Seleucid conquest of the Land of Israel under Antiochus III in 198 B.C.E. Throughout the years of warfare between the Seleucids and the Ptolemies each empire had its partisans among the aristocracy of Jerusalem. When the Seleucids firmly established their dominion over Judea, the pro-Ptolemaic party was left disenfranchised. The high priest Onias III had supported the Ptolemies during the reign of King Seleucus IV Philopator (187–175 B.C.E.). The pro-Seleucid party, therefore, denounced him to the Seleucid rulers. In an effort to exonerate himself, Onias set out for Antioch to meet with the king.

Meanwhile Seleucus IV died, and the infamous Antiochus IV Epiphanes (175–164 B.C.E.) succeeded to the throne. Onias, unable to convince him of his loyalty, was forced to remain in

Antioch. His brother Jason then bought the high priesthood from Antiochus. This disruption of the hereditary succession of the high priests set a precedent that would hasten the decline of this office in the years to come.

In addition to purchasing the office of high priest, Jason also bought the right to establish a gymnasium and ephebion in Jerusalem, and, on the basis of these institutions, to turn the city into a Hellenistic polis to be named Antioch in honor of Antiochus IV. The right to live according to the Torah, granted to the Judeans by Antiochus III, was now rescinded. In its place, the Jews were to live under the laws of a Greek city. Among other things, this meant that the majority of those who previously had enjoyed full rights under the laws of the Torah now found themselves second-class citizens in an oligarchy. In addition, Greek-style athletic activities began and the Gerousia was probably purged of members who did not support the reform.

It is not surprising that the already Hellenized aristocracy of Judea so willingly undertook these changes. Throughout the Hellenistic world rulers were encouraging ancient cities to become up-to-date Greek poleis (plural of polis). The poleis were allied closely with the kings and could be depended upon to control the less Hellenized rural areas. Citizenship in Greek cities held out many pluses: the commercial benefits of trade with other such cities, the minting of coins, and other advantages that would have been particularly attractive to the aristocracy. Further, the polis afforded its citizens the opportunity to see themselves as part of a wider and more open world.

THE MACCABEAN REVOLT
(all dates are B.C.E)

175–171	Jason high priest
ca. 175	Hellenistic reform
171–167	Menelaus high priest
168–164	Maccabean Revolt
167–166	Antiochus decrees persecution
166–160	Judah Maccabee leads rebellion
164	Judah conquers Jerusalem and rededicates Temple
160	Judah defeated and killed
152	Jonathan establishes independence

Jason and his followers were not extremists. Although they introduced the political and commercial changes mentioned above, they did not seek to change the Jewish faith. They maintained the Temple and its rituals according to the tradition, even if they compromised with the Hellenistic way of life in other spheres. They were seeking a way to live as Jews within the wider Hellenistic world without abandoning the age-old traditions of Israel.

Jason's brand of Hellenization was apparently not enough for some. As a member of a family which had been pro-Ptolemaic, he soon found himself opposed by the pro-Seleucid Tobiad family, and by the three brothers Simeon, Menelaus and Lysimachus. The Tobiads plotted to have Menelaus replace Jason as high priest. Menelaus succeeded in buying the office from Antiochus in 171 B.C.E., as Jason himself had done only a few years earlier. After an armed battle, Jason was forced to flee Jerusalem. Now in control, Menelaus appropriated funds from the Temple treasury to present gifts to Antiochus.

Menelaus's misappropriation of Temple funds and his lack of Oniad family ties turned the people bitterly against him. Violence broke out in Jerusalem, and Lysimachus, who had taken over in his brother's absence, himself fell in the fighting. Despite an appeal from representatives of the Gerousia that Menelaus be replaced, Antiochus allowed him to continue in office, and the representatives were executed. It was not long before, under new leaders, popular discontent became full-scale revolt.

Antiochus had for some time been trying to conquer Egypt. His first attempt against the Ptolemies failed, but his second, in 168 B.C.E., almost succeeded. The Romans, however, already looking toward the East, forced him to abandon Egypt. The false rumors of Antiochus's death which spread in the aftermath of this humiliation led Jason, the deposed former high priest, to leave his hiding place in Transjordan and mount an assault on Jerusalem. He managed to drive Menelaus and his supporters into the citadel, but was not able to reassert his rule. Apparently, popular forces arose against him, remembering that he had begun the Hellenistic reform, and forced him to again flee the holy city. Despite a slaughter led by Antiochus himself, the insurrection in Jerusalem continued. An attempt by the Seleucid

DEFENSIVE TOWER AT DOR. During the Hellenistic period Dor was known for its massive fortifications. Shown here is a tower on the western side of the city, north of the city gate area. In the middle was a circular staircase leading up to the top. Part of the city wall can be seen at the bottom of the picture. The city withstood the attack of Antiochus III in 219 B.C.E. Tryphon (142–138 B.C.E.) fled there after murdering Jonathan the Hasmonean in 143 B.C.E. and withstood the seige of Simon the Hasmonean and Antiochus VII Sidetes. *Courtesy of Professor Ephraim Stern.*

general Apollonius to bring the situation under control by establishing a fortress, known as the Akra, at the center of the polis, and by stationing a Hellenistic garrison there, led only to further popular opposition and to a massive flight of Jews from the city, some of whom had been dispossessed to make room for the garrison.

It was probably at this time that foreign deities were introduced into the Temple, creating further friction. The Jewish Hellenizers, Menelaus and his party, saw these gods as equivalent to the God of Israel, and thus in their view this was not really foreign worship. They regarded the ancestral God of Israel as simply another manifestation of the supreme deity known in Syria as Baal Shamin (Master of Heaven) and in the Greek world as Zeus Olympius. In this way they rationalized their behavior.

The earliest attempts at an organized uprising were probably led by the Ḥasidim ("pious"), a group of pietists who found the religious compromises in Hellenistic Jerusalem totally unacceptable. Rebellion was mounting; determined to stem it, Antiochus conceived of the infamous persecutions, which, far from being the beginning of our story, come after years of struggle and insurrection fueled by the attempt of Hellenistic Jews to foist their way of life on the entire nation of Israel. There is no evidence whatsoever that Antiochus pursued a similar policy anywhere else in his kingdom. He took up the Hellenizing banner in Judea in response to the nature of the rebellion confronting him there. As he saw the situation, the way to defeat the rebels was by an onslaught against the forces that propelled them, the Torah, the commandments, and the culture of the Jewish people.

The persecutions were enacted in the winter of 167/66 B.C.E. To begin with, the decree of Antiochus III which had granted the Jews extensive rights of religious freedom was formally rescinded. Moreover, in December of 167 foreign idolatrous worship and cultic prostitution were introduced into the Temple. In addition, throughout Palestine the Sabbath and festivals were to be violated, high places (outdoor shrines) were built where unclean animals were to be offered, circumcision was outlawed, and the dietary laws could not be observed. The penalty for violating these ordinances was death. In every part of the land Jews found themselves facing royal officials who sought to enforce the regulations with a vengeance, burning Torah scrolls and executing those who hid them. Antiochus had instituted this brutal program in order to deprive the Jewish uprising of a purpose by forcing the Jews to become normal citizens of the Seleucid Empire. Thanks to his short-sighted scheme, the stage was now set for the confrontation of two opposing forces, the Jewish people and the Seleucids. The appearance of the Hasmonean (Maccabean) family would ignite the flames of full-scale revolt.

We cannot be sure whether the accounts of the beginning of the revolt in I and II Maccabees are historical. Nonetheless, Mattathias, the priest of Modiin, and men and women like him bravely refused to submit to the persecution and repaired to the forests. Several thousand soon coalesced around the Hasmonean family, led by Judah the Maccabee ("hammer"), and his brothers John, Simon, Eleazar, and Jonathan. Together with elements of the Hasidim they began to take control of villages throughout the countryside. By Mattathias' death in 166/65 B.C.E. they had taken control of Judea.

Under Judah the Maccabee the Jewish army defeated a series of Seleucid generals who attempted to put down the uprising. Having defeated the best of Antiochus's generals, Judah soon was master of the entire country. Menelaus and the Hellenizers sought a peaceful settlement, asking that the Jews be allowed to return to their homes and that the persecution be officially suspended. The Seleucid government recognized the need for a political compromise. On October 15, 164 B.C.E. it restored the rights of the Jews as granted by Antiochus III, providing amnesty as well. While some may in fact have taken advantage of the amnesty, the soldiers of Judah did not. In December of that year Judah and his men captured Jerusalem, although a Seleucid garrison continued to hold the Akra, the Hellenistic fortress. On the 25th of the Hebrew month of Kislev Judah purified the Temple and reorganized the sacrificial cult to conform to the Jewish tradition. This event is commemorated in the holiday of Hanukkah ("rededication"). The main objective of the revolt, ending the persecutions and restoring Judaism, had been achieved.

Throughout the period of persecution and revolt, the Hellenistic pagans in the Land of Israel had sided with the Seleucids and had participated in the persecutions. It was therefore natural that Judah now turned on these enemies as well as on the Hellenizing Jews who had brought on the horrible persecutions. The Hellenizers, many of them of aristocratic origins, had fought on the side of the Seleucids against Judah. Their center was the Akra, and it was here that they finally took refuge when Judah conquered Jerusalem.

Judah undertook wars throughout the Land of Israel to defend the Jews from their pagan neighbors and at the same time to extirpate paganism from the country. After Antiochus IV died in 164 B.C.E., his son Antiochus V Eupator advanced on Judea, came to terms with Judah, and again restored the rights of the Jews. He executed Menelaus, the Hellenizing high priest, blaming him for embroiling the Seleucid Empire in the persecutions and the war with the Jews, and appointed Alcimus, a moderate Hellenizer, as high priest. By 162 B.C.E. Judah and his party had barred Alcimus from taking office. Alcimus sought the help of the Seleucids, and they confirmed him in office. The Ḥasidim hastened to compromise with Alcimus, but the Hasmoneans continued to resist his rule. After a brief honeymoon, the Ḥasidim were back in Judah's camp. The Syrians had again succeeded in putting the Hellenizers in power over Judea.

Alcimus sought Seleucid help to maintain his regime against Judah. The force dispatched to aid him was defeated, and Alcimus fled to Syria. He returned with the Seleucid general Bacchides, and Judah fell in battle against him in 160 B.C.E. The Hasmoneans now rallied around Jonathan, Judah's brother. Again the Hellenized Jews sought to rule and again the Hasmoneans plagued them on all sides. For several years, as the war raged, the post of high priest remained vacant. Finally, Bacchides entered negotiations with Jonathan. The two signed a treaty that gave Jonathan, based in his stronghold at Michmash, control over most of Judea.

In 152 B.C.E., when internal affairs in Syria led to a civil war over the succession to the throne, both sides began wooing

Jonathan. He gave his backing to Alexander Balas and on Tabernacles of 152 B.C.E appeared in the Temple in the robes of the high priest, having been appointed to the office by Balas as a quid pro quo. Judea was now united under the rule of a Hasmonean high priest. A dynasty had dawned which would rule the Jewish people until the coming of the Romans in 63 B.C.E.

SUMMARY

The rising Hellenistic influence over the Jews of the Land of Israel eventually led to a major confrontation between the radical Hellenizers and the majority of the Jewish people, who sought to maintain their ancestral ways. Even with the help of the Seleucid armies, the radical Hellenizers failed once and for all to sway the Jewish people. Extreme forms of Hellenization had been rejected, and the Jews would now seek other approaches to living in the new cultural ambience. Even in the Greco-Roman Diaspora, as will be seen in the next chapter, the attempt to synthesize Judaism with Hellenism would not be carried to such extremes.

5
Judaism in the Hellenistic Diaspora

Since biblical times many Jews had been living in places beyond the boundaries of the Land of Israel. As early as the time of King Solomon, commercial efforts must have led some Israelites abroad for extended periods of time, and some may even have settled abroad permanently. Yet the notion of Diaspora, a dispersion of Jews exiled from their homeland, did not become central until 722 B.C.E., when Shalmaneser V, the king of Assyria, carried off part of the population of Northern Israel into exile in Assyria. This was followed soon after by the population movements that took place under Babylonian domination, first in 597 B.C.E., when the upper strata of Judean society were exiled, and then in 586 B.C.E., when the First Temple was destroyed and many other Judeans were led into captivity. These population movements led to the establishment of a sizable Jewish community in Mesopotamia, one that was destined, as we shall see, to lay the foundations for much of medieval Jewish life. At the same time other Jews fled to Egypt, where some of their coreligionists had already relocated in the years leading up to the destruction of the Land of Israel and its Temple, and here too a substantial Jewish community was established.

By Second Temple times the Diaspora had spread throughout the Hellenistic world as well. Jews were to be found along the coasts of the Mediterranean basin as well as in Mesopotamia and many other lands of the East. Wherever they settled, they carried Judaism to the land of their dispersion, each separate Jewish community developing its own distinctive style.

THE EARLY HISTORY OF BABYLONIAN JEWRY

From the accounts in Ezra and Nehemiah it is certain that only a small minority of Babylonian Jewry returned to rebuild the Land of Israel. The Murashu Tablets, the records of a prominent family of Babylonian bankers which mention numerous Jews, are usually taken as evidence of Jewish business activity in Nippur during the reigns of Artaxerxes I (465/4–424 B.C.E.) and Darius II (423–404 B.C.E.). That Jews attained positions of importance is indicated by the biblical account of Nehemiah, who was a high official of the Persian king, and this state of affairs provides the backdrop for the books of Esther and Daniel.

After Alexander's conquest of Babylon in 331 B.C.E., Mesopotamia was ruled by the Seleucids for some two centuries. They soon founded new cities, which, together with the garrisons they established, fostered the Hellenization of Babylonia. We have no evidence regarding the effects of this process on the Jewish communities. The privileges accorded to the Jews by the Persians were reconfirmed by the new rulers. In the late third century B.C.E. Jews serving in the Seleucid army were excused from certain duties for religious reasons. One heritage of the Seleucid period in Babylonia was the use of the Seleucid era as a means of counting years (taking 312 B.C.E. as the year 1), a pattern that some Jewish communities continued well into the Middle Ages.

By 129 B.C.E. the decline of Seleucid power made possible the westward expansion of the Parthians (Parthia is located east and north of the Caspian Sea), and Babylonia now came under Parthian rule. The Parthian Empire allowed the native populations to continue their indigenous traditions, leaving the Greek colonies intact and granting favorable treatment to the Jews. Some contacts between the Parthians and the Hasmonean rulers of Palestine must have occurred. We know that in 41/40 B.C.E. the Parthians deposed Herod and supported the Hasmonean

Judah Antigonus, only to be chased back across the Euphrates by the Romans in 38 B.C.E.

Little is known of the position of the Jews in the Parthian Empire during the Hellenistic period, but the evidence indicates that the majority of them were farmers and tradesmen with a small upper class of nobility. Attachment to the Land of Israel, especially to Jerusalem, and pilgrimage to the Temple are attested. From the story of the conversion to Judaism (ca. 40 C.E.) of the royal house of Adiabene, a Parthian vassal state in the upper Tigris region, we gather that Jews and Judaism were a regular part of Mesopotamian culture and life in this period. There was even a short-lived Jewish state in Babylonia from about 20 to 35 C.E.

JEWS IN THE HELLENISTIC WORLD

Much more is known about the Jewish communities of the western Diaspora in this period. We have already met the small colony of Jewish troops that was based in Elephantine in Upper Egypt after the Persian conquest in 525 B.C.E. Jews probably first immigrated to Egypt from Judea in the difficult years following the Babylonian conquest in the early sixth century B.C.E., and some Babylonian Jews must have come there in connection with the Persian conquest. Large-scale Jewish emigration from Palestine to Egypt, however, is first attested in the reign of Ptolemy I (323–283 B.C.E.), although accounts differ as to whether the Jews who came to Egypt at this time did so voluntarily or as captives. The Egyptian priest Manetho, in the reign of Ptolemy II Philadelphus (283–246 B.C.E.), may be credited with being the author of the first known anti-Semitic tract. His writings show familiarity with the exodus and indicate that there were enough Jews in Egypt to make attacking them worthwhile. At the same time, Ptolemy II is credited with having arranged the liberation of many Jews still held captive from his father's day.

The reign of Ptolemy VI Philometor (181–146 B.C.E.) began the golden age of Egyptian Jewry. It was near the end of his reign that the Temple of Onias was built. Onias IV, as legitimate successor, had expected to be appointed high priest after the

STAMPED JAR HANDLES. Rhodian stamped jar handles, such as these found at Dor, Israel, are in evidence throughout the Hellenistic world. They indicate the extent of international trade and commerce and the manner in which the Mediterranean basin and the coast of Palestine were linked economically, even before the rising cultural tides of Hellenism engulfed the Near East. *Courtesy of Professor Ephraim Stern.*

death of Menelaus, the usurper, and left Jerusalem between 162 and 160 B.C.E. when Alcimus was appointed instead. He and his relatives eventually constituted a military colony (katoikia) at Leontopolis, where they established a temple to provide for orderly worship in their community, and, possibly, to advance their candidacy to assume the rule of Palestine in the event of a Ptolemaic victory there. Needless to say, if sacrifices were actually offered in this temple, it would have been a major deviation from what Diaspora Jews did elsewhere, for in virtually all other cases they seem to have been convinced that sacrifice was permissible only at Jerusalem. On the other hand, a sacrificial cult was certainly part of the worship of the Jews of the Elephantine military colony in the fifth century B.C.E.

Onias's role in Egyptian political and military affairs shows the extent to which Jews were already penetrating the life of the country as a whole. As a result of Onias's support for Cleopatra II, the widow of Ptolemy VI, Ptolemy VII Physcon (145–116 B.C.E., also called Euergetes II) unleashed a pogrom against the Jews, the first such event documented in history. Peace was eventually restored when Ptolemy VII married Cleopatra. Good relations with the Jews must have been quickly restored, since a synagogue was eventually dedicated in his honor.

Onias's descendants continued to serve in the Ptolemaic military under Cleopatra III (ruled jointly with Ptolemy VIII and IX, 116–102 B.C.E.). His sons Helkias and Hananiah were among her commanders. They are credited with having persuaded the queen to abandon her plan to conquer and annex the territory of the Hasmonean king, Alexander Janneus. Here we see the loyalty of Egyptian Jewry to their coreligionists in Palestine and their support for the Hasmonean dynasty.

Accounts of the remainder of Jewish history in Hellenistic Egypt are scanty, but they reveal the continued role of Jews in Egyptian affairs up to the Roman period. The center of the Egyptian Jewish community was Alexandria, where Jews had settled as early as the beginning of the third century B.C.E. Before long, two of the city's five quarters were predominantly Jewish and synagogues were scattered everywhere. Jews were also to be found throughout both Upper and Lower Egypt and constituted a substantial and recognizable group within the population. Many of their communities had originally been military colonies.

The earliest reliable evidence for the spread of the Jewish Diaspora to Asia Minor dates from the reign of Antiochus III, who, around 210–205 B.C.E., transferred Jews from Babylonia to the area that is now Turkey to serve as military colonists. By the time of Simon the Hasmonean (142–134 B.C.E.), a circular letter published by the Roman consul regarding the rights of Jews was sent to nine different regions and cities on the mainland of Asia Minor and four Greek islands. Numerous other locales in Asia Minor are mentioned as having Jewish communities in the Hellenistic and Roman periods. By the first century C.E. Jews were to be found in every part of Asia Minor.

Especially significant in light of its role in the history of the spread of Christianity was the Syrian Diaspora. It size is partly to be accounted for by its proximity to Palestine. The Jewish community of Antioch, Syria's largest city, was established around 200 B.C.E. Jews dwelled also in Apameia, and in the year 70 C.E. there was a pogrom against the Jews of Damascus. Tyre and Sidon (in present-day Lebanon) were centers of Jewish population from Hasmonean times. By the turn of the era Jews were spread throughout the towns and cities of Syria.

The Jewish community of Cyrene, in North Africa, was founded by immigrants from Egypt in the time of Ptolemy I. The letter from the Roman consul also confirmed the rights of the Cyrenaican Jews. In the mid-second century B.C.E. their number included Jason, the author of a five-volume history which was excerpted in 2 Maccabees. By the first half of the first century B.C.E. the Jews were a distinct population group in Cyrene. The community would continue to grow in Roman times, only to suffer destruction during the revolt of the Diaspora Jews against Trajan in 115–117 C.E..

Jews also settled in Greece, Macedonia, Crete, and Cyprus. The first influx of Jews to Greece may have consisted of captives brought there as slaves during the Maccabean revolt. Presumably many of them remained in Greece after having obtained their freedom. By the second century B.C.E. Greek authors were claiming that Jews were to be found throughout the world.

The population figures which they put forward for the Jewish population of Greco-Roman times were vastly exaggerated, but by how much cannot be said precisely.

The size of the Jewish community was no doubt swelled by many proselytes (converts) who were attracted to the ancient Mosaic faith as belief in the traditional deities of the Greek pantheon declined. We cannot be sure what processes of conversion were obligatory in order to join fully the Jewish communities of the Hellenistic world, although there is no question but that circumcision was required. At the same time there was a large class of semi-proselytes who did not formally become part of the Jewish people but kept many Jewish customs, such as attending the synagogues and abstaining from pork. This group of "God-fearers," as they were called, must have appeared to the pagans to have converted to Judaism, but they did not consider themselves to have become full-fledged members of the Jewish people, nor were they considered by the Jewish people to have become Jews.

POLITICAL, SOCIAL, AND ECONOMIC DEVELOPMENTS

The survival of the Jews and Judaism as a distinct entity in the Greco-Roman world, and, for that matter in every other time and place, depended on the organization of Jewish communal structures. With the exception of a few who were so Hellenized that they disassociated themselves from their coreligionists, virtually all Diaspora Jews were members of the Jewish communal organization, termed in Greek either *politeuma* ("political body," "citizens"), *katoikia* (the designation for a separate settlement or body of residents within a city), or *synagoge* ("community"). The Jews were organized into autonomous bodies of this kind because they were seen as foreigners born abroad. Other ethnic groups in the Hellenistic world were similarly organized either as foreign ethnic communities or as religious corporations. All such organizations required royal permits and, in the case of the Jewish community, were guaranteed the right to conduct their affairs in accord with their ancestral laws. Thus, the Jewish communities had complete freedom to build synagogues, set up independent courts of justice and other institutions, educate their youth in the tradition, and elect their own officials.

Various officials are known to have existed in the Jewish communities. The archons, from the Greek for "chief, head," were the members of the Gerousia. The head of the Gerousia was the gerousiarch. There were also the archisynagogos, or head of the synagogue (i.e., the Jewish community, not the house of worship), and various other officials. The synagogue, or temple, was the central building, providing facilities for the instruction of children, the dispensing of justice, and the lodging of visitors, and, of course, serving as the house of worship. Throughout the Diaspora the synagogue became the major institution for the preservation of the Jewish tradition, a role it would soon come to occupy even in the Land of Israel with the destruction of the Temple. Because Jews tended to live in proximity to the synagogue, and would not eat or intermarry with non-Jews, anti-Semites often accused them of exclusivity. From later sources it seems that Jews were not granted equal rights as citizens of the Greek cities, except for small numbers who were considerably Hellenized and were admitted to citizenship as individuals.

In the Hellenistic and Roman eras Jews constituted distinct communities within the larger society. Foremost among their particular needs was exemption from the requirement to worship the local deities, which usually constituted the formal cult of the city. This was usually forthcoming, but it had to be granted informally and is never directly mentioned even in the many documents relating the privileges of the Jews in this period. This unspoken privilege seems to have had the effect of restricting the entry of Jews into full citizenship in most Greek cities.

Yet numerous other privileges are documented. The Jews were permitted to live according to their ancestral laws. Sabbath observance was made possible by excusing them from appearing in court or in municipal offices on the seventh day. Further, Jewish military units were exempted from marching on the Sabbath. Despite the strong resentment of their non-Jewish neighbors, Jews were permitted to send money to the Jerusalem Temple, and later to the patriarchate in the Land of Israel.

These seemingly minor privileges amounted to a recognition that Jews could live in the Greco-Roman world only at some distance from their neighbors. At the same time, this bit of tolerance made possible their entry further and further into Hellenistic life, and may have sown the seeds for the eventual assimilation of the Hellenistic Jews and the disappearance of Hellenistic Judaism.

The Jews of the Western Diaspora engaged in manifold occupations. They originally came to Egypt, Cyrene, and Asia Minor as soldiers, a role Jews played in many parts of the Hellenistic world. They were generally assigned land which eventually became their private property, thus creating a class of Jewish small farmers throughout the region. Some Jews leased royal lands, while others worked as tenants for large landholders. Agriculture had been important in Palestine, so it is not surprising that Jews continued to be farmers in the Diaspora.

The various literary sources lead us to believe that Jews practiced a wide range of crafts, and that Jewish craftsmen were organized into guilds. There was a large middle class, made up of Jewish traders, including some who owned their own ships and others who were involved in investment. A few Jews amassed tremendous wealth and lent money on interest. Under the Ptolemies Jews occupied government posts in Egypt, including tax collecting. All in all, Jews reflected the occupational distributions of the societies in which they lived and cannot be said to have attained the role of "economic catalyst" to which the Middle Ages, with its restrictions on Jewish occupations, would bring them.

RELIGIOUS LIFE

Only a few Jews in the Hellenistic Diaspora went so far as to apostasize from Judaism. A somewhat larger group seems to have become involved in syncretism, identifying the God of Israel with the chief pagan diety, a phenomenon which had grievous consequences in Judea. Some scholars have mistakenly considered the religion of the syncretists to have been the dominant Judaism of the Diaspora, but in fact this approach had few adherents, and for the most part, the Diaspora Jews were loyal to their ancestral ways and faith. At the same time, however, they eagerly sought to adapt and accommodate to the surroundings in which they lived, especially when they came to have the same educational background and occupations as their neighbors, a process that was abetted by the many shared ethical concepts of Judaism and the Greek philosophical tradition.

The writings of numerous Greek and Latin authors testify that the Jews of the Greco-Roman world observed such central commandments as the Sabbath, the laws regarding forbidden foods, and circumcision. The influence of the synagogues on many Greco-Roman pagans leads us to believe that they were well attended. Here Jews gathered to worship and to hear homilies which taught them how to synthesize Judaism with the prevailing culture. Synagogues were found throughout the Diaspora, often more than one in a community. Some were magnificent structures which were part of the complex of public buildings of their respective cities.

We cannot be certain of the language of prayer in Hellenistic synagogues. In all probability, at least the greatest part of the worship service was conducted in *koine* Greek, the dialect of the Hellenistic world. Evidence points to the use of psalms as part of the service, clearly in imitation of the Temple ritual. As for the reading of the Torah, it is virtually certain that Greek Bible texts, of which the Septuagint is an example, were in use. It is not known for sure, though, whether the formal Torah reading was conducted in Greek or took place from the Hebrew text with the Greek, much like the later Aramaic targums, serving as a translation. Tombstones indicate that Diaspora Jews had at least some knowledge of Hebrew. Moreover, a process of Hebraization can be observed in the later Roman and Byzantine periods as Hellenistic Judaism was pulled in two contradictory directions, toward Palestinian tannaitic Judaism on the one hand, and toward assimilation to the Christianized Roman world on the other.

Jews in the Greco-Roman world celebrated the Sabbath, as well as the annual cycle of festivals and new moons, just as did their brethren in Palestine. They gathered for festive communal meals and erected booths for the festival of Sukkot. Some communities observed local commemorative days as well. Strong ties to the Land of Israel were maintained. In the years before the destruction of the Temple, Jews from great distances streamed to the holy city for the pilgrimage festivals. Various Temple furnishings were donated by Diaspora Jews. Regular Temple taxes were collected throughout the Diaspora and sent to Palestine. After the destruction of the Temple, Diaspora communities continued to support the patriarchate in Palestine.

Nevertheless, some scholars have argued that an attenuation of ritual observance did occur in the Hellenistic world. A more serious threat to traditional Judaism came from philosophically oriented Jews who explained the Torah as an allegory and therefore maintained that the commandments did not have to be observed. Philo Judaeus, the Alexandrian, forcefully objected to this approach.

All in all, the Judaism of the Greco-Roman Diaspora set patterns of communal organization that would carry Jews through the next two thousand years. The collapse of Hellenistic culture and the rise of Christianity ultimately led to its decline. Yet in its heyday Hellenistic Judaism was vibrant and committed; its strength is best demonstrated by the many semi-proselytes who flocked to its institutions and by the rich literature it left.

ANTI-SEMITISM IN THE HELLENISTIC WORLD

The Hellenistic period saw the rise of many of the elements of classical anti-Semitism. From a later perspective, anti-Semitism has two basic features; one is economic and social, and the other is the motif of the Jew as Christ-killer. While the second, quite obviously, had to await the rise of Christianity to begin its ignominious career, the economic and social aspects began to surface in the Hellenistic Diaspora. Judaism was regarded as a barbarous superstition, and various canards were circulated describing its allegedly disgraceful beginnings. Among the main targets were Moses and the commandments, especially circumcision. Jews were said to be misanthropes who hated all other people, and it was claimed that there was an idol of an ass in the Holy of Holies. Even more damaging was the first blood libel, an accusation that Jews sacrificed a foreigner every seven years for ritual purposes.

It is always possible to advance explanations for anti-Semitism. We may speak of the economic role of the Jews, an aspect to some extent retrojected from medieval Jewish history. We may also note that many non-Jews saw their Jewish neighbors as strangers and resented the special privileges they enjoyed without becoming full members of the polis. Perhaps even more unacceptable was the Jewish refusal to worship the pagan gods, and, therefore, to join in the local city cults.

Yet anti-Semitism seems to transcend history; and no explanation suffices to explain it. New circumstances change some of its details from time to time, but the dominant motifs and accusations persist no matter how often they are shown to be false and no matter how much Jews may assimilate. In Hellenistic times, Jews lived in close relations with their neighbors, but they were soon to confront the most serious blood libel accusation of all, that of deicide. Ultimately, these tensions would lead to the Diaspora revolt of 115–117 C.E.

THE LITERATURE OF THE HELLENISTIC DIASPORA

The Jewish communities of the Greek-speaking world had an active cultural and religious life. Accordingly, they produced numerous literary texts, only some of which have been preserved for us, mostly through the efforts of the church fathers. These texts are of many different kinds, but a common thread runs through them, for they all represent an attempt to synthesize the ancient traditions of the people of Israel with the new "modern" life of the Hellenistic world.

The Septuagint

The Septuagint (often abbreviated LXX, "seventy") is the Hellenistic Greek version of the Bible. Its name derives from a legend, preserved in both the Letter of Aristeas (probably to be dated to the late second century B.C.E.) and talmudic sources, attributing its translation to seventy-two elders brought from Jerusalem to Alexandria by Ptolemy II Philadelphus (283–246 B.C.E.). This translation was preserved by the church and for most early Christians constituted what they termed the "Old Testament." The canon of the Septuagint was wider than that of the Hebrew Bible in that it included various apocryphal works, some of which will be taken up below. Greek Bibles were organized into sections based on a distinction between the genres of law, history, poetry, and prophecy. For this reason the Septuagint's order of books is radically different from that of the Hebrew Bible. The order of the Hebrew Bible is based on the date of canonization of each book and its subsequent placement in the Torah, Prophets, or Writings, and this reflects the degree of divine inspiration which the book or later tradition claims for its author.

The Septuagint began to take shape in the third century B.C.E. in response to the needs of the Alexandrian Jewish community. Initially all that was translated was a version of the Torah for worship and study. The translators may have included Palestinian scholars, and the project may even have been encouraged by the king. On the other hand, the text may have come about more informally, as an oral translation used in worship services, which later was edited and committed to writing. By the second century the books of the latter prophets, then the former, were translated as well. Some of the Writings had also been translated by the beginning of the second century B.C.E., whereas others were rendered into Greek only in the first century. The translations of the various biblical books circulated independently and in many differing manuscripts. The lack of a fixed, standard text may have been one of the factors that ultimately led the Greek-speaking Jews to abandon the Septuagint for other translations that emerged later. The differences between the Septuagint translation and the Hebrew text, which was taken as authoritative by the rabbis of the Yavnean period (ca. 80–100 C.E.), must have led to more strenuous objections to the use of this translation as time went on.

The Septuagint was not simply a literal translation. In many areas, the translators used Hellenistic Greek terms that made the text easier for Greek readers to understand but changed its meaning subtly. Elsewhere, the translators introduced Hellenistic concepts into the text. At times, they translated from Hebrew texts which differed from those current in Palestine, a

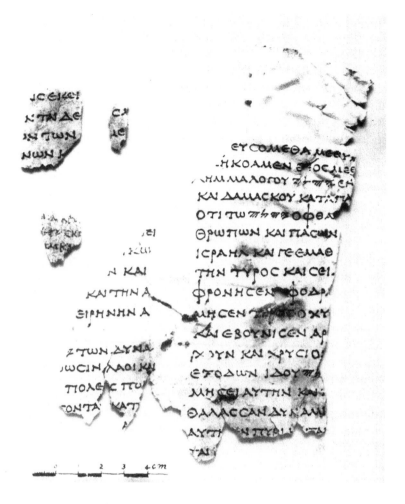

TWELVE PROPHETS SCROLL FROM NAḤAL ḤEVER. Among the many finds from the Judean Desert from the first part of the second century C.E. were fragments of a Greek translation of the Twelve Prophets found at Naḥal Ḥever, 7 km. south of Ein Gedi. Texts such as this were in use even in Palestine, indicating the presence there of some Greek-speaking, and perhaps considerably Hellenized, Jews. Note the writing of the Tetragrammaton (four lettered divine name) in ancient Hebrew script (in the 3rd and 5th lines). From Plate XX in E. Tov, *The Greek Minor Prophets Scroll from Naḥal Ḥever*, Discoveries in the Judaean Desert VIII (Oxford: Clarendon Press, 1990), *Courtesy of the Israel Antiquities Authority and Professor Emanuel Tov.*

matter now much clearer thanks to the evidence provided by the Dead Sea Scrolls. At other points, the Septuagint reflects knowledge of Palestinian exegetical traditions which are enshrined in rabbinic literature.

Some modern scholars have maintained that the Hebrew text of the Bible should be revised on the basis of the textual differences in the Greek translation. It is indeed true that certain readings of the Septuagint have been confirmed by the discovery of ancient manuscripts. Yet care must be exercised in view of the complex history of the Greek biblical text and the fact that differing biblical texts are known to have existed in ancient times. In recent years scholars have emphasized the significance of the Septuagint as a document of Hellenistic Judaism. Seen from this perspective it offers evidence of a long tradition of biblical exegesis in the Alexandrian Jewish community, shows the spiritual links between the Egyptian Diaspora and the Palestinian homeland, and illustrates how Greek-speaking Jews read and studied their sacred Scriptures in order to preserve their Jewishness in an alien environment.

Two new Greek translations were produced in the second century C.E. by Aquila the Proselyte and Theodotion, both of whom were Jews. These translations were faithful to the Hebrew texts declared authoritative by the Palestinian rabbis and to the emerging tannaitic exegesis. Evidence from the Dead Sea Scrolls shows that there had been earlier attempts to revise the Septuagint. Symmachus, who somewhat later translated the Hebrew Bible into more idiomatic Greek, may have been a Samaritan or a Christian or may have been Jewish. All of these translations illustrate the new requirements of the common era. The Jews needed a translation in accord with the now dominant rabbinic approach to Judaism; the Christians sought one that would mirror their interpretation of the Hebrew Scriptures.

Philo Judaeus

Hellenistic Jewish literature is dominated by a unique and overarching figure, the Alexandrian Jew Philo Judaeus (ca. 20 B.C.E.–ca. 50 C.E.). It was he who seized the opportunity to fuse Judaism systematically with the thought of the Hellenistic world in a corpus which today occupies some twenty-five hundred printed pages. This contribution would be passed on by the church fathers and virtually ignored by the Jewish people, only to be rediscovered by them during the Italian Renaissance.

Philo was born into a noble family in Alexandria and received an education both Jewish and Greek. In 38 or 39 C.E., when the Jewish community of Alexandria sent an embassy to the emperor Caligula in Rome because of the anti-Jewish riots that had taken place in the city, Philo was appointed the delegation's leader. Although their mission was unsuccessful, this shows the high regard in which he was held by his compatriots and his willingness to stand up for his people. Thereafter he continued his literary work until his death in about 50 C.E.

Philo wrote in an extremely discursive style, jumping back and forth between biblical exegesis, which endows most of his treatises with their form, and philosophical exposition, which provides the intellectual backdrop for his interpretations. His philosophy, much of it in the Platonic mold, is a blend of the personal God of the Hebrew Bible and the abstract, perfect deity required by Greek metaphysics. Both of these merge in the divine logos, the Word and Wisdom of the Supreme Being. The notion that the logos was the firstborn son of the deity led to the popularity of Philo among the early Christian fathers.

A number of Philo's works concern biblical narratives and are a mixture of legal and philosophical expositions. His *On the Creation* argues that the laws of the Bible accord with those of nature. The patriarchs Abraham, Isaac, and Jacob, as well as Joseph, are the subject of special treatises in which Philo deals with them as embodiments of the law and archetypes of virtue. In the *Life of Moses* Philo casts Moses as the ideal lawgiver, priest, and prophet in Platonic terms. His *On the Decalogue* and *Special Laws* are expositions of Jewish law and practice interpreted in Greek philosophical terms.

In *Allegorical Interpretation* Philo's Greek philosophical background is put to best use, for here he interprets the first seventeen chapters of Genesis as presenting a set of philosophical and even quasi-mystical concepts. Purely philosophical issues are raised in a number of treatises, such as *On the Eternality of the World* and *On Providence*. *Against Flaccus* details the pogrom against the Jews in 38 C.E., and *On the Embassy to*

Gaius reports on Philo's above-mentioned trip to Rome to protest the pogrom, a journey which coincided with the emperor's order to erect a statue in the Jerusalem Temple.

Philo believed in a transcendent God. His concept of the logos bridges the gap between man and God, making possible the close relationship of the Jewish people to God, as described in the Bible. The search for an understanding of God becomes the goal of Jewish piety. The Bible, allegorically understood, is an account of the soul's striving for God. Accordingly, Philo explains the Bible on two levels, the literal and the symbolic. When the literal was unacceptable to him, he used only the allegorical. This method allowed him to radically recast the biblical narratives in Hellenistic garb. Throughout his work Philo calls for the strict observance of Jewish law, which he sometimes interprets in a unique manner and sometimes in accord with views also evidenced in Palestinian sources of his day.

Also significant is his view of the soul. According to Philo, the soul has descended into the world of matter, and it is up to each individual, by stripping himself of earthly passions, to bring about the his soul's ascent to God. This process is helped by the striving for intellectual appreciation of God, but it is clear from Philo's descriptions that the final stage is that of a mystical experience of union with the Divine. Indeed, for him, prophecy is an act of ecstasy, in which man receives the effulgence of divine light.

SUMMARY

Diaspora Judaism in the Greco-Roman world was a rich and flourishing culture for some four or five centuries. It attempted, in a variety of social, economic, and religious spheres, to attain a synthesis of the Jewish and the Hellenic that would enable it to thrive in a Hellenistic setting while yet preserving and nourishing the Jewish tradition. Ultimately, the communities of the Hellenistic Diaspora disappeared, some to Christianity, some to assimilation, some as casualties of the Diaspora revolt, and more to the emerging rabbinic tradition which was spreading beyond the borders of Palestine. By contrast, the Babylonian Dispersion, virtually unexposed to Hellenism and its pressures, became the crucible from which eventually emerged the Babylonian Talmud, the greatest monument to rabbinic teaching.

6
Sectarianism in the Second Commonwealth

The years immediately following the Maccabean revolt and victory are known, after the name of the victorious dynasty, as the Hasmonean period. Like the Roman period, which immediately followed, it was distinguished by a tendency toward what, for want of a better term, we call sectarianism. By this we mean a tendency to split into competing ideologies (sects) each vying with the others to win over the wider Jewish community to its own brand of Judaism. The designation of these groups as "sects" and of this phenomenon as "sectarianism" is admittedly problematic, since these two terms usually assume a dominant or normative stream from which others have diverged. Rabbinic tradition claimed such a status for Pharisaic Judaism but it is difficult to consider a minority, no matter how influential, to be a mainstream. Nevertheless, the alternative of identifying these various ideologies as independent "Judaisms" ignores the vast body of commonality which united them around adherence to the law of the Torah. Indeed, what divided the groups from one another was only a small part of their faith and practice; what brought them together as a nation, civilization, and religion far outweighed the differences, which tend to be exaggerated in the sources, so often written as polemics rather than as objective appraisals. With these considerations in mind, then, we will examine the problem of sectarianism in this chapter. First, however, we will sketch the political history which serves as the background for these developments.

THE HASMONEAN DYNASTY

By 152 B.C.E. Jonathan the Hasmonean had firmly established himself as ruler over Judea. From then until the Roman conquest of Judea in 63 B.C.E., the descendants of Judah the Maccabee ruled over the Land of Israel. Jonathan took advantage of the instability in the Seleucid Empire to expand his territory beyond Judea proper to include southern Samaria and the southern coastal cities of Ekron and the environs, originally centers of Hellenistic culture. In 143 B.C.E. he was murdered by Tryphon, a pretender to the Seleucid throne.

Jonathan was succeeded by his brother Simon. In 142 B.C.E. Simon gained recognition from the Seleucid king Demetrius II Nicator (145–138 and again in 129–125 B.C.E.). Demetrius's grant of tax exemption to the Hasmonean state, by which he intended to secure its support, was the final step in the process whereby Judea gained total independence. Like his brother Jonathan before him, Simon served as both temporal ruler and high priest. A public assembly in 140 B.C.E. gave formal legal standing to this arrangement and to the hereditary succession of his sons to the same offices. He continued the expansionist policy begun by Jonathan, taking the harbor at Jaffa in order to ensure Judea's access to the sea. He also continued the extirpation of paganism from the land. His crowning achievement was

THE HASMONEAN PERIOD
(all dates are B.C.E.)

152	Jonathan established as high priest
143	Jonathan murdered
142	Simon assumes rule
141	Capture of Akra by Simon
140	Public assembly confirms Simon as high priest and ruler
134	Murder of Simon
134–104	John Hyrcanus
104–3	Aristobulus I
103–76	Alexander Janneus
76–67	Salome Alexandra
67–63	War between Hyrcanus II and Aristobulus II
63	Roman conquest by Pompey

the dislodging of the Seleucid garrison which had continued to occupy the Akra in Jerusalem. When Antiochus VII Sidetes (138–129 B.C.E.), the Seleucid king, attempted to force Simon to give up the territories he had conquered, Simon defeated him squarely. Simon's reign came to an end in 134 B.C.E., when his son-in-law, apparently with the help of the Seleucids, murdered him and two of his sons.

Simon's surviving son, John Hyrcanus (Yohanan in Hebrew), succeeded him. In the first two years of his reign, John was involved in a war with the Seleucids. Because they needed his help in their campaign against the Parthians, they offered to negotiate and the two sides came to terms, the Seleucids recognizing John's rule and the Hasmoneans indemnifying them for territory they had conquered. After the death of Antiochus VII in 129 B.C.E. the ensuing collapse of the Seleucid Empire allowed John to regain complete independence and assert his authority over the entire Land of Israel. Expanding to the south, he conquered Idumea and forced its people to convert to Judaism. He also captured territory in Transjordan, defeated the Hellenistic cities, and conquered the Samaritans. He died in 104 B.C.E.

Simon's son Aristobulus I succeeded him, but reigned only for one year, from 104 to 103 B.C.E. He continued his father's conquests, subduing the Itureans in the north and converting them to Judaism, and gaining control over the Galilee. After treating his mother with the utmost cruelty, imprisoning three of his brothers, and having another brother, Antigonus, killed, he died of remorse and a painful disease. He was the first of the Hasmoneans to style himself "king."

Alexander Janneus (Yannai), the brother of Aristobulus, came to power in 103 B.C.E. when he married Aristobulus' widow, Salome Alexandra (Shelomzion). During his reign, which ended with his death in 76 B.C.E., the remaining non-Jewish cities in Palestine were conquered. He and John Hyrcanus, the rulers whose conquests truly exemplified the Hasmonean achievement, together expanded the borders of Judea to encompass the entire Land of Israel.

There was another side to the story, however. The Maccabees had not fought only to free the Jews from foreign domination, or

The Hasmoneans (2nd-1st cent. B.C.E.)

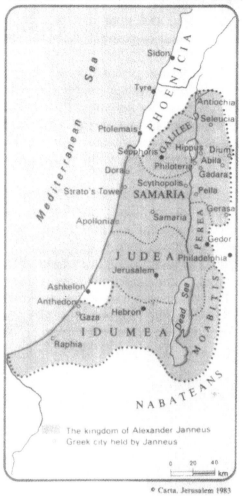

for power and wealth. They had risen initially against elements in the Jewish population who sought to Hellenize themselves and their countrymen. Their struggle was transformed into a war of independence against the Seleucid Empire only when it sought to aid the Hellenizers by persecuting Jews and Judaism. Yet gradually, the Hasmonean descendants of the Maccabees themselves acquired the trappings of Hellenism. They began to conduct their courts in Hellenistic fashion and were estranged from Jewish observance. This transition went way beyond the need of any monarch at that time to make use of Hellenistic-style coinage, diplomacy, and bureaucracy. The Hasmoneans employed foreign mercenaries to protect them from their own people.

Opposition to the Hasmonean house came from a variety of corners. First, they had never made peace with remnants of the old-line Hellenizers among the landed aristocracy. Second, the Pharisees (about whom more will be said later in this chapter) opposed the concentration in Hasmonean hands of both temporal and religious power, demanding that the Hasmoneans relinquish the high priesthood, since they were not of the proper high priestly lineage. Third, other groups, whose point of view is represented in some of the Dead Sea Scrolls, accepted the legitimacy of the Hasmoneans as high priests but condemned them for also holding political power.

All these factors had already led Alexander Janneus to prepare his wife, Salome Alexandra, for the succession and to recommend to her that she compromise with the dynasty's opponents. This she did effectively for some nine years until her death in 67 B.C.E.. Yet she failed effectively to designate her successor, and her sons, Hyrcanus II and Aristobulus II, fought

THE HASMONEAN FAMILY

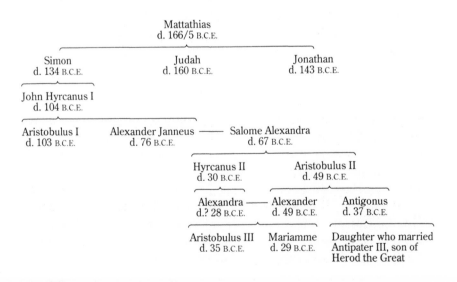

one another for the crown. Both eventually appealed to the Romans. By this time Rome was already in Syria and positioned to swallow up Judea. Aristobulus was remembered by later sources as a great hero, a man possessed of the spirit of the Maccabees, seeking nothing less than freedom from foreign rule. Hyrcanus was pictured as a weakling, desiring power for power's sake, at any cost to himself and his nation. In 63 B.C.E., as the two fought with one another, each turned to the Roman general Pompey, in Syria. After a series of negotiations, Pompey decided to capitalize on the situation by satisfying the long-standing Roman desire to dominate Palestine, the strategic land bridge between Africa and Asia. He played the brothers off against each other for a time, then marched on Jerusalem and took it by storm.

Thus ended the Hasmonean dynasty. The Romans were now the country's real rulers. They awarded the high priesthood to Hyrcanus II and imprisoned Aristobulus II. He and his sons would for years show themselves to be true Maccabean descendants, repeatedly escaping Roman imprisonment to seek against all odds to wrest Judea back from the Romans. But the Hasmonean star had set.

PHARISEES AND SADDUCEES

It is against the background just sketched that the phenomenon of religious sectarianism came to fruition. There had been divergences in Israelite religion even in the biblical period, and in many cases the very same issues that had led to conflicts in biblical times became the basis for disagreements and strife in the Hasmonean period. Yet the nature of the sectarianism of which we are speaking is very different. In biblical times, the fundamental question was whether the God of Israel was to be worshipped exclusively, or whether a syncretistic identification of Him with Canaanite gods and cult was to take place. To the Judeans, the same point was at stake in their rejection of the Samaritans and the subsequent schism. It had resurfaced earlier in the Hellenistic period, in the years leading up to the Hellenistic reform and the persecutions of Antiochus IV. The nation had rallied behind the Maccabees precisely because, like the biblical prophets and the deuteronomic editors of the historical books of the Bible, they would not tolerate any tinkering with the exclusive monotheism to which they adhered.

Now, however, the debates would all take place within a new context. Matters would revolve around two axes. First, while it was now accepted without question that the canonized Torah was authoritative, there were many differences of opinion as to its interpretation. Second, while extreme Hellenism had been rejected, the exact parameters of assimilation or Hellenization and of separatism and pietism were still to be determined. Ultimately, these questions would be resolved only after the destruction of the Temple with the rise of Rabbinic Judaism. For the present they would be played out, not in the ivory tower of religious disputation, but in the political, social, and even economic affairs of the Hasmonean period.

Our sources suggest that the Hasmonean priest-kings relied on a body of advisors or councilors called the Gerousia. This body was composed of a shaky coalition of Pharisees and Sadducees, the two groups which were most active in the political life of the state. Like the other groups to be described here, they also had distinct religious ideologies, as well as social characteristics.

The Pharisees

The Pharisees derived their name from the Hebrew *perushim*, "separate." This designation most probably refers to their separation from ritually impure food and from the tables of the common people, later termed the *'am ha-'areṣ* ("people of the land") in rabbinic sources, who were not scrupulous regarding the laws of levitical purity and tithes. The term may originally have been a negative designation used by the opponents of the Pharisees. Tannaitic sources describe those who observed the laws of purity as *haverim*, "associates," and groups of such people as *havurot*. The *haverim* are contrasted with the *'am ha-'areṣ*. Although most historians assume these groups to have been Pharisaic, the sources never associate the terms "Pharisee" and *haver*. In rabbinic sources, the Pharisees are sometimes designated as "the sages," an anachronism resulting from the view of the rabbis that they were the continuators of the

Pharisaic tradition. Although the influence of the Pharisees grew steadily until they came to dominate the religious life of the Jewish people, they are said to have numbered only six thousand in Herodian times.

By and large, the Pharisees had three major characteristics. First, they represented primarily the middle and lower classes. Second, and perhaps as a consequence of their social status, they were really not Hellenized and seem to have remained primarily Near Eastern in culture. To be sure, they may have adopted certain Greek words or intellectual approaches, but they viewed as authoritative only what they regarded as the ancient traditions of Israel. Third, they accepted what they termed the "tradition of the fathers," nonbiblical laws and customs said to have been passed down through the generations. These teachings supplemented the written Torah and were a part of what the rabbis would later call the oral law. They are said to have been extremely scrupulous in observing the law and to have been expert in its interpretation.

In a number of significant teachings the Pharisees appear to have espoused views that were later incorporated in the rabbinic tradition. The Pharisees accepted the notions of the immortality of the soul and of reward and punishment after death, both of which the Sadducees denied. The Pharisees are said to have believed in angels, another belief which the Sadducees denied. The Pharisees accepted the idea of divine providence, believing that God allowed human beings free will but could play a role in human affairs. The Sadducees rejected totally the notion of divine interference in the affairs of man. To them free will was complete and inviolable. In contrast, the Essenes maintained a belief in absolute predestination, as did the sect of the Dead Sea Scrolls. Although these views are recounted in Greek philosophical garb by Josephus, our only source for the theological disputes between the two groups, the actual points of view emerge from varying interpretations of the biblical tradition, and, therefore, the basic outlines of the controversy may be accepted as authentic.

From the accounts available to us, it appears that the Pharisees were divided over one of the most burning issues of the period. Some advocated an accommodationist policy toward the government, so long as it allowed them to practice Jewish traditions in the manner required by the Pharisaic view. Others maintained that no government was acceptable, whether controlled by non-Jews or by nonobservant Jews, so long as it was not built on the Pharisaic notion of Torah observance, and they called upon their compatriots to rise in revolt. This dispute can be traced throughout the history of Pharisaism and continued in Rabbinic Judaism, becoming central in the two Jewish revolts against Rome.

In the extant sources, the Pharisees first appear by name during the reign of Jonathan, brother of Judah the Maccabee (ca. 150 B.C.E.). Many scholars have attempted to identify the Pharisees with, or to locate their origins in, the Ḥasidim who were allies of Judah in the Maccabean Revolt. This theory, however, cannot be substantiated. Further, our knowledge of the Ḥasidim is very limited. It is probable that they were not really a sect or a party, but rather a loose association of pietists, as denoted by this term in later talmudic literature.

Rabbinic sources trace the Pharisees back to the Men of the Great Assembly, who are said to have provided Israel's religious leadership in the Persian and early Hellenistic periods. Some modern scholars have associated the Soferim ("Scribes") with the Men of the Great Assembly. The Soferim would then be forerunners of the Pharisaic movement. Unfortunately, the historical evidence does not allow any definite conclusions here. All that can be said is that the Pharisees could not have emerged suddenly, full-blown, in the Hasmonean period. Their theology and organization must have been in formation somewhat earlier. How much earlier and in what form, we cannot say.

In any case, the Pharisees appear in Hasmonean times as part of the Gerousia in coalition with the Sadducees and other elements of society. Here they sought to advance their vision of the way the Jewish people should live and govern themselves. Under John Hyrcanus and Alexander Janneus, conditions led them further and further into the political arena. As the Hasmoneans became increasingly Hellenized, the Pharisees expressed greater opposition to them. Under John Hyrcanus, there was a decisive Hasmonean tilt toward the Sadducees. In the time of Alexander Janneus the Pharisees were in open warfare with the king, who was consequently defeated by the Seleucid Demetrius III Eukairos (96–88 B.C.E.) in 89 B.C.E. This rout led to a reconciliation between the king and the Pharisees. During the reign of Salome Alexandra they were the dominant element, in control of the affairs of the nation, although the extent of their influence has been exaggerated by many scholars.

There has been considerable controversy regarding the extent to which the later rabbinic claims that the Pharisees dominated the ritual of the Jerusalem Temple ought to be taken at face value. Recently, the trend has been to discount these reports as a later reshaping of history in light of post-destruction reality. Sources soon to be published from the Dead Sea Scrolls now require reevaluation of the entire question. These texts indicate that the views assigned to the Pharisees in a number of mishnaic disputes are precisely those which were in practice in the Jerusalem Temple. Whether the dominance of the Pharisaic view was due to the political power of the Pharisees, or whether their positions were indeed commonly held views in the Hasmonean period, cannot be determined with certainty.

Over and over Josephus stresses the popularity of the Pharisees among the people. This must certainly have been the case in the last years of the Second Temple period, for which Josephus had first-hand experience, although his pro-Pharisaic prejudices must be acknowledged. Their popularity, together with the unique approach to Jewish law which they espoused, laid the groundwork for the eventual ascendancy of the Pharisees in Jewish political and religious life. The oral law concept which grew from the Pharisaic "tradition of the fathers" provided Judaism with the ability to adapt to the new and varied circumstances it would face in talmudic times and later. As such, Pharisaism would become Rabbinic Judaism, the basis for all subsequent Jewish life and civilization.

The Sadducees

The Sadducees also were a recognizable group by about 150 B.C.E. They were a predominantly aristocratic group. Most of them, in fact, were apparently priests or those who had intermarried with the high priestly families. They tended to be moderate Hellenizers whose primary loyalty was to the religion of Israel but whose culture was greatly influenced by the environment in which they lived. The Sadducees derived their name from that of Zadok, the high priest of the Jerusalem Temple in the time of Solomon. The Zadokite family of high priests had served at the head of the priesthood throughout First Temple times, except when foreign worship was brought into the Temple, and during Second Temple times until the Hasmoneans took control of the high priesthood. Ezekiel 44:9–16 had assigned the priestly duties exclusively to this clan.

The Sadducees rejected the "tradition of the fathers" which the Pharisees considered as law. For this reason the later rabbinic sources picture them as rejecting the oral law. The notion of some church fathers that the Sadducees accepted only the Torah as authoritative, rejecting the Prophets and the emerging corpus of Writings, is unsubtantiated by any earlier sources.

It is difficult to date the many differences which tannaitic texts ascribe to the Pharisees and Sadducees. Some of these are preserved only in very late post-talmudic sources, but those in the mishnaic materials are of greater interest. The Sadducees required compensation for injuries done by a person's servant, whereas the Pharisees required it only in the case of one's animals, according to their interpretation of Exod. 21:32, 35–36. The Sadducees required that false witnesses be executed only when the accused had already been put to death because of their testimony (Deut. 19:19–21). The Pharisees imposed this penalty only when the accused had not been executed. The Sadducees criticized the inconsistencies in the Pharisaic interpretations of the purity laws, and the Pharisees regarded Sadducean women as menstrually impure as a result of following improper interpretations of these laws. In general, the Sadducees saw the purity laws as referring to the Temple and its priests, and saw no reason for extending them into the daily life of all Israel, a basic pillar of the Pharisaic approach.

A fundamental question is why the Sadducees disagreed so extensively with the Pharisaic tradition and, therefore, how they came to disagree on so many matters of Jewish law. Later Jewish tradition sought to claim that all the differences revolved

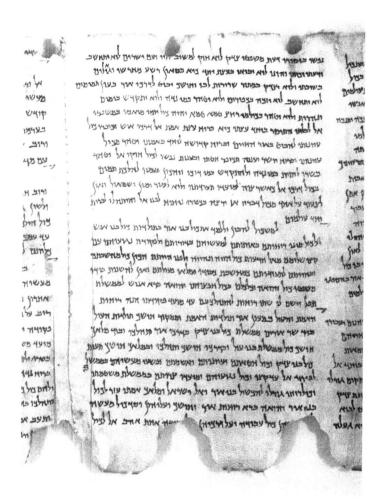

MANUAL OF DISCIPLINE. The Dead Sea sectarians, identified by many scholars at Essenes, were guided in their lives by a text entitled the *Manual of Discipline* or the *Rule of the Community*. This text set out how members were accepted, their obligations, the conduct of the affairs of the sect, basic theological beliefs, and the code of punishments. This scroll was one of the original group of scrolls found in 1947 by Bedouin in the Qumran Caves and serves as a basic text for study of the Qumran sect. *Courtesy of the Shrine of the Book of the Israel Museum.*

around the Sadducean rejection of the oral law. Based on this assumption, modern scholars have argued that the Sadducees were strict literalists who followed the plain meaning of the words of the Torah. Yet such an approach would not explain most of the views on legal matters that were attributed to the Sadducees.

Recent discoveries from the Dead Sea caves have aided greatly in this respect. One text, written in the form of a letter purporting to be from the founders of the Dead Sea sect, who were apparently closely related to the Sadducees, to the leaders of the Jerusalem establishment, lists some twenty-two areas of legal disagreement. Comparison of these with the Pharisee-Sadducee disputes recorded in rabbinic literature has led to the conclusion that the writers of this "letter" took the views attributed to the Sadducees while their opponents in the Jerusalem priestly establishment held the views attributed later to the Pharisees. Examination of this document and related materials leads to the conclusion that Sadducees had their own methods of biblical exegesis and accordingly derived laws which were different from those of the Pharisees and their supporters.

The Sadducees also differed with the Pharisees on theological questions. As already mentioned, they denied the notion of reward and punishment after death as well as the immortality of the soul, ideas accepted by the Pharisees. They did not believe in angels in the supernatural sense, although they must have acknowledged the many divine "messengers" mentioned in the Bible. To them, since man had absolute free will, God did not exercise control over the affairs of mankind.

The Sadducean party cannot be said to have come into being at any particular point. The priestly aristocracy, which traced its roots to First Temple times, had increased greatly in power in the Persian and Hellenistic periods, since the temporal as well as the spiritual rule of the nation was in its hands. Some priests had been involved in the extreme Hellenization leading up to the Maccabean revolt, but most of the Sadducean lower clergy had remained loyal to the Torah and the ancestral way of life.

In the aftermath of the revolt, a small and devoted group of Sadducean priests probably formed the body that eventually became the Dead Sea sect. They were unwilling to tolerate the replacement of the Zadokite high priest with a Hasmonean which took place in 152 B.C.E. Further, they disagreed with the Jerusalem priesthood on many points of Jewish law. Recent research indicates that soon after the Hasmonean takeover of the high priesthood, this group repaired to Qumran on the shore of the Dead Sea. (The complex question of the identification of the Qumran sect is taken up below.) Other moderately Hellenized Sadducees remained in Jerusalem, and it was they who were termed Sadducees, in the strict sense of the word, by Josephus in his descriptions of the Hasmonean period and by the later rabbinic traditions. They continued to be a key element in the Hasmonean aristocracy, supporting the priest-kings and joining with the Pharisees in the Gerousia. After dominating this body for most of the reign of John Hyrcanus and that of Alexander Janneus, they suffered a major political setback when Salome Alexandra turned so thoroughly to the Pharisees. Thereafter the Sadducees regained power in the Herodian era, when they made common cause with the Herodian dynasty. In the end, it was a group of Sadducean lower priests, by deciding to end the daily sacrifice for the Roman emperor, who took the step that set off the full-scale revolt against Rome in 66 C.E.

Closely allied to the Sadducees were the Boethusians, who seem to have held views similar to those of the Sadducees. Most scholars ascribe the origin of the Boethusians to Simeon ben Boethus, appointed high priest by Herod in 24 B.C.E. so that he would have sufficient status for Herod to marry his daughter Mariamme (II). This theory is completely unproven, and certain parallels between Boethusian rulings and material in the Dead Sea Scrolls argue for a considerably earlier date. There certainly were some differences between the Sadducees and the Boethusians, but the latter appear to have been a subgroup or an offshoot of the Sadducean group.

The most central of the disputes recorded in rabbinic literature as having separated the Boethusians from the Pharisees pertained to the calendar. The Boethusians held that the first offering of the Omer (barley sheaf, see Lev. 23:9–14) had to take place on a Sunday rather than on the second day of Passover, in accord with Lev. 23:11, "on the morrow of the Sabbath." To ensure that this festival be observed on the proper day of the week, a calendar was adopted which, like the one known from the Dead Sea sect and the pseudepigraphical Book of Jubilees, was based on both solar months and solar years. Following this calendar, the holiday of Shavuot (Pentecost) would always fall on a Sunday. While this approach seemed to accord better with the literal interpretation of the words "on the morrow of the Sabbath," the Pharisees could accept neither the innovative solar calendar (the biblical calendar was based on lunar months) nor the interpretation on which it was based. To them, "Sabbath" here meant festival. (The attribution of this Boethusian view to the Sadducees by some scholars results from confusion in the manuscripts of rabbinic texts.)

The Sadducean approach certainly had a major impact on political and religious developments in the Judaism of the Second Temple period. Sadducean offshoots played a leading role in the formation of the Dead Sea sect, which will be discussed below. There is evidence that some Sadducean traditions remained in circulation long enough to influence the Karaite sect, which came to the fore in the eighth century C.E. Yet otherwise, with the destruction of the Temple in 70 C.E., the Sadducees ceased to be a factor in Jewish history. The sacrificial system, in which they had played so leading a role, was no longer practiced. Their power base, the Jerusalem Temple, was gone, and their strict constructionism augured poorly for the adaptation of Judaism to the new surroundings and circumstances of the years ahead.

APOCALYPTICS AND ASCETICS

The Pharisees and the Sadducees were the major participants in the Jewish religious and political affairs of Greco-Roman Palestine. In fact, the gradual transfer of influence and power from the priestly Sadducees to the learned Pharisees went hand in hand with the transition from Temple to Torah which characterized the Judaism of this period. At the same time, a number of sects with apocalyptic or ascetic tendencies were part of the texture of Palestinian Judaism. Some of these had a profound role in creating the backdrop against which Christianity arose. Others encouraged the messianic visions that twice led the Jews into revolt against Rome. Still others served as the locus for the development of mystical ideas that would eventually penetrate Rabbinic Judaism. Each of these groups was characterized by the extreme dedication of its members to its own interpretation of the Torah and associated teachings it had received.

Essenes

The Essenes, a sect noted for its piety and distinctive theology, were known in Greek as *Essenoi* or *Essaioi*. Numerous suggestions have been made regarding the etymology of the name, among which are derivations from Syriac *ḥase'*, "pious," Aramaic *'asaia'*, "healers," Greek *hosios*, "holy," and Hebrew *ḥasha'im*, "silent ones." The very fact that so many suggestions have been made, and that none has carried a scholarly consensus, shows that the derivation of the term cannot be established with certainty. The most recent theory, and also the most probable, holds that this name was borrowed from the designation of a group of devotees of the cult of Artemis in Asia Minor because their demeanor and dress somewhat resembled those of the group in the Land of Israel.

Until the twentieth century, the Essenes were known only from Greek sources, primarily from Philo and Josephus. Since the discovery of the Dead Sea Scrolls in 1947, a consensus has developed which identifies the sect of the scrolls with the Essenes described by the two Greek authors. Although the term "Essene" does not appear in the Qumran scrolls, this view has led many scholars to interpret the Greek texts describing the Essenes in light of the scrolls, and the scrolls in light of the Greek texts. This circular method does not allow for an objective view of the Essenes. Only after the evidence regarding them is presented can we compare it with what is said in the Dead Sea Scrolls.

There were about four thousand Essenes according to the testimony of Philo and Josephus. Apparently, they were scattered in communities throughout Palestine, although there is some evidence that they avoided the larger cities. According to the Roman author Pliny, there was an Essene settlement between Jericho and Ein Gedi on the western shore of the Dead Sea. This location in the vicinity of Qumran, which immediately brings to mind the settlement adjacent to the caves where the

Dead Sea Scrolls were unearthed, has led many scholars to identify the Essenes of Philo and Josephus with the sect which copied and hid the Dead Sea Scrolls.

Only adult males could enter the Essene sect, although children were educated in the ways of the community. The Essenes were organized under officials to whom obedience was required. Members who transgressed could be expelled from the community by the court of one hundred. Aspiring members received three items, a hatchet, an apron, and a white garment, and had to undergo a detailed initiation process which included a year of probation. They were then eligible for the ritual ablutions. Subsequently, candidates had to undergo a further two years of probation, after which time they were to swear an oath, the only oath which the Essenes permitted. In the final stages of their initiation, the candidates bound themselves by oath to be pious toward God, just to men, and honest with their fellow Essenes, to properly transmit the teachings of the sect, and to maintain the secrecy by which the doctrines of the sect were guarded from outsiders. Among the teachings to be kept secret were the names of the angels. The initiants were then able to participate in the sect's communal meals and were considered full-fledged members.

The Essenes practiced community of property. Upon admission, new members turned their property over to the group, whose elected officials administered it for the benefit of all. Hence, all members shared wealth equally with no distinctions between rich and poor. Members earned income for the group through various occupations, including agriculture and crafts. The Essenes avoided commerce and the manufacture of weapons. All earnings were turned over to officials who distributed funds for the purchase of necessities and for taking care of older or ill members of the community. Not only did the Essenes provide aid to their own members, but they also dispensed charity throughout the country. Traveling members were taken care of by special officers in each town.

Characteristic of the Essenes was their moderation and avoidance of luxury. Wealth was only a means for providing the necessities of life. They applied this approach to their eating and drinking habits and their clothes, and for this reason they did not anoint themselves with oil. Asceticism manifested itself most strongly among those Essenes who were celibate. On the other hand, it appears that in many cases celibacy was not absolute, but was embarked upon later in life, after the individual had had children.

The Essenes began their day with prayer. Their attitude toward the Jerusalem Temple was ambivalent. While they accepted the notion of a central place of worship in Jerusalem, they disagreed with the manner in which the purity and sacrificial laws were understood by the Temple authorities. Thus they sent voluntary offerings to the Temple but did not themselves participate in its sacrificial worship. After praying, they worked at their occupations. Later, they assembled for purification rituals and a communal meal which was prepared by priests and eaten while wearing special garments. After the members took their places in silence, the baker and cook distributed the food in order of status. A priest would recite Grace before and after the meal. The community then returned to work and came together once again in the evening for another meal. At the setting of the sun, they recited prayers to God.

Ritual purity was greatly emphasized. Ablutions were required not only before communal meals but also after relieving oneself and after coming in contact with a nonmember or a novice. Members were extremely careful about attending to natural functions modestly. They bathed often in order to maintain ritual purity and refrained from expectorating. They customarily wore white garments and regarded modesty of dress as very important.

The Essenes are said to have believed in unalterable destiny. They studied the Bible and interpreted it allegorically. Noteworthy was their stringency in matters of Sabbath observance. Essene teachings were recorded in books which the members were duty bound to pass on with great care. They were reported to be experts on medicinal roots and the properties of stones, the healing powers of which they claimed to have derived from ancient writings.

Most notable among their doctrines was the belief in the immortality of the soul. According to Josephus they held that only the soul survived after death, a concept of Hellenistic origin. Josephus asserts that in this respect their belief was very close to that of the Pharisees, but many scholars have seen the Essenes as strongly influenced by such contemporary Hellenistic trends as Pythagorianism.

Josephus first mentions the Essenes in his account of the reign of Jonathan the Hasmonean (152–143 B.C.E.) as part of a short description of the religious trends at that time. According to Josephus, Essenes participated in the war against Rome in 66–73 C.E., and some were tortured by the Romans during the revolt. With the destruction of the country following the unsuccessful uprising, the Essenes disappeared from the stage of history.

The Dead Sea Sect

The Dead Sea or Qumran sect claimed to have the only correct interpretation of the Torah. Like other apocalyptic movements of the day, the sect believed that the messianic era was about to dawn. Only those had been predestined to share in the end of days and had lived according to the ways of the sect would fight the final victorious battle against the forces of evil. In order to prepare for the coming age, the members of the sect led what they considered to be a life of purity and holiness at their center near the caves at Qumran on the shore of the Dead Sea.

According to the sect's own description of its history, it had come into existence when its earliest members decided to separate themselves from the corrupt Judaism of Jerusalem. The founders of the sect, apparently Zadokite priests, left Jerusalem to set up a refuge at Qumran.

The sect was organized along rigid lines. There was an elaborate initiation procedure lasting several years during which members were progressively admitted to the sect's ritually pure banquets. Members were expected to abide by detailed rules in addition to living according to the sect's interpretation of Jewish law. Decisions regarding the sect's laws and ordinances were made by the sectarian assembly. The sect had a prescribed system of courts to deal with violations of its law. New laws were derived through regularly occurring sessions of biblical exegesis which the sect believed to be divinely inspired.

Annual covenant-renewal ceremonies took place in which the

members were mustered in order of their status in the chain of sectarian authority. A similar mustering was part of the sect's preparations for the eschatological battle. The Qumran sect believed that in the end of days, which was to dawn immediately, it and the angels would defeat all the nations and the evildoers of Israel. Two messiahs would then appear, a Davidic messiah who was to be the temporal authority, and a priestly messiah descended from Aaron, who was to take charge of the restored sacrificial cult. They were both to preside over a great messianic banquet. The sect's members periodically ate meals in ritual purity in imitation of this final banquet.

The scrolls refute the common view that the sectarians of Qumran were celibate. The sect maintained a strictly solar calendar rather than the solar year–lunar month calendar utilized by all other Jews. Although the principle of private ownership of property was maintained, members of the sect could freely use each other's possessions.

We have already noted that after the discovery of the Dead Sea Scrolls, most scholars took the view that these documents were the library of Essenes who had settled at Qumran. Indeed, there are many parallels between the sect described by the Greek sources and the sect of the scrolls from Qumran. The two groups had similar initiation ceremonies, although the procedure described in the classical sources diverges in some respects from that of the Qumran texts. According to our sources, the Essenes seem to have eaten communal meals regularly. The Qumran texts, however, envisage only occasional communal meals. The Essenes held all property in common, whereas at Qumran property was used in common but owned privately. The purity observances of the Essenes, although paralleled at Qumran, were not unusual among the sects of this period.

The main weakness of this identification is that the word "Essene" or its equivalent is not present in the Qumran scrolls, whereas the phrase "Sons of Zadok" which often designates the sect links it with the Sadducees. In addition, there are many small discrepancies between the texts describing the Essenes and the Dead Sea Scrolls, and there is no evidence that the Essenes had any apocalyptic beliefs. Nor do we know that they used a calendar of solar months like the one the Qumran sect

THE QUMRAN RUINS. This view shows part of the ruins of Qumran, occupied from after 135 B.C.E. until 68 C.E. by the group of Jews who left the Dead Sea Scrolls in the surrounding caves. This is the room which was the storge area for the vessels which were used to serve the several hundred inhabitants at the communal meals of the group. These meals were open only to those who fulfilled a rigorous set of qualifications regarding piety and knowledge and who adhered to the sect's laws of ritual purity. This room was part of the complex which functioned as the main center for the Qumran sect, members of which were also located throughout the Land of Israel. *Photo by Lawrence H. Schiffman.*

followed. Those who identify the Dead Sea sect with the Essenes reconcile these minor differences by claiming that Josephus and Philo had the sensibilities of their Greek-speaking audiences in mind when they described the Essenes and therefore omitted apocalypticism because it could be connected with sedition against the Roman Empire.

If the two groups are to be identified as one and the same, then the Qumran evidence may be used to fill in the picture derived from the classical sources. If not, we would have to reckon with two sects, with similar teachings and ways of life. Palestine in the Second Commonwealth period was replete with sects and movements, each contributing to the religious ferment of the times. Josephus himself makes clear that what he calls the Essene "philosophy" was composed of various groups. If, indeed, the Dead Sea community was an Essene sect, perhaps it was an offshoot of Essenes who differed in many ways from those described in the sources.

SUMMARY

The groups we have studied were the major sects of Second Temple times. Along with the minor groups whose literature survived in the apocrypha and pseudepigrapha, as well as some whose names alone are known, the major sects participated in a political and religious ferment throughout their existence. Clearly, Second Temple Judaism included a variety of competing political and religious ideologies. The destruction of the nation and its Temple and the attendant loss of Jewish political independence in the Great Revolt of 66–73 C.E. once and for all settled many of the issues in conflict. The Sadducees had lost their power base, and the Essenes and Dead Sea sectarians had been decimated, and their centers destroyed. Extreme apocalypticism had been discredited. Some sectarian teachings contributed to the rise of Christianity, but we will not discuss this until we have examined the literature of Second Temple Judaism in greater detail. The medieval Jewish movement of Karaism was also nourished, indirectly, by some elements of the Sadducean and sectarian heritage. It was the Pharisaic approach, however, which shaped the later development of Rabbinic Judaism as well as its medieval and modern reflections.

7
Apocrypha, Pseudepigrapha, and the Dead Sea Scrolls

In the preceding chapter several of the groups or sects of the Second Commonwealth period were surveyed. These and a variety of other less well known groups left a vast literature which has come down to us in a number of forms and languages. Before investigating the nature and origins of this literature, it will be helpful to begin with a few definitions. The term "apocrypha" refers to those books which are found in the Hellenistic Jewish Bible canon of Alexandria, Egypt, but not in the Palestinian Jewish canon. The Hellenistic canon was preserved by the Christian church in the Septuagint and Vulgate Bibles, and the Palestinian canon was handed down in the form of the traditional Hebrew Bible. "Pseudepigrapha," strictly speaking, are books ascribed by their authors to others, in this case to ancient and venerable biblical heroes, but the term also designates writings from the Second Temple period, preserved mostly by Eastern churches, in such languages as Greek, Slavonic (a medieval Slavic dialect), Ethiopic, and Syriac. The term "apocalyptic" refers to books which present revelations in a narrative framework in which an otherworldly being discloses mysteries to a human being. These revelations usually concern both eschatological salvation and a supernatural world. The Dead Sea Scrolls are a collection of manuscripts from the caves of Qumran on the western shore of the Dead Sea among which are many writings from this period as well as much material from the Hebrew Bible. Among these scrolls are biblical texts, apocryphal and pseudepigraphal texts, and various sectarian compositions.

THE APOCRYPHA

The apocrypha, as mentioned earlier, consists of a body of texts that form part of the standardized corpus of the Septuagint and other Greek Bibles. Our presentation here will discuss the various genres and books included in it.

The desire to supplement Scripture was part of a general tendency in the Greco-Roman period toward "rewritten Bible." In such works the authors, out of reverence for the Bible, sought to extend the biblical tradition and often applied it to the issues of their own day. One of the books of this type is 1 Esdras (3 Esdras in Latin and Roman Catholic Bibles). It begins with a description of the great Passover held by Josiah, king of Judah, in Jerusalem in 621 B.C.E. according to 2 Chronicles. It then reproduces an alternative version of the whole of Ezra and parts of Nehemiah, ending in the middle of the account of Ezra's reforms. The author wanted to emphasize the contributions of Josiah, Zerubbabel, and Ezra to the reform of Israel's worship. From the confused chronology, it is clear that the author did not have access to superior historical texts. He sought to "correct" the canonical text based on his own analysis, a process in which he was not successful to judge from the remaining inconsistencies. The work appears to have been adapted in Greek from the more literal version in the Septuagint, although some argue for composition in late biblical Hebrew. It is most probable that the book is to be dated to the second half of the second century B.C.E. and assigned to a Hellenistic provenance. Josephus relied heavily on this book.

Tobit is a short didactic story. It is set in Nineveh in Assyria after the exile of 722 B.C.E. Tobit son of Tobiel, a righteous man who has become blind, sends his son Tobias to Media to seek some money belonging to him. Tobias is guided by the angel Raphael. In Media, with the angel's help, he weds Sarah, whose previous seven husbands had died on their wedding nights at the hand of the demon Asmodeus. The couple returns home to Nineveh, where, again with the angel's help, Tobias cures his father's blindness. As the names show (*tov* = "good"), the book points out the rewards for ritual and ethical righteousness, emphasizing that a life of piety is possible even in the Mesopotamian Diaspora. Most likely, the book is to be dated to the third century B.C.E., when it was composed in either Hebrew or Aramaic. Fragments of four manuscripts of Tobit from the Qumran caves are in Aramaic and one is written in Hebrew. It appears that Aramaic was the original language of Tobit and that the Hebrew texts are translations. The full text, however, was preserved only in the Greek translation.

Similar in style is the Book of Judith. This tale is set in the last years of the First Temple period, although names and details are drawn from the Persian period as well. In reality the book addresses the Maccabean era. It tells how the Jews of the Judean fortress of Bethulia (probably an imaginary name) were saved when Judith, a pious and observant Jewish woman, captivated the enemy general Holophernes with her beauty and killed him, thus redeeming her people. The book emphasizes that it was the heroine's piety that led to her success. Judith is assumed to have been composed in Hebrew and survives in Greek and in secondary translations from the Greek. The various Aramaic and Hebrew versions of the story which circulated in the Middle Ages are either retranslations, probably from Latin, or derive from Jewish folklore and tradition.

The Septuagint's versions of several biblical books include supplementary passages that are not found in the Hebrew originals of these texts. The Greek Esther, for instance, has six additions of this kind which fill in details presumably deemed necessary for the Hellenistic reader, whether for dramatic or religious reasons. The additions tell how Mordecai saved the king's life and how Esther appealed to the king. The text of the king's order to massacre the Jews is provided as well as his second letter calling on his people to support and defend the Jews. Most importantly, the prayers uttered by Mordecai and Esther are included, thus filling what some readers must have seen as an obvious spiritual lacuna in the canonical version of the book. Some of these additions were no doubt introduced by Lysimachus, an Alexandrian Jew living in Jerusalem, who translated Esther around 114 B.C.E., according to the book's colophon.

There are similar additions to the Book of Daniel. Jewish tradition saw the book as authored by Daniel, who lived in the last years of the Babylonian Empire in the seventh century B.C.E. Modern scholars have argued that the first half of the book, dealing with the experiences of Daniel at the Babylonian court, dates to the third century B.C.E., while the remainder, describing the Maccabean period and its aftermath in apocalyptic terms, dates to the reign of Antiochus IV Epiphanes, 167–163 B.C.E. The book survives in the original Hebrew and Aramaic and is preserved in a number of Qumran manuscripts.

Greek texts of Daniel as found in the Septuagint include three additions: (1) The Prayer of Azariah and the Song of the Three Young Men in the Furnace provide the otherwise missing prayers in Daniel 3. (2) The story of Susanna is a beautiful didactic tale in which the pious Susanna resists the desires of two old men only to be accused by them of adultery. When his wisdom proves her innocent, Daniel's greatness is first recognized. This tale is intended not only to teach the virtue and reward of piety and the sinfulness of adultery, but also to explain how Daniel's wisdom came to be recognized while he was but a youth. (3) The tales of Bel and the dragon picture Daniel as proving the emptiness of these false gods and their worship. Similar compositions, related to the Book of Daniel, are known from Qumran manuscripts, especially the Prayer of Nabonidus and Pseudo-Daniel materials. Clearly composed by the time Daniel was translated into Greek around 100 B.C.E., since otherwise they would not have been included, the original language of these additions and their provenance cannot be determined.

Baruch (1 Baruch) is a hortatory work which was treated as a supplement to Jeremiah. It is a pseudepigraphon, purporting to have been written by Baruch, the scribe of Jeremiah. In the book, the Jews confess their transgressions, particularly that of rebelling against the Babylonians, which resulted in the destruction of the Temple. The book further asserts that all wisdom is from God, and that He will eventually return His people to their land. Baruch seems to be a composite of two or more parts and was probably written in Aramaic or Hebrew. Palestine is the most likely place of composition. The first part had to have been written by the onset of the first century B.C.E., but the date of the second half cannot be established. It may postdate the destruction of the Second Temple in 70 C.E., in which case the finished book would address the tragedy of the destruction. The book was read by some Hellenistic Jews on the Ninth of Av, the commemoration of the destruction of both Temples.

The Letter of Jeremiah claims to be a letter written by the prophet to the exiles from Judah who were taken to Babylonia in 597 B.C.E. A condemnation of idolatry, it was probably composed in Greek in the second century B.C.E., and a first-century B.C.E. Greek fragment was found at Qumran. The Prayer of Manasseh supplements 2 Chronicles, providing the words Manasseh, king of Judah (698–643 B.C.E.), supposedly uttered in asking God's forgiveness for his sins.

Two wisdom texts are the books of Ben Sira and the Wisdom of Solomon. Ben Sira is a wisdom anthology, much in the style of the biblical Proverbs. It provides practical advice on interpersonal relations, especially with family, the conduct of business, and a variety of ethical teachings. This wisdom comes from God, the Creator and Ruler of all, who rewards and punishes. Ben Sira identifies God's wisdom with the Torah, the observance of which he demands, and clearly opposes the rising tide of Hellenism. He praises all of Israel's biblical heroes, concluding with the stately high priest Simeon the Just. The author, Joshua (or according to some manuscripts Simeon) ben Sira (or Sirach in the Greek texts), wrote in Hebrew around 180 B.C.E., and his grandson translated the work into Greek around 130 B.C.E. Some parts of the book have been preserved in the Qumran and Masada scrolls, and large parts survive in medieval manuscripts descended from the original Hebrew text.

The Wisdom of Solomon draws its inspiration from biblical sapiential texts (a technical term for wisdom materials) and their ancient Near Eastern setting as well as from Hellenistic ideas and motifs and Greek philosophical notions. This work is entirely an argument for the foolishness of ungodliness and idolatry. Although Solomon is never named in the book, its message is placed in his mouth. The message is applied first to the individual, then to the king, and finally to the entire people of Israel. Wisdom is pictured here as an emanation from God, a great light, a concept similar to the logos (divine wisdom) of Philo. At the same time the imagery used to describe wisdom is

BEN SIRA SCROLL FROM MASADA. The apocryphal book of Ben Sira, composed ca. 180 B.C.E., was known only from its Greek translation until medieval manuscripts were identified in the Cairo *genizah*. In the excavations of Masada a manuscript of this scroll was unearthed preserving chapters 39–44 in the original Hebrew. The photograph above is of Ben Sira 42:15–43:8 with parts of the preceding and following columns visible. Note the stitching between the sheets visible on the left. Fragments of this book were also found at Qumran indicating that it was widespread in the Second Temple period. *Courtesy of the Shrine of the Book of the Israel Museum.*

that of Proverbs. The Wisdom of Solomon was probably written in Alexandria in the Roman period, although we cannot be at all certain.

2 Esdras, also known as 4 Ezra, is the only truly apocalyptic book in the apocrypha. The angel Uriel reveals to Ezra the secrets of the approaching end of days in which the messiah will destroy all evildoers in a cataclysm. Most probably the work dates to 81–96 C.E. Originally written in Hebrew or Aramaic, a no longer extant Greek text served as the basis for the later translations which survive. This text reflects the tragedy of the destruction of the Temple and the land in the Great Revolt of 66–73 C.E. The apocalyptic, cataclysmic messianism of this work contrasts sharply with the messianism of mishnaic literature.

Finally, the apocrypha provides us with two of the most important historical sources for the Second Temple period, 1 and 2 Maccabees. 1 Maccabees is an account of the history of Judea from 175 to 134 B.C.E. It describes the background of the Maccabean revolt, the revolt itself, the exploits of Judah the Maccabee, and the efforts of his brothers Jonathan and Simon to permanently reestablish Jewish national independence and religious practice. The author paints the Hasmoneans as loyal Jews fighting against extremist Hellenizing Jews and their Seleucid supporters. 1 Maccabees was written in Hebrew in the early decades of the first century B.C.E. It survives only in the Greek text, which served as a major source for the first-century C.E. historian Josephus.

2 Maccabees is an abridgement of a lost five-volume work by Jason of Cyrene. Jason's work and the abridgement were both composed in rhetorical Greek. 2 Maccabees details the events which led up to the Maccabean revolt and the career of Judah, concluding with his death in 160 B.C.E. As it stands now, the purpose of the book is to encourage the observance of the holiday of Hanukkah. Jason wrote not long after 160 B.C.E., and the abridger probably did his work before 124 B.C.E. Josephus did not have access to this book. To a great extent it serves as a complement to 1 Maccabees, since the two books emphasize different aspects of the revolt and the events surrounding it. On the other hand, there are many chronological and historical inconsistencies between the two works.

3 Maccabees (considered by some to be part of the apocrypha) is an unhistorical account of the deliverance of the Jews of Egypt from religious persecution, including the demand that they abandon their religion. The book draws on motifs from the biblical Book of Esther, 2 Maccabees, and other sources, and attempts to explain the existence in Hellenistic Egypt of a festival similar to Purim but celebrated in the summer.

PSEUDEPIGRAPHA

All in all, the apocrypha are a varied group of texts that have in common little more than their approximate dates of composition and their preservation in the Septuagint Bible. There is little of literary or historical significance to distinguish these texts from the pseudepigrapha except that the latter did not constitute a closed collection. Many of the pseudepigrapha found their way into the canons of various Eastern churches, usually in translations (often from earlier Greek texts) into such languages as Ethiopic, Slavonic, Syriac, and Armenian. A few of the pseudepigrapha are of major significance either for what they tell us about the period in which they were written or because they exerted influence on the later history of Judaism.

1 and 2 Enoch are totally separate works. Each, however, takes its cue from the biblical statement that God "took" Enoch (Gen. 4:24). Enochic literature, texts containing revelations to or about this enigmatic biblical figure, appeared quite early in the Second Temple period, certainly by the second century B.C.E. The impact of these traditions on later Jewish esoteric and mystical literature is significant.

1 Enoch (the Ethiopic Enoch) is an apocalyptic book in which Enoch reports his vision of how God will punish the evildoers and grant eternal bliss to the righteous. Enoch describes the angels and the heavenly retinue. He also has visions regarding the Elect, the Son of Man, and reveals a collection of astronomical data which provide the secrets of the natural order. Visions of the destruction of the sinners then occur, followed by a recounting of the history of the world as a series of "weeks." An account of the birth of Noah and the flood concludes the book. The work is preserved in extensive manuscripts from Qumran,

covering virtually all of it except chapters 37–71 (there are 105 chapters). Qumran evidence and the Greek manuscripts for parts of the book indicate that 1 Enoch is a composite of materials, mostly from the second century B.C.E., the final redaction of which must be dated after the completion of the Parables section (chaps. 37–71) sometime in the late first century C.E. Qumran versions included the so-called Book of the Giants, which is not included in the Ethiopic book.

2 Enoch (the Slavonic Enoch) is to some extent related to 1 Enoch. It is essentially a description of Enoch's life and the lives of his descendants up to the flood. Enoch's journey to the seven heavens is described, followed by God's revelation of the history of the world up to Enoch's time and the prediction of the flood. Then Enoch returns to earth, where he instructs his children in matters of belief and behavior, emphasizing the importance of his books. Finally there is a description of Enoch's ascension to heaven. It is impossible to determine whether the book was composed in Hebrew or in Greek, or is a composite of both. The text must have been complete by the end of the first century C.E. It was passed down in two separate Slavonic recensions, one longer than the other.

The Book of Jubilees is a prime example of the genre of rewritten Bible in which Second Temple authors recast and retold biblical stories in order to teach their own lessons. Jubilees is a reworking of biblical history from the start of Genesis until the commandment of Passover in Exodus 12. The book purports to represent the revelation of an angel to Moses on Mount Sinai. Its chronology is based on the counting of years by sabbatical cycles (seven-year periods) and jubilees (forty-nine-year periods). The author fixes the dates of the Jewish festivals and gives them special significance by claiming that they were first observed by the patriarchs in commemoration of events in their lives. Indeed, the biblical heroes are pictured throughout as observing Jewish law. This work was mentioned in the Dead Sea Scrolls, and fragments of the original Hebrew text were preserved in the Qumran caves. We should note the links with the *Genesis Apocryphon* from Qumran. The book must have been completed in the second century B.C.E. It clearly springs from a group of Palestinian Jews who influenced the Qumran sect or were in some way related to it, but no great certainty is possible. The traditions of Jubilees played an important role in the development of the Judaism of the Falashas of Ethiopia.

The Testaments of the Twelve Patriarchs are a pseudepigraphic group of works in which the twelve sons of Jacob present exhortations to their children, as their father Jacob had done at the end of his life according to Genesis 49. The Testaments were preserved in their entirety in Greek and were known to the church fathers. The final text may have been worked over by a Christian editor, but the Jewish base can be easily uncovered. Each testament includes an account of the protagonist's life in which he confesses his sins and praises his virtues, admonitions to avoid these transgressions, a prediction of the future of each tribe, including sin, punishment, and exile, and exhortation to follow the leadership of Judah and Levi. Fragments of the Testament of Levi in Aramaic and the Testament of Naphtali in Hebrew exist from both Qumran and medieval times. It seems, therefore, that the author of the Greek text used various Aramaic and Hebrew testaments (probably composed in the second century B.C.E. in sectarian circles related or antecedent to the Dead Sea sect) as a basis for his work, sometime between 100 and 63 B.C.E. His Greek text was in turn Christianized during the second century C.E. The testaments quote Enoch repeatedly and have parallels with Jubilees and the Qumran literature.

The Letter of Aristeas represents the Hellenistic milieu. In reality it is not a letter but a Hellenistic Jewish wisdom treatise presented in the guise of a report on the translation of the Torah into Greek. The work purports to have been written by the non-Jew Aristeas, an official of Ptolemy II Philadelphus (283–246 B.C.E.). The text is a tribute to Jewish law and Jewish wisdom. It tells the story of how the high priest in Jerusalem sent seventy-two scholars to Alexandria to translate the Pentateuch at the king's request, describes how they went about their work, and affirms the validity of the translation thus produced. Much of the account is not historical. A series of embellishments from Greek philosophical traditions in fact constitutes the bulk of the text. The work is generally dated to the beginning of the second century B.C.E. It was composed in Greek, probably by an

Alexandrian Jew. The very same legend is related by Philo, Josephus, talmudic literature, and the church fathers.

4 Maccabees is likewise a product of the Hellenistic Jewish world and proposes a Judaism anchored in Platonic and Stoic philosophy. The work is a discourse addressed directly to the reader and intended to encourage a Judaism in which reason ruled over the passions. Its title derives from the fact that it details the sufferings of the martyrs of the Maccabean period. In this respect it parallels 2 Maccabees. The author believes in immortality, that is, an eternal life in heaven for the pious immediately after their death. The text is probably to be assigned to the mid-first century C.E., but its place of composition cannot be determined. It was known to the church fathers, some of whom mistakenly attributed it to Josephus.

This brief survey of a few of the works of the Second Temple period, from both Palestine and the Diaspora, opens a window on the various approaches to Judaism in this important period and demonstrates the highly variegated texture of its literature. Many of these texts, and a whole host of others, were found in the Qumran caves. It is to these works that our attention now turns.

DEAD SEA SCROLLS

The term Dead Sea Scrolls designates a corpus of manuscripts which have been discovered in the last forty years in the Judean Desert in caves along the Dead Sea. The main body of materials comes from Qumran, an area situated near the northern end of the Dead Sea, 8½ miles south of Jericho. The scrolls were collected by a sect of Jews in the Greco-Roman period. They were hidden in ancient times and rediscovered in 1947, when a young Bedouin shepherd entered what is now designated as cave 1 and found several pottery jars containing leather scrolls wrapped in linen cloths. Starting in 1951 a steady stream of manuscripts was brought to light.

Actually, this was not the first discovery of its kind, for several accounts preserved by the church fathers indicate that scrolls were unearthed in the Dead Sea region as early as Roman and

The Dead Sea Sect

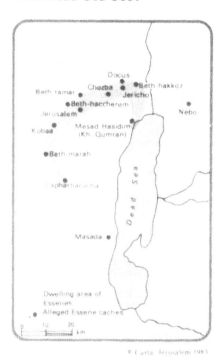

© Carta, Jerusalem 1983

Byzantine times. Medieval accounts speak, as well, of an ancient Jewish sect of cave dwellers in the area.

The dating of the Dead Sea Scrolls was a subject of controversy from the very beginning. Some regarded the new texts as medieval Karaite documents. Others held that they dated from the Roman period, and some even thought they were of Christian origin. The dating question was resolved by means of several kinds of evidence.

Of primary importance was the archaeological excavation of the building complex on the plateau immediately below the caves. In the view of most scholars, this complex was connected with the scrolls. The residents of the complex copied many of the scrolls and were part of the sect described in some of the texts. Numismatic evidence has shown that the complex flourished from around 135 B.C.E. to 68 C.E. Occupation was interrupted only briefly by an earthquake in 31 B.C.E.

Similar conclusions resulted from carbon-14 dating of the

QUMRAN CAVE 11. A total of eleven caves in the area of Qumran, on the western shore of the Dead Sea, south of Jericho, yielded scrolls or fragments. Photograph A shows the entrance to Cave 11. Inside this cave (photograph B) were found numerous scrolls, including the *Temple Scroll* and the *Psalms Scroll*. The small size and inaccessibility of the caves make it extremely unlikely that the Dead Sea sect lived in them, or that they functioned as the stacks of a sectarian library. *Photo by Lawrence H. Schiffman.*

cloth wrappings in which the scrolls were found. Studies of the paleography (the form of the Hebrew letters in which the texts are written) have supported much the same dating. Scholars have identified the scrolls, therefore, as the library of a sect which occupied the Qumran area from after the Maccabean revolt of 168–164 B.C.E. until the Great Revolt of 66–73 C.E.

The many scrolls found in the Qumran caves can be divided into three main categories: biblical manuscripts, apocryphal compositions, and sectarian documents. Fragments of every book of the Hebrew Scriptures (Old Testament) have been unearthed at Qumran with the sole exception of Esther. Among the more important biblical scrolls are the two Isaiah scrolls (one is complete), and the fragments of Leviticus and Samuel (dated to the third century B.C.E.). The study of the biblical texts from Qumran has given rise to a theory of local texts. This theory maintains that at the root of the variations are three recensions of the Hebrew Bible: One is the Palestinian, from which the Samaritan Pentateuch is ultimately descended. A second is the Alexandrian, upon which the Septuagint is based. Finally, there is the Babylonian, which is the basis of the Masoretic (received and authoritative) Hebrew text fixed by the tannaim (the Mishnaic rabbis) in the late first century C.E. While the division of biblical manuscripts into three basic families has much to recommend it, it is unlikely that these text types originated outside of the Land of Israel. Further, recent studies show that the proto-Masoretic texts are the most common and that only a few proto-Samaritan or Septuagintal texts can be identified. In addition, there are a substantial number of manuscripts written in a form peculiar to the Qumran sect.

The contribution of the biblical scrolls to our understanding of the history of the biblical text and versions cannot be overstated. We now know of the fluid state of the Scriptures in the last years of the Second Temple. With the help of the biblical scrolls from Masada and the Bar Kokhba caves, it is possible to trace the early stages of the standardization process that ultimately led to the final acceptance of the Masoretic (received) Hebrew text as authoritative by the first-century rabbis. We can understand as well the manner in which local texts played a role in this history, and finally, the nature of the Hebrew texts which served as the basis for the ancient translations of the Bible.

By far the most interesting materials among the Dead Sea Scrolls are the sectarian compositions. These are the writings of the sect which inhabited Qumran. They consist of biblical commentaries and documents outlining the regulations by which the sect was governed, its approach to Jewish law, and its messianic yearnings.

The *Pesharim* were the sect's biblical commentaries. They seek to show how the present pre-messianic age (i.e., the era in which the scrolls were written) is the fulfillment of the words of the prophets. As such, they provide an important source for an understanding of the sect's self-image and view of its own history and place in the general society. These *Pesharim* include commentaries to Habbakuk, Nahum, and some of the psalms. It is only in the commentaries that we find the names of actual historical figures who lived in the period during which Qumran was occupied.

Another of the manuscripts in the Qumran collection was the *Damascus Document*, also known as the *Zadokite Fragments*. Two copies of this work, dating from the tenth and twelfth centuries C.E., had been among the Hebrew manuscripts that Solomon Schechter had found in the *genizah* ("storehouse") of the Ben Ezra synagogue in Cairo, Egypt, and brought to Cambridge University in England in 1896. Until the discovery at Qumran the Damascus Document, which detailed the life and teachings of an otherwise unknown Jewish sect, had been regarded as a strange composition of quite uncertain provenance. It now became apparent that it had been written by the Qumran sect and thus that at least one Dead Sea text had continued to circulate in the Middle Ages.

Admission into the Qumran sect, the conduct of daily affairs, and the penalties for violating its law are the subjects of the *Manual of Discipline (Rule of the Community)*. This text makes clear the role of ritual purity and impurity in defining membership in the sect, and, as well, details the annual mustering ceremony and covenant renewal. Appended to it are the *Rule of the Congregation*, which describes the community at the end of days, and the *Rule of Benedictions*, which contains praises of the sect's leaders.

The *Thanksgiving Scroll* contains a series of poems describing the beliefs and theology of the sect. Many scholars attribute its authorship to the so-called teacher of righteousness (or "correct teacher") who led the sect in its early years.

The *Scroll of the War of the Sons of Light against the Sons of Darkness* details the eschatological war. In it, the sect and the angels fight systematically against the nations and the evildoers of Israel for forty years, after which the end of days dawns. This scroll is notable for its information on the art of warfare in the Greco-Roman period.

Unique is the *Temple Scroll*, an idealized description of the Jerusalem Temple and its cult, including, as well, various other aspects of Jewish law. The text takes the form of a rewritten Torah, and the various verses dealing with the subjects at hand are harmonized into one consistent whole. Debate surrounding this text concerns the question of whether it is actually a sectarian scroll or simply part of the sect's library like the biblical and apocryphal compositions described above. Numerous smaller texts throw light on mysticism, prayer, and sectarian law. Many of these texts have not yet been published or await thorough study.

Exceedingly significant is a still unpublished text called the *Miqsat Ma'aseh Ha-Torah* (literally, *Some Matters Relating to the Torah*), referred to in chapter 6 in connection with the Sadducees. Described as a "halakhic letter," it is written in the form of a letter from the leaders of the sect to the Jerusalem establishment, outlining the disagreements over Jewish law and Temple practice that had caused the sectarians to secede. The text indicates that there were close connections between the founders of the sect and the Sadducean priesthood, and demonstrates, as we have noted, that views later attributed to the Pharisees governed actual practice in the Jerusalem Temple in Hasmonean times.

The Dead Sea Scrolls have illuminated the background for the emergence of Rabbinic (Mishnaic) Judaism and early Christianity. While many of the detailed comparisons that have been suggested do not have adequate support, the more general

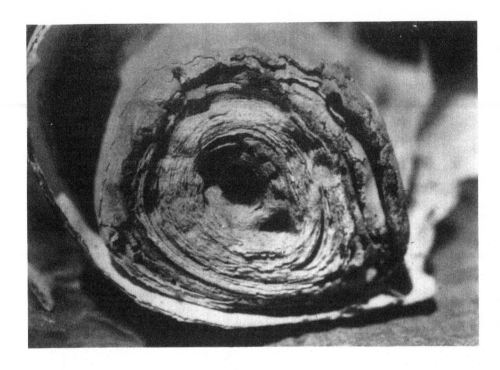

THE TEMPLE SCROLL. The 66-column *Temple Scroll* is the largest text of Jewish law known from the Dead Sea Scrolls. Here it is pictured from the top, showing the manner in which scrolls were rolled in Antiquity. Because most scrolls were deposited in the Qumran caves rolled in this manner, the damage done to the scrolls is usually along regular patterns, allowing scholars to reconstruct the order of the fragments in some cases. The full length of this scroll was almost 9 m. *Courtesy of the Shrine of the Book of the Israel Museum.*

conclusions reached by scholars are very important. We now know that as a result of the Great Revolt of 66–73 C.E., and to some extent even in the years preceding it, Judaism was moving toward a consensus that would carry it through the Middle Ages. As Talmudic Judaism emerged from the ashes of the destruction, groups like the Dead Sea sect fell by the wayside. Nonetheless, the scrolls allow us an important glimpse of the nature of Jewish law, theology, and eschatology as understood by one of these sects.

The scrolls show us that the Second Commonwealth period was an era in which Jews engaged in a vibrant religious life based on study of the Holy Scriptures, interpretation of Jewish law, the practice of ritual purity, and messianic aspirations. Jewish practices known from later texts, such as the putting on of tefillin (phylacteries), daily prayer, and grace before and after meals, were regularly practiced. Rituals were seen as a preparation for the soon-to-dawn end of days which would usher in a life of purity and perfection.

The scrolls, therefore, have shown us that Jewish life and law were already considerably developed in this period. Although we cannot expect a linear development between the Judaism of the scrolls and that of the later rabbis, since the rabbis were heir to the tradition of the Pharisees, we can still derive great advantage from the scrolls in our understanding of the early history of Jewish law. Here, for the first time, we have a fully developed system of postbiblical law and ritual.

At the same time, it is now clear that the sect, emphasizing as it does the apocalyptic visions of the prophets, provides us with a background for understanding the emerging Christian claims of messiahship for Jesus. The Dead Sea Scrolls are especially illuminating with regard to the world-view of early Christianity. This is true despite the fact that the Dead Sea sect, and for that matter all the known Jewish sects of Second Temple times, adhered strictly to Jewish law as they interpreted it.

SUMMARY

This survey of the literary heritage of Second Temple times gives only a small indication of the religious and intellectual

ferment of the age. Varying interpretations of the biblical tradition were constantly interacting with each other and with
Hellenistic notions in the marketplace of ideas. While this process must have involved intimately only a minority of the Jewish
population of the Land of Israel and the Diaspora, events soon
to burst upon the scene would bring ideological differences to
center stage. Many ideas found in the texts surveyed here would
become central to the ongoing debate among Jews regarding
freedom from foreign domination, revolt, messianism, and redemption. Jews would soon face the challenges of Roman rule
and the rise of Christianity.

8
The Jewish-Christian Schism

From the perspective of the later history of Western Civilization, no aspect of Jewish history in this period is more important than the series of events and developments which led to the rise of Christianity. The new religious faith was rooted in the Judaism of the Second Temple period. Yet it was ultimately to diverge radically from its mother religion. It is therefore especially important to understand both the historical background of this period and the exact process by which the Jewish and Christian communities separated.

JUDEA UNDER ROMAN RULE

We have already traced the history of the Hasmonean dynasty through the days of Salome Alexandra to its end in recrimination and civil war in 63 B.C.E. The decline of this great dynasty resulted, as was noted, from the very same Hellenizing forces against which the Maccabees had risen so valiantly. The last gasp of freedom was breathed as Aristobulus II and Hyrcanus II fought the fratricidal war which handed Judea over to the Romans.

Aristobulus was led off in chains to Rome, and Hyrcanus II was installed as high priest, entrusted with managing the internal affairs of the nation. For all intents and purposes, Judea was reduced to the status of a Roman tributary. It was ruled by a Roman procurator who managed its political, military, and fiscal affairs. Its governmental structure was reorganized by Gabinius, the Roman governor of Syria from 57 to 55 B.C.E., who

divided the country into five *synhedroi*, or administrative districts. This arrangement was clearly intended to eliminate the
age-old system of toparchies (administrative districts made up
of central towns and the rural areas surrounding them), dating
from the reign of Solomon, and taken over in turn by the
Assyrians, Babylonians, and Persians, and then by the Ptolemies and Seleucids. The intent of this reorganization was to
destabilize the nation and thus make certain that popular resistance would be impossible. Julius Caesar restored certain territories to Judea and appointed Hyrcanus ethnarch (Greek for
"ruler of the nation").

Hyrcanus was a weak figure who on his own could neither
administer the affairs of Judea nor collect its taxes. For this
reason, it became possible for the Idumaean Antipater, whose
father had been forcibly converted to Judaism in the time of
John Hyrcanus, to insinuate himself into the halls of power. He
soon took control of virtually all matters of state, thus exercising the authority that technically belonged to Hyrcanus as high
priest, and combined with this the powers delegated to him by
the Romans, who clearly saw him as their agent. Antipater's
decision to install his sons as governors, Herod over Galilee and
Phasael over Jerusalem, sowed the seeds of the Herodian dynasty.

Herod, then a man of twenty-five, set about ridding the Galilee
of what his official court historian, Nicolaus of Damascus, called
"robbers" but who in reality may have been a kind of resistance
movement against Roman rule. By 47 or 46 B.C.E., Herod's
summary methods of justice had led him into a confrontation
with the Sanhedrin. Only the intervention of his father, Antipater, prevented him from taking revenge for their having called
him to account. Herod's difficulties with his brethren had no
impact on his relations with the Romans, who appointed him
strategos (governor and general) of Coele-Syria, a Greek designation for the area of Palestine and southwest Syria.

In 43 B.C.E. Antipater was poisoned, leaving the fate of
Palestine open. Herod and Phasael managed to retain power,
even after the accession of Antony as ruler over the entirety of
Asia in 42 B.C.E. Despite the complaints of their countrymen,

THE HERODIAN FAMILY

Antipater I

Antipater II, d. 43 B.C.E. (Cyprus I)

- Phasael I d. 40 B.C.E.
- Joseph II d. 36 B.C.E.
- Joseph I, d. 35/4 B.C.E. (Salome)
- Pheroras d. 5 B.C.E.
- Salome I d. 10 C.E. (1. Joseph, d. 35/4 B.C.E. 2. Costobar, d. 28 B.C.E. 3. Alexas)

Herod the Great d. 4 B.C.E.

(Doris of Jerusalem [Idumean])
- Antipater III d. 4 B.C.E. (daughter of the Hasmonean Antigonus)
  - Phasael II (Salampsio)
  - Cyprus II (Agrippa I)

(Mariamme [Hasmonean]), d. 29 B.C.E.
- Alexander (d. 7 B.C.E. Glaphyra)
- Aristobulus IV d. 7 B.C.E. (Berenice I)
  - Herod of Chalcis (Berenice II)
  - Agrippa I d. 44 C.E. (Cyprus II)
    - M. Iulius Agrippa II d. before 93 C.E. (or 100 C.E.)
    - Berenice II (1. Herod of Chalcis 2. Polemon of Cilicia)
    - Drusilla (1. Azizus of Emesa 2. Antonius Felix the Procurator)
      - Agrippa d. 79 C.E.
  - Herodias (1. Herod Philip 2. Herod Antipas)
- Salampsio (Phasael II)
- Cyprus III (Antipater IV)

(Mariamme II)
- Herod Philip (Herodias)
- Salome II (Philip)

(Malthace [Samaritan])
- Herod Archelaus (1. Mariamme IV 2. Glaphyra)
- Herod Antipas (1. daughter of Aretas IV of Nabataea 2. Herodias)

(Cleopatra of Jerusalem)
- Philip d. 34 C.E. (Salome II)

(by Costobar)
- Antipater IV
- Berenice I (Aristobulus IV)

who dispatched embassies to Antony, Herod and Phasael each acquired the title of tetrarch.

Their fate, and that of Palestine as well, changed markedly with the Parthian invasion in 40 B.C.E. The Parthians allied themselves with Antigonus II (Mattathias) the Hasmonean, the youngest son of Aristobulus II (and nephew of Hyrcanus II), who as the last of the Hasmonean princes had long been seeking to reassert Hasmonean rule over Judea. Unable to stem the invasion, Phasael and Hyrcanus II were lured into a Parthian trap. Hyrcanus was maimed in the ear in order to disqualify him from serving as high priest and Phasael took his own life. Only the wily Herod had foreseen the trap and escaped.

Now once again Judea had a Hasmonean king. Herod determined that in order to regain power he had no option but to seek Roman support. He set sail for Rome, where he persuaded the Senate to declare him king of Judea despite his lack of an army and of any real claim to the throne. He knew that the Roman desire to see the Parthians expelled from the province would lead the Senate to support his claims. In 39 B.C.E. he landed in Ptolemais (present-day Akko) and quickly gathered some northerners around his banner, alongside the Roman troops ordered by the Senate to assist him. His first attack on Jerusalem was unsuccessful, with Antigonus still holding his own in the city. But the tide was turning against the Parthians, who had been expelled from most of Syria and were on the run in Palestine as well.

By 37 B.C.E. Herod had subdued virtually all of the country. By order of Antony, Sossius, the Roman governor of Syria, gave Herod aid which ultimately enabled him to take Jerusalem. Antigonus was captured by the Romans and was beheaded at the wish of Herod. Thus Hasmonean rule over an independent Jewish nation in the Land of Israel was finally brought to an end.

HERODIAN RULE

What follows is but a brief summary of the life and dynasty of the most famous and infamous of Judean kings, known to history as Herod the Great. From the beginning of his reign, popular discontent, which he had already faced as governor of the Galilee, reached high proportions, led by certain Pharisees and some of the nobility. Only with harsh and brutal measures did Herod succeed in bringing it under control. In 35 B.C.E., to shore up his hold on the throne, he installed the Hasmonean Aristobulus III as high priest and married Mariamme, his sister. However, realizing that Aristobulus, as a descendant of the Maccabees, was very popular, Herod soon had him drowned. This was only the first of a chain of killings he perpetrated, often against members of his own family regarding whom he harbored the darkest and most irrational of fears.

Having set to rest the internal challenges to his control, Herod soon faced other problems from abroad. Called before Antony in 34 B.C.E. to defend himself for the death of Aristobulus,

THE HERODIAN PERIOD

63–40 B.C.E.	Hyrcanus high priest and ethnarch
57–55	Gabinius governor of Syria
47 or 46	Herod's confrontation with the Sanhedrin
43	Antipater poisoned
42	Accession of Antony as ruler of Asia
40	Parthian invasion
39	Herod lands in Palestine
37	Siege and capture of Jerusalem
37–34	Herod rules Judea
34	Herod defends himself before Antony
31	Herod's victory over Nabatean Arabs
31	Earthquake in Palestine
29	Mariamme put to death
22–9	Caesarea built
20/19	Building of Herodian Temple begins
7	Execution by Herod of his sons Alexander and Aristobulus
4	Execution by Herod of his son Antipater
4	Death of Herod
4 B.C.E.–6 C.E.	Archelaus ethnarch
6	Archelaus deposed
26–36	Pontius Pilate
29	John the Baptist executed by Herod Antipas
30	Jesus crucified by Romans

Herod was acquitted. Yet Cleopatra VII, the queen of Egypt, persuaded Antony soon afterwards to give her possession of certain territories in the region of Jericho that were among the best agricultural lands in Herod's kingdom. Rather than resist and alienate this powerful woman, Herod cleverly arranged to lease back his own land. In this way, paying what amounted to a small tribute, he retained his territory intact. Although Herod's war with the Nabatean Arabs ended in victory in 31 B.C.E., his army suffered great casualties. That same year an earthquake killed some thirty thousand people and Herod had to undertake massive relief works in its aftermath. When Antony was defeated at the battle of Actium, Herod quickly changed sides in the Roman civil war and allied himself with Octavian, now known as Augustus Caesar. In gratitude, Augustus confirmed Herod in office in 30 and returned to him the territories taken by Cleopatra.

Domestic, internecine jealousies led Herod to put his wife Mariamme to death in 29 B.C.E. The resulting psychological depression and recriminations led in turn to the execution of other family members and courtiers. Among them were other Maccabean descendants, killed for fear that they might reassert the claims of the Hasmonean house.

The consolidation of Herod's power made possible a variety of massive building projects that befitted his status as a Roman client king. Theaters and amphitheaters were constructed. He built a palace in the upper city of Jerusalem, as well as the Antonia fortress north of the Temple. In non-Jewish areas, both within his kingdom and outside, he built temples to pagan gods and in honor of Caesar and funded athletic games. Although quite Hellenized, and born of a non-Jewish mother, hence not Jewish according to the predominant view, he often sought to avoid offending his Jewish subjects. At other times, however, he completely violated Jewish laws and sensibilities. From 22 to 9 B.C.E. he built the port of Caesarea on the Mediterranean coast, intended as a shipping point to foster his role in the international grain trade. Many fortresses were rebuilt, including Masada, where he had hidden his family when he fled to the Roman Senate in 40 B.C.E.

Herod's largest and most beautiful project was the rebuilding

Herod's Kingdom (1st cent. B.C.E.)

Nuts
Forests
Olives
Wheat
Sheep/Goats
Figs/Dates
Wine
Camels
Tyrian purple
Pottery
Copper

0   20   40
km

© Carta, Jerusalem 1983

of the Jerusalem Temple. He began in 20/19 B.C.E., yet work on
the details was still proceeding long after his death when the
Temple was destroyed by the Romans in 70 C.E. Although Herod
adhered to Pharisaic demands regarding many aspects of the
Temple's construction, he ignored them in other respects. In
consequence, the Pharisees continued to be hostile to him, and
it is even doubtful that the Sanhedrin functioned in his time.
Herod appointed and removed high priests at will. The Sadducean elements, therefore, were also opposed to him, as were the
heavily taxed common people. He was able to maintain control

only because of his extremely close relations with Augustus and the Roman authorities and because of the repressive tactics he used to subjugate the populace.

The last years of his reign were dominated by family intrigues. (He had had a total of ten wives.) Herod's son from his first marriage, Antipater, schemed successfully against the sons of Mariamme, Alexander and Aristobulus. Eventually, Herod accused them of treason before Augustus, then had them tried and executed, probably in 7 B.C.E. When Antipater sought to gain control of the kingdom, he was accused of plotting to kill Herod and was imprisoned. As Herod's domestic situation deteriorated, so did his health. In 4 B.C.E. he executed Antipater and gave instructions that a large group of leaders of the country were to be put to death after he died, a plan that never took effect. Five days after his son's execution, he died. The entire country breathed a sigh of relief as the reign of this despot and murderer came to an end.

JUDEA UNDER THE PROCURATORS

After his death, Herod's kingdom was divided in three. The largest part, comprising Judea, Samaria, and Idumaea, was placed under the rule of his son Archelaus, who was appointed ethnarch. (Antipas and Philip received territories in the north and were made tetrarchs.) Immediately, a revolt against Archelaus broke out in Judea, as the people found him brutal and his tyrannical rule intolerable. In 6 C.E. he was deposed by the Romans and the country was reorganized as a Roman province.

Thus began the period of the Roman governors. These officials are customarily called procurators by modern scholars, but initially their true title was prefect, and it was only during the reign of the emperor Claudius (41–54 C.E.) that the term procurator came into use to designate them.

Since the garrison stationed in Judea was made up only of auxiliary troops, the procurators were dependent on the legions of the governor of Syria, who accordingly functioned as their immediate superior. Under procuratorial rule the Jews were granted substantial autonomy and were allowed to maintain their own courts and to arrange for the collection of taxes. In

SOUTHERN WALL OF THE HERODIAN TEMPLE. King Herod rebuilt the Second Temple beginning in 20/19 B.C.E. In so doing, he constructed beautiful pillared streets on the sides of the Temple Mount which he enlarged and reinforced. This is a view of the excavations of the southern wall of the Temple Mount showing remnants of the pillars and the stairs leading up to the entrance. The doorway leading into the Temple precincts can still be seen in the lower levels of the wall. *Photo by Steven Fine.*

matters of religion and worship the procurators did not interfere with Jewish practice.

The early procurators seemed to govern wisely and peace-fully. With the appointment of Pontius Pilate (26–36 C.E.), the procurator who executed Jesus, conflict and bloodshed began. From that point on relations deteriorated for a number of reasons: Roman insensitivity to Jewish religious requirements, high taxes, the stationing of troops in Jerusalem, and the rising messianic yearnings of the Jews. Problems escalated during the reign of the emperor Caligula (37–41 C.E.), who demanded that the Jews erect an image of him in the Temple. His timely death prevented a tragic and violent confrontation between Rome and the Jewish people.

Soon after his accession as emperor in 41 B.C.E., Claudius (41–54) C.E. appointed Agrippa I, the grandson of Herod and Mariamme, as king of the entire Land of Israel. From 41 to 44 Judea was no longer a province but functioned again as a kingdom. Agrippa loved his people and their ancestral way of life, and sought, within the limits imposed on client states by the Roman Empire, to renew the ancient glory of Israel. He enjoyed widespread support among the Jews, who gave him the same respect and devotion they had given the Hasmoneans, but the non-Jewish residents of the land were arrayed against him.

THE ROMAN PROCURATORS
(all dates are C.E.)

6–9	Coponius
9–12	Marcus Ambibulus
12–15	Rufus Tineus
15–26	Valerius Gratus
26–36	Pontius Pilate
36–37	Marcellus
37–41	Marullus
44–46	Cuspius Fadus
46–48	Tiberius Julius Alexander
48–52	Ventidius Cumanus
52–60	Antonius Felix
60–62	Porcius Festus
62–64	Albinus
64–66	Gessius Florus

When Agrippa unexpectedly died, the Romans judged his son too young to succeed him and returned Judea to procuratorial rule. From this point on, there was constant strife between the procurators and their Jewish subjects. The Roman officials displayed little concern either for Judaism and its dictates or for the economic well-being of the country. Economic decline proceeded quickly, as did the activities of the growing rebel factions. Anarchy was fast approaching, and soon the nation would be aflame with rebellion and then destruction.

THE RISE OF THE EARLY CHURCH

The earliest years of Christianity unfolded during this period of decline and unrest. In these years what would later be called the "church" was in reality a Jewish sect, and that is how it is treated here. The difficult economic and political situation in Judea during the career of Jesus and in the period of the emerging church tended to encourage the rise of religious movements. In addition, the multiplicity of sects and movements in Second Temple Judaism provided a rich legacy which could serve as the basis for the Christian apocalyptic movement. These two factors together constituted the major influences on the rise of the new religious group and the schism that eventually followed. Further, scholars have long noticed the propensity for religious ferment in the area where Christianity began, the region of Galilee in the northern part of the Land of Israel.

Christianity was firmly anchored in the heritage of Second Temple sectarianism. Various documents from the corpus of materials discovered in the Qumran caves tell us of the extreme apocalypticism of some groups of Jews in this period. These groups hoped for the immediate revelation of a messiah who would redeem them from their misfortunes and tribulations. As time went on, and political and economic conditions worsened, they became more and more convinced that the messianic deliverance would be accompanied by a cataclysm. The forces of evil, usually identified both with Israelite transgressors and with the non-Jewish powers that dominated the Jewish people, would then be totally destroyed. This view took its cue from the prophetic idea of the Day of the Lord. The destruction of evil would be accompanied by a utopian messianism wherein an ideal society would come into existence with the restoration of the Davidic monarchy. When Christianity came to the fore in the first century C.E., its adherents saw themselves as living in the period of the fulfillment of these visions. They identified Jesus as the Davidic messiah who would usher in the eventual destruction of all evil.

Any study of the career of Jesus and the rise of the Christian church must acknowledge that Palestine in this period gave rise to occasional messianic and prophetic figures. Among these was John the Baptist, who, according to the New Testament, was the teacher and inspiration of Jesus. John preached repentance as well as the need for baptism (immersion) in the Jordan River as a one-time experience designed to bring about true repentance. (John was put to death around 29 C.E. by Herod Antipas, son of Herod the Great, who ruled Galilee and Peraea in Transjordan from 4 B.C.E. to 39 C.E.) Statements about Jesus by certain modern writers to the effect that he studied among the Essenes or the Dead Sea sectarians must be rejected as purely speculative. Rather, Jesus was affected, as was early Christianity, by a variety of ideas in the air among the various sectarian groups, of which by chance only certain texts survive. The Qumran materials, if properly understood, provide the background for Christianity, showing that it was on the foundation of this type of Judaism, and not that of the Pharisees, that the church was erected. Yet at the same time, some Pharisaic tendencies had a great impact on the church, as did Second Temple sectarian trends on Rabbinic Judaism.

It is difficult to date with precision the exact point, sometime around the turn of the era, when Jesus was born. Christian traditions placing his birth in Bethlehem, the birthplace of King David, must be seen as an attempt to identify Jesus as the messiah son of David whom the Jewish people expected to redeem them from Roman domination. Jesus grew up in Galilee, where he became a preacher. Many of his ideas were similar to those of his brethren in the various sects, including the Pharisees and the Dead Sea and apocalyptic sects. Yet already in his early career, as portrayed in the Gospels, he disagreed with the Pharisees on matters of Jewish law. The New Testament ac-

PONTIUS PILATE STONE. Pontius Pilate, Roman procurator of Judea in 26–36 C.E., presided over the trial and execution of Jesus. This limestone block, found in secondary use in the ampitheater at Caesarea, contains the following inscription: . . . TIBERIEUM/ . . . [PO]NTIUS PILATUS/ . . . [PRAEF]ECTUS IUDA[EAE], probably to be understood as a dedicatory inscription refering to the gift of a building in honor of Tiberius by Pontius Pilate, Prefect (i.e. procurator) of Judea. *Courtesy of the Israel Museum and the Israel Antiquities Authority.*

counts presage the later Jewish-Christian schism and may even be a reflection of it. In any case, Jesus's teachings apparently raised the ire of some of the Hellenized Jews in the leadership of the high priesthood, as well as of the Romans, who decreed his crucifixion. It is impossible from the incomplete accounts we have to determine exactly what led to the execution of Jesus, yet we know the tragic results of the widespread Christian assumption that the Jews were responsible for it. The challenge posed by Jesus to the Jewish authorities cannot have been of such significance as to warrant a demand for his execution. The Romans, however, had both a vested political interest in his death and the authority to execute him. To a large extent, however, it was the fact that his followers came to believe that he had been resurrected from his grave that gave impetus to the emerging faith.

The followers of Jesus in the early days of his career and soon afterwards gathered together in Jerusalem and formed (according to the Acts of the Apostles) a small group which sought both to live as Jews and to accept the messiahship of Jesus. It was only later that the notion of the divinity of Jesus appeared, toward the end of the New Testament redactional process in the second half of the first century C.E. Thus the early Christian sect began as a coterie of Jews seeking to propagate the belief in Jesus as messiah and evolved into an apostolic group seeking to convert the world. Following the lead of Peter, Paul convinced the fledgling church to formally open itself to gentile converts and brought to it the notion of a mission to the gentiles, transforming Christianity in the process. He also encouraged the notion of abandoning the law. His literary legacy greatly intensified the anti-Jewish notions in the New Testament.

PARTING OF THE WAYS

The split between Judaism and Christianity did not come about simply or quickly. It was a complex process which took some one hundred years, starting from the crucifixion, and which had different causes and effects depending on whether it is looked at from the point of view of Judaism or Christianity.

Further, the question of legal status as seen through Roman eyes also had some relationship to the issue.

From the standpoint of Christianity, the schism is not difficult to trace. In the earliest Gospel texts, which picture Jesus as debating issues of Jewish law with the Pharisees, no hostility is observed. The crucifixion is said to have been carried out by the Romans with the support of some (apparently Hellenized) priests. As we trace the history of the New Testament traditions, they move from disputes with Pharisees, scribes, and chief priests to polemics against the Jews and Judaism, from the notion of some Jews as enemies of Jesus to the demonization of the Jewish people as a whole. By sometime in the first century the New Testament redactors had clearly decided that they were no longer part of the Jewish people. Therefore, they described Jesus as disputing with all the Jews, not just some, as would be appropriate to an internal Jewish dispute. Once Christians saw Jews as the "other," it was but a short step to the notion that all Jews were responsible for the rejection of Jesus and, hence, for the failure of his messianic mission to be fulfilled.

From the Jewish point of view, the matter is more complex. By this time, tannaitic Judaism was already the dominant form of Judaism, for the Pharisees had emerged from the revolt against Rome as the main influence within the Jewish community. After the destruction, the tannaim immediately recognized the need to standardize and unify Judaism. One of their first steps was to standardize the Eighteen Benedictions, which, along with the Shema, constituted the core of the daily prayers. At the same time, they expanded an old prayer to include an imprecation against the *minim*, Jews with incorrect beliefs. In this period, this could only have meant the early Jewish Christians, who observed the laws of Judaism but accepted the messiahship of Jesus. Although the rabbis continued to regard the early Christians as Jews, they reformulated this prayer in order to expel them from the synagogue, as testified to by the Gospel of John and the church fathers. In addition, the tannaim enacted laws designed to further separate the Jewish Christians from the community by prohibiting commerce and certain other interrelationships with them.

Hereafter, it is possible to trace the process of separation

from the end of the first century C.E. until the period of the Bar
Kokhba Revolt (132–135 C.E.), when the tannaim outlawed the
writings of the early Christians, declaring that Torah scrolls or
texts with divine names copied by Christians had no sanctity.
This was clearly a polemic against the Gospels, which must have
been circulating in some form by now.

In the time of Paul, about 60 C.E., the decision to open
Christianity to gentiles had taken place, and the tannaim gradually found themselves facing a church whose members were
not Jews from the point of view of halakhah. To the rabbis, they
were not Jews with incorrect views about the messiah but
gentiles who claimed to be the true Israel. For this reason, the
tannaim began to see the Christians as the other, not as Jews
who had gone astray. This process was complete by the Bar
Kokhba period. Jewish Christianity had been submerged, while
Gentile Christianity had gained the ascendancy. Since it was
now virtually the only form of Christianity the rabbis encountered, they termed the Christians *noṣerim* ("Nazarenes"), regarding them as a completely separate and alien religious group.

The third point of view, that of the Romans, can be traced as
well. The Romans at first regarded the Christians as part of the
Jewish people. When Christianity spread and took on a clearly
different identity, as acknowledged by both Jews and Christians, the Roman government modified its view. The emperor
Nerva (96–98 C.E.) freed the Christians (probably including the
Jewish Christians) from paying the *fiscus judaicus*, the Jewish
capitation tax decreed as a punishment in the aftermath of the
revolt of 66–73 C.E. Clearly, the Romans now regarded the
Christians as a separate group. The way was paved for the
legitimization of Christianity as a licit religion. The decline of
the old pagan cults, coupled with the tremendous success of
Christianity, would eventually lead to the acceptance of the new
faith as the official religion of the Roman Empire in 324 C.E.

JEWISH–CHRISTIAN RELATIONS IN THE
EARLY CENTURIES

How did Jews and Christians relate once the final break had
come about? There are several kinds of evidence for an answer

to this question, all of which point to a deterioration of relations and a rise of hostility. The early days of the schism were marked by questioning and debate. This is clear from accounts in both rabbinic literature and the writings of the church fathers. Jews and Christians discussed such matters as the interpretation of the Hebrew Bible and the authority of their respective traditions. Even in this literature, however, one can trace the rising tensions that would ultimately prevail between the two groups. At some point, probably connected with the Christianization of the empire in the fourth century, the Christians began to approach their Jewish neighbors with a much greater degree of antagonism, especially in Byzantine Palestine. Physical attacks against Jews and their houses of worship were not unknown in this period. Whereas in earlier times, there had been coexistence and harmony, by the fifth century much anti-Semitic legislation had been enacted. Jews were forbidden to build synagogues and to study the oral law. The Jews were said to be Christ-killers, and anti-Judaism was the norm in Christian preaching.

In the very same period groups within the Christian church were persecuted for being "Jewish-Christians." In fact, they were Judaizing Christians, gentiles who sought to observe Judaism as part of their Christianity because they believed in the continued authority of what they called the Old Testament. This position, declared heretical by the church, ought not to be seen as a direct continuation of the early Jewish-Christian church of Jerusalem. These were new groups seeking to imitate what they thought the early church had been. They were not Jews by the standards of Jewish law. The old form of Jewish Christianity had disappeared.

By the end of the talmudic period, Christianity had taken up the classical anti-Semitic views that were to inform its relations with the Jews in the Middle Ages. Jews were able to resist only by comforting themselves with the belief that they were correct and that their suffering would end with the messianic redemption. It was not until the Middle Ages, however, that the violence we have come to associate with anti-Judaism became a significant factor.

SUMMARY

The difficult circumstances of the Herodian period and the years of Roman procuratorial rule, combined with the apocalyptic messianic tendencies of some Second Temple manifestations of Judaism, created a background against which Jesus's followers could consider him to be the messiah. They constituted themselves as a messianic community which soon was identified as a separate religion by its own members, the Jewish community, and the Roman government. Relations between Jews and Christians steadily deteriorated as Christianity marched steadily toward control of the Roman Empire. It is no wonder, then, that with the final ascendancy of Christianity, anti-Semitic legislation was enacted which would set the stage for the tragic history of Jewish-Christian relations in medieval and modern times.

9
Revolt and Restoration

The destruction of the Second Temple in 70 C.E. was the culmination of some seven decades of Jewish unrest and anti-Roman agitation. Certain families had a continuous tradition of opposition to Roman rule which can be traced from the earliest years of the Herodian dynasty through the period of the procurators. The constant efforts of various groups seeking an end to Roman domination and persecution eventually led to the full-scale revolt of 66–73 C.E.

The opposition to Rome was fueled by a number of factors. First, many Palestinian Jews, from the Maccabean Revolt on, had steadfastly fought against foreign domination. For these predecessors of the later revolutionaries, this was not a question of religious liberty; the issue was not whether a foreign power would allow the Jews to follow the Torah but rather a question of national pride and the ideal of complete freedom and independence. Indeed both the prophets of old and the visionaries of Second Temple times looked forward to an independent Jewish nation. Moreover, many of those who took part in the Great Revolt of 66–73 C.E. were motivated by messianic expectations, and some of the leaders of the factions involved in the revolt had messianic aspirations.

Throughout the Second Temple period, the concept of messianism was central to many of the groups whose surviving writings we know from the apocrypha, the pseudepigrapha, and the Dead Sea Scrolls. Stimulated by the biblical hope for the restoration of the Davidic monarchy and the destruction of the wicked on the Day of the Lord, numerous authors elaborated the idea of messianic redemption. By the first century C.E. it was widely agreed that at some future date the Jews could expect a renewal of the Davidic dynasty's rule over the Land of Israel, a purification of religious life, and freedom from foreign domination. While some groups expected this redemption to evolve naturally, others believed that the new order would be born out of a series of great messianic battles and catastrophes.

The two motivating forces, the heritage of the Maccabean uprising and messianism, were set in motion in an atmosphere of rule by Roman procurators who were increasingly capricious and cruel. The procurators paid little or no attention to the needs or sensitivities of the Jews of Palestine during the years leading up to the revolt. Rome would eventually reap the results of this callous approach.

THE GREAT REVOLT

The revolt, as we have already observed, can be said to have been going on from the day the Romans first set foot in the Land of Israel. The previous chapter traced the growing discontent and resistence of segments of the Jewish people in the Herodian period and in the time of the procurators. Yet full-scale revolt did not break out until 66 C.E.

The proximate cause was a series of acts by the procurator Gessius Florus (64–66 C.E.) which displayed disrespect for Jewish religious sensibilities. Widespread strife broke out in Jerusalem, and, as a consequence, some of the priests decided to suspend the offering on behalf of the emperor, an action tantamount to declaring open revolt. The efforts of King Agrippa II, the leading priests, and some of the Pharisees to stem the incipient revolt failed. Jerusalem was soon in the hands of the rebels. This led, in turn, to uprisings throughout the country, where Jews battled their non-Jewish neighbors for the upper hand. Cestius Gallus, the governor of Syria, attempted to put down the revolt, but his forces were routed by the Jews.

Military commanders were now assigned to the entire country, to prepare for the expected Roman attack. Among them was the future historian Josephus, who commanded Jewish forces in the Galilee. Judging from his experiences, duly ap-

DESTRUCTION AND ITS AFTERMATH
(all dates are C.E.)

66–73	Great Revolt
67	Roman conquest of Galilee
68	Destruction of Qumran
70	Destruction of the Temple
73	Capture of Masada
75–79	*Jewish War* written by Josephus
ca. 80	Sanhedrin at Yavneh
93 or 94	Josephus's *Antiquities* completed
ca. 100	Death of Josephus
115–117	Diaspora revolt
132–135	Bar Kokhba revolt
135–138	Hadrianic persecutions
ca. 140	Sanhedrin at Usha
ca. 170	Sanhedrin at Beth Shearim
ca. 200	Sanhedrin at Sepphoris
ca. 200	Redaction of the Mishnah

pointed commanders had to contend with competition from a variety of popular, even semi-messianic, leaders. As this illustrates, the rebels did not constitute a uniform group. Many different forces were involved in the revolt. Among them were the Sicarii, known in the years before the war for having assassinated collaborators with the Romans with short daggers (Latin *sica*) which they kept hidden under their garments. The followers of Simeon bar Giora regarded their leader as a messianic figure, and in his name seem to have committed violent acts not only against the Romans but against other groups of rebels. The Zealots may have had their origins in the groups that had continuously struggled against Rome since the beginning of Roman rule in Palestine, but according to many scholars they only became an organized faction at the start of the revolt. The inability of the various rebel forces to work together was one of the major reasons why the revolt did not succeed. At the same time, it must be recognized that ultimately, even if united, the Jews could not have stood up to Rome's superior military forces and unlimited resources.

The Roman emperor Nero (54–68 C.E.) appointed the experi-

Revolt Against the Romans
(1st-2nd cent. C.E.)

enced general Vespasian to lead the attack on Judea. With the
help of his son Titus, Vespasian assembled three legions and
several contingents of auxiliary forces totaling some sixty thousand men. By the end of 67 C.E., Vespasian had taken Galilee.
Josephus himself surrendered to the Romans at Jotapata.

When the Galilee was lost, some of the rebel groups led by
popular messianic figures moved south to join the forces defend-
ing Jerusalem. They soon took a leading role there, displacing
the aristocratic leaders whose policies had led to the loss of
Galilee. Before long, however, civil strife broke out among the
various factions in Jerusalem. Meanwhile, Vespasian was busily
subjugating the rest of the country. In 68/69 there was a brief

respite while Vespasian awaited the outcome of the death of the emperor Nero and the struggle for succession which then took place. In 69 C.E. the Roman legions of the East decided to declare Vespasian emperor. Soon afterwards he was accepted at Rome as well. He returned there and left his son Titus to prosecute the war in Palestine. All the while, those besieged within Jerusalem continued to undercut their own position by their inability to join together.

By Passover of 70 C.E. Titus had massed a large force around Jerusalem while Jewish factions inside the city were killing one another. As Titus's battering rams began to strike, the factions finally came together. One by one the Romans breached the walls of the city, gaining control of the entire city except for the Temple area. By building siege ramparts, Titus was finally able to take the Temple Mount itself. According to Josephus, Titus planned to spare the Temple from destruction, but it was nonetheless engulfed in a conflagration and could not be saved. The ensuing slaughter of men, women, and children and the leveling of the city which followed dealt a lasting blow to Jewish life in the Land of Israel.

This was not the end of the war. While the Temple treasures and the rebel leaders were paraded in Rome, the Romans still had to mop up small bands of Jewish fighters who had taken refuge in other areas of the city, and to take several fortresses scattered through the land where rebel forces were holding out. With the capture of Masada in 73 C.E., the last resistance to Rome was crushed. As the Roman commemorative coins stated, "Judea had been captured."

DESTRUCTION AND ITS AFTERMATH

If anything is remarkable in the events and developments we have been surveying here, it is the resilience of the Jewish people and the Land of Israel in the face of the catastrophic outcome of the revolt. Despite the destruction of the Temple and the city of Jerusalem, and the near devastation of the land, including the agrarian basis of the economy, it was not long before Jews were again flourishing in Palestine. Although the tendencies toward liberty and independence were strong, and to a great extent messianic in motivation, the traditional Jewish sense of pragmatism reigned supreme, even in the face of defeat and desperation. The Jews and their civilization adapted to the new circumstances and tried to live normally under the Romans in a restored and rebuilt land. Yet their messianic hopes would not die and ultimately reemerged in the Bar Kokhba revolt (132–135 C.E.) only a few generations later.

It is important that the spiritual consequences of the destruction of Jerusalem and its Temple be put into proper perspective. As was the case in the era leading up to the destruction of the First Temple in 586 B.C.E., most Jews apparently had thought that the Temple was impregnable. They saw it as a sign of God's presence and accessibility among them and could not believe that the sanctuary might at any time fall and be taken from them. Its destruction must have precipitated a major spiritual crisis. Indeed, in view of the tragedy's magnitude, the sources from the early tannaitic period are extremely reticent about the destruction, just as Jewry was reticent for the first thirty years after the Holocaust in modern Europe. The silence in Late Antiquity stemmed from several factors. Among them were a lack of preparation for a tragedy of such dimensions, as well as an inability to accept the inevitable traditional explanation for all such suffering—that it was due to the transgressions of the people. It is often stated that there was no reaction at all, but this is not true; it was merely delayed. Numerous midrashim later refer to the tragedy and there are many areas in which halakhah, Jewish law, adapted itself to the new circumstances. Further, a reaction is also observable in pseudepigraphical works like 2 Baruch (preserved in Syriac), which bemoans the destruction.

In the rabbinic tradition, it is in the area of halakhah that expressions of fundamental thought processes occur. For this reason, although there are few direct references to the impact of the destruction in tannaitic sources, many changes occurred in the area of Jewish law and practice. In some cases, Temple-oriented rituals were transferred to the home or synagogue. In other instances, it had to be decided how to deal with rituals that simply had no place but the Temple. The problem was so complicated that there is evidence of uncertainty and transition at first. By the mid-second century, however, many of these questions had been decided, although some were not settled until the time of Rabbi Judah the Prince, with the editing of the Mishnah at the beginning of the third century.

The problem of how to observe holidays and festive occasions in the absence of a Temple must have existed even before the destruction. Many Jews in the Diaspora and even in the Land of Israel did not journey to Jerusalem for festivals like Passover but still celebrated them to the extent possible. Their ritual practices provided some precedent for the transformations that had to take place once the Temple was destroyed.

In the case of Passover, since the paschal sacrifice was no longer possible, the ritual was transformed into a festive Seder meal to take place in the home. For Sukkot (Tabernacles) the requirement to dwell in a booth (sukkah) still applied, but the procession with lulav and etrog (palm branch and citron), originally conducted outside of the Temple on the first day of the festival only, became a week-long ritual (omitted on the Sabbath, however) as a replacement for the Temple observance. Moreover, the procession with the willow branches, a mainstay of the ritual in the Temple, was now transferred to the emerging synagogue, where instead of the willow branches, the lulav and etrog were carried, a practice still central to the celebration of Sukkot.

The problem presented by the priestly dues and tithes, the offerings the people contributed for the support of the priests and the Levites, was most complex. For a short period the people still set aside the full dues and tithes, but left them unused. Later, symbolic amounts were set aside. This compromise was meant to ensure the sanctity of the land and its produce by not consuming that which could rightly be used only for holy purposes, now that it could no longer be eaten in the manner required by the law.

According to tannaitic sources, some Jews in this period, believing that the destruction meant that the spiritual connection between Israel and its God had been permanently interrupted, engaged in mourning practices of various kinds, such as abstention from wine and meat and the elimination of joy from wedding festivities. The tannaim were opposed to such excesses.

By and large they succeeded in taming these tendencies, but some circles maintained such practices until well into the Middle Ages, and the Karaite movement eventually inherited them.

The tannaim succeeded in suppressing such behavior because they provided a ritual for commemorating and mourning the Temple which, like the rabbinic rituals for mourning after the death of a loved one, were designed to allow the mourner to live with the loss and move back to normal life. The fast-day cycle of the tenth of Ṭevet, the seventeenth of Tammuz, the ninth of Av, and the Fast of Gedaliah served the rabbis as an opportunity to commemorate the losses of both the First and the Second Temples. These days were already observed as remembrances of the destruction of the First Temple, and it was natural to add the tragedy of the Second Temple to the commemoration. In tannaitic times the liturgy, laws, and regulations of the fast-days were fixed. These rituals gave the tannaim a means of expressing grief for the destruction of the Temple and the cessation of its sacrificial service within the context of the ritual calendar of Rabbinic Judaism.

FROM TEMPLE TO SYNAGOGUE

The most central aspect of the transition from pre-destruction to post-destruction times was the change of the center of worship from Temple to synagogue. This change must be fully understood to grasp the essence of Rabbinic Judaism. In Temple times, the Jerusalem Temple was understood to be a place where the Divine Presence could always be approached. In other words, it was the locus of God's abiding in Israel, in fulfillment of the biblical statement, "I will dwell among them" (Exod. 25:8). The sudden disappearance of this avenue of communing with God was a tragedy of awesome dimensions.

The question of the discontinuance of animal sacrifice is more complex. In the years leading up to the revolt and the destruction, animal sacrifice was certainly regarded as the highest form of worship. Yet it was not the only form. Evidence of various kinds, including that of the Dead Sea Scrolls, demonstrates that the role of prayer was constantly increasing in Second Temple times. In the last years of the Second Commonwealth, prayer

SYNAGOGUE AT MASADA. Only three synagogues have been identified from first century C.E. Palestine, at Masada, Herodion and Gamla. This aerial photograph shows the synagogue at Masada with the bleacher-type seating which typifies these early synagogues. This synagogue was adapted by the defenders of Masada from a preexisting building in the northeast wall of the fortress built by Herod. In these early synagogues the congregation sat higher than the cantor who was said to "go down before the reader's desk." No Torah ark existed and the scrolls were brought from an adjoining room for public reading. *Courtesy of the Institute of Archaeology of the Hebrew University.*

had so extensively found its way into the Temple service that it was assigned a special place, or *proseuche* (Greek for "prayer room"), in the Jerusalem Temple.

We should not be surprised at the development of the synagogue at this time. There is no evidence for the synagogue as an institution in Palestine before the first century C.E. The *synagoge* mentioned in Greek inscriptions in the Diaspora from Hellenistic times was not a prayer area (*proseuche*) but, rather, the organization that managed the affairs of the local Jewish community. Synagogues in the sense of a place for prayer may first be observed in Palestine in the first century C.E. (Masada, Herodion, and Gamla), and probably somewhat earlier in the Diaspora. From then on we can trace the development of the synagogue up through the end of the talmudic period.

Where did Jews pray before the rise of synagogue buildings? We cannot be sure. Many scholars theorize that the synagogue had its origins in the Babylonian exile when the Jews first had to adapt to the lack of a Temple and animal sacrifice. Yet there is absolutely no evidence, literary or archaeological, for this theory. On the other hand, the history of postbiblical prayer begins early in the Hellenistic period, and perhaps even before. There must have been places for prayer, maybe in the town squares, but this is simply speculation.

Clearly, however, the concomitant development of the synagogue as an institution, along with the gradual ascendancy of prayer over sacrifice as a means of worship, prepared Judaism for the new situation brought about by the destruction of the Temple. By the time the Temple was taken away, its replacement had already been created. From that time on the daily prayers would serve in place of sacrifice, and the synagogue, the "Temple in miniature," would replace the central sanctuary in Jerusalem. Jews would look forward to the rebuilding of the Temple and the restoration of its system of worship. But the Jewish people was equipped with a portable system of worship which it could carry throughout its wanderings, and which would preserve the closeness to God that had once been symbolized and embodied in the Jerusalem Temple.

RESTORATION OF AUTONOMY: THE AUTHORITY
OF THE RABBIS

In the aftermath of the Great Revolt of 66–73 C.E., a total realignment of Jewish political and religious groups took place. It must be remembered that the constellation of approaches known from Second Temple times was radically affected by the events of the Roman conquest.

The Sadducees lost their power base when the Temple was destroyed. While some of their traditions probably survived among non-rabbinic Jews and may have influenced the medieval Karaite movement, the Sadducees ceased to be a factor in Palestinian life after the revolt. They may even have been perceived as in some way responsible for the debacle. Some of the high priests had been close to the Romans, and other priests had actually started the open revolt by refusing to offer the sacrifices provided by the emperor. Accordingly, they incurred the wrath of both pro- and anti-Roman forces. Further, some Jews may have taken the destruction of the Temple as indicative of divine impatience with the way in which the sacrificial worship had been conducted. In any event, the Sadducees exited the stage of history.

The Essenes and the various sects allied to or similar to them also disappeared. The Essenes themselves were leaders in the failed military revolt, according to Josephus, and were decimated by the Romans. Qumran, the center of the Dead Sea sect, was attacked and destroyed in 68 C.E. as part of Roman operations in the Judean Desert. Groups like the Essenes may have contributed to the streams of tradition leading to the medieval Karaite opposition to Talmudic Judaism. Indeed, the parallels between Karaism and the Dead Sea materials are quite striking. With this exception, sectarian groups of the Essene type became insignificant, although in certain ways they seem to have influenced the development of Rabbinic Judaism.

The more extreme and messianically inspired revolutionaries were in the main wiped out. Yet their traditions and approach reemerged again in the Bar Kokhba Revolt sixty years later. From the political point of view, however, these groups were not

a factor in Jewish life in Palestine after the war. The victorious
Romans saw little reason to make common cause with defeated
enemies, especially with enemies who had wreaked so much
havoc on the Roman armies sent to destroy them. Accordingly,
they had no interest in deals with the remnants of the rebel
groups.

The only serious factor left in Palestinian Judaism in the
aftermath of the war was the Pharisaic, rabbinic group. This
group had survived the war relatively intact. Some of the
Pharisaic leaders, perhaps including Rabbi Simeon ben Gamaliel
(I), had taken an active part in the revolt. Yet other rabbis, as
would also be the case in the time of Bar Kokhba, had opposed
the revolt and advocated a negotiated settlement with the Romans. The striking difference in Pharisaic attitudes reflected
the long-standing debate over the question of whether Judaism
demanded national independence or simply freedom of religion,
an issue which may also have been the basis of the disagreement
between Judah Maccabee and the high priest Alcimus. In any
case, the Romans saw at least some of the rabbis, most notably
Yoḥanan ben Zakkai, as leaders with whom they could deal.

Nonetheless, the Roman decision to regard the Pharisaic
rabbis as representative of the Jewish nation cannot be explained simply as a proclivity to deal with those whom they
perceived to be more sympathetic. The Romans came to see the
tannaim as ideally suited to be the country's internal leaders.
Several factors contributed to this decision, most notably the
popularity of the Pharisees and the fact that elements of this
group had preached accommodation with the Romans. The
Romans therefore decided to countenance the establishment of
the patriarchate as Palestinian Jewry's internal self-governing
body. In this way they hoped to solve the problems that had led
to the large-scale revolt against procuratorial government.

Large segments of the Jewish people came to accept this
arrangement, not only for "civil" matters, but for matters of
religion as well. The few sources that we have indicate that the
approach and personalities of the Pharisees were most appealing
to the 'am ha-'areṣ, literally "the people of the land," the
common people, who increasingly followed their lead in matters
of religious practice. In view of the ease with which the rabbinic

tradition established itself after the destruction, the tannaim must indeed have captured the hearts of many of the populace. Tannaitic Judaism provided the best means for the adaptation of tradition to the new reality without Temple and without sacrifice. This ability to adapt to the circumstances was made possible by the rabbis' unique approach to Jewish law, the notion of an oral law given at Sinai along with the written. The interpretation and reinterpretation of the Torah which their approach allowed brought about the unique combination of tradition and change which characterized tannaitic Judaism.

The establishment of tannaitic, rabbinic authority did not take place immediately or without difficulty. The earliest attempts to assert control seem to have occurred in the immediate aftermath of the war, when the sages gathered together at Yavneh under the leadership of Yoḥanan ben Zakkai. His claim to authority was based only on learning and respect. Soon, however, the Hillelite patriarchal house came back into power after Rabban Gamaliel II reasserted his authority at Yavneh around 80 C.E. Rabban Gamliel traced his descent to Hillel, the prominent Pharisaic sage of the end of the first century B.C.E. and beginning of the first century C.E. At Yavneh, under Rabban Gamliel's direction, the rabbis engaged in standardizing, recording, and gathering traditions. This process, and its extension to the entire Jewish people, would take centuries to complete. In addition, Rabban Gamliel undertook, perhaps with specific Roman authority, to establish the patriarchate as the system of self-government for the Jews of Palestine. He acted out of a sense that this measure was the only way to bring about the Jewish people's economic and political restoration in their own land and to unite the whole nation under the authority of one Judaism, tannaitic Judaism.

Rabban Gamaliel's efforts in this direction went too far at times, and he was almost removed from office by his colleagues. Yet his overzealousness was part and parcel of the effort to establish his authority on a firm basis. Had that authority not been established, and the tannaim, in consequence, not been able to play their crucial leadership role, it is doubtful that the Jewish people would have been adequately prepared for future catastrophes and for the vicissitudes of medieval life in the Near East and in Europe.

JOSEPHUS: HISTORIAN OF THE GREAT REVOLT

Most of what we know about Jewish history in the era of the revolt and the Hasmonean dynasty is known from the works of the historian Josephus. He was born in 37/38 C.E. to a priestly family. After acquiring an excellent education in Jerusalem, he tells us, he studied in the schools of the Pharisees, Sadducees, and Essenes, and then with a desert hermit named Bannus. When he returned to Jerusalem at nineteen, he took up the approach of the Pharisees. In 64 C.E. he was sent to Rome to secure the release of certain priests imprisoned by the procurator. During the war against Rome he served as commander of the Galilee, where he was unsuccessful, either because he only half-heartedly supported the revolt or for objective military reasons. After his surrender he took the side of the Romans, later claiming that he had believed that only some form of accommodation could end the ill-advised war and save the nation and its Temple from destruction. When the war ended he went to Rome. There he received from Vespasian a place to live, Roman citizenship, a pension, and lands in Judea. He must have died around 100 C.E.

There are some important things to keep in mind about Josephus as a historian. First, he did not in fact author most of what his works preserve. The great bulk of it comes from various sources, including Jewish materials, documentary evidence (some forged), and some of the best-known historians of Antiquity, which he compiled, sometimes even slavishly, ignoring contradictions with his own words or with his other sources. Second, he had a specific ax to grind. He sought to demonstrate to the Jews that life under Rome was not so bad as long as religious freedom was guaranteed. He also wanted to show the Romans that the war had been brought about by a minority of the Jews and had not reflected the attitude of the people at large. This was certainly one of the main functions of his *Jewish War*, written toward the end of Vespasian's reign, between 75 and 79 C.E. He also attempted to relate the story of the war as if he had not been among those to blame for its failure. This is especially evident in his *Life*, a work which cannot be precisely dated. His *Antiquities of the Jews*, completed in 93 or 94 C.E., is a history of the Jews from earliest times to the end of the first century C.E. This work also has a purpose, to show the hoary antiquity and, hence, legitimacy of the Jews and Judaism within the Greco-Roman world. In his *Against Apion*, written after *Antiquities*, the purpose is to respond to anti-Semitic propaganda and to maintain that Jews had not set themselves apart from the human race by their religion, as their enemies alleged, and did not believe the ridiculous things often attributed to them.

Josephus's works, written in Greek (one may originally have been composed in Hebrew or Aramaic) served to educate both Greek-speaking Jews and non-Jews about the nature and history of the Jews and Judaism. These books were quickly lost to the Jewish people, as assimilation and conversion to Christianity led to the decline of the Greek-speaking Jewish community whose members would have read Josephus's works. In the Middle Ages some of his writings circulated again in the form of the book of *Josippon*, a medieval Hebrew translation of a Latin adaptation. Without Josephus, the entire Herodian period and the story of the Great Revolt would be, historically speaking, virtually unknown.

THE BAR KOKHBA REVOLT

The debacle of the first revolt against Rome was followed by a period of relative calm. Yet during the years of rule by the autonomous Hillelite patriarchs and the leaders of the tannaitic academies, problems were brewing, both inside and outside the Land of Israel. These developments took place despite the separation of Judea from the province of Syria and the appointment of higher-level Roman governors of senatorial rank. In particular, the need to pay a capitation tax to the Temple of Jupiter in Rome must have made the Jews very unhappy.

It was not until the reign of the Roman emperor Trajan (98–117 C.E.) that the problems came to the surface. In 115–117 C.E., while Trajan was occupied in Mesopotamia, Jews through-

THE ROMAN EMPERORS

44 B.C.E.	Assassination of Julius Caesar
27 B.C.E.–14 C.E.	Augustus
37–41	Caligula
41–54	Claudius
54–68	Nero
69	Galba, Otho, Vitellius
69–79	Vespasian
79–81	Titus
81–96	Domitian
96–98	Nerva
98–117	Trajan
117–138	Hadrian
138–161	Antoninus Pius
161–180	Marcus Aurelius
193–211	Septimus Severus
222–235	Alexander Severus
284–305	Diocletian

out the Diaspora rose up against their non-Jewish neighbors in a violent confrontation. Before long pitched battles were being fought in Egypt. The Jews of Cyrene (in North Africa) were said to have massacred their neighbors. Similar disturbances followed in Cyprus and Mesopotamia. The Roman general Lucius Quietus, ferocious in putting down the Mesopotamian revolt, was rewarded with the governorship of Palestine. When Hadrian became emperor in 117 C.E. he had to spend his first year mopping up the last of the rebels. The Land of Israel seems to have been involved in these battles only to a limited extent.

What is especially significant in these disturbances is the evidence that they were fueled by the very same messianic yearnings that had helped to fan the flames of the Great Revolt and would soon lead to the Bar Kokhba Revolt. To be sure, other social, economic, and political causes were at work, especially a general decline in relations between Jews and their neighbors in the Hellenistic world, but when these finally led to the outbreak of a rebellion, it was the belief in a messianic future that made possible the leap of faith to the belief that the revolt might succeed.

Early in the time of Hadrian there was an abortive attempt to rebuild the Jerusalem Temple, believed by some scholars to have had Hadrian's support. The failure of this effort was another great disappointment for the Jewish community of Palestine. Soon after, Hadrian founded a city of his own in Jerusalem called Aelia Capitolina, where he erected a temple to Zeus. It is also probable that Hadrian prohibited circumcision even before the Bar Kokhba Revolt, although some see the outlawing of circumcision as a measure enacted after the uprising had begun, much like the persecutions of Antiochus IV. It was in this context, as well as on the basis of the strong messianic yearnings we have observed already, that some elements in the Jewish population of Palestine began preparing for revolt in the 120's.

The revolt did not begin until it had found its leader. From letters and documents unearthed in the Judean Desert we know the real name of the leader to have been Simeon bar Kosiba. The sobriquet Bar Kokhba, "Son of a Star," was given to him in accord with Num. 24:17 ("A star shall go forth from Jacob"), taken to refer to the messiah. The tannaim were divided, some supporting his rebellion, others not. Those who supported him saw him as a messianic figure.

The war began as a guerilla struggle against Rome in 132 C.E. Within a short time it had spread throughout the country, and the rebels took Jerusalem, which had not been heavily fortified by the Romans. It is possible that sacrifices were now reinstituted and that work was begun on rebuilding the sanctuary. From the coins Bar Kokhba struck we know of his high priest, Eleazar, who must have taken the lead in efforts to reestablish sacrificial worship. Here we see a reflection of the ancient concept of two messiahs, a lay and a priestly figure, prominent in the Testaments of the Twelve Patriarchs and in certain Qumran scrolls.

We know from the documents that the country was organized into administrative districts, that taxes were collected, and that governmental operations were carried out by Bar Kokhba's supporters. Bar Kokhba observed Jewish law, and it may be stated that the documents confirm the close relationship between this "messiah" and tannaitic Judaism. Parenthetically,

the texts also show that Hebrew was very much a living language at this time, and that, along with Aramaic and Greek, it
served a large segment of the population.

Little is known of the actual course of the revolt and of Rome's
successful attempt to regain control. Hadrian sent one of his
finest generals, and he succeeded in turning the tide by means
of a series of sieges, starving out the rebels in their strongholds
and places of refuge. Jerusalem was retaken and future Jewish
settlement there was prohibited by Hadrian. The last fortress
to fall was Betar, not far to the southwest of Jerusalem, which
was captured by the Romans during the summer of 135 C.E. By
the end of the war many Jews had been massacred, the land had
been devastated again, and distinguished rabbis had been mar-
tyred. Indeed, the execution of these rabbis, together with the
biblical story of the binding of Isaac, would serve as a paradigm
for Jewish martyrdom (termed *qiddush ha-shem*, "sanctification
of God's name") in the medieval and modern periods. Once again
a Jewish attempt to defeat the Romans and to bring the messianic era had failed.

REBUILDING FOR THE FUTURE

As if history were repeating itself, recovery and the reinsti-
tution of Jewish self-government ensued once again. With the
accession of the emperor Antoninus Pius (138–161 C.E.), virtually all of Hadrian's decrees were rescinded. The patriarchate
and the high court were reconstituted at Usha, in the Galilee.
Indeed, the two revolts contributed greatly to encouraging the
Jewish population of Palestine to move from Judea to the north,
settling primarily in the Galilee. Under Rabban Simeon ben
Gamaliel II, (first half of the second century C.E.) and later
under Rabbi Judah the Prince (latter half of the second and
beginning of the third century C.E.), the editor of the Mishnah,
the patriarchate and the other institutions of the Jewish community reached their height. Taxes poured into the patriarchal
coffers even from the Diaspora, where the emissaries of the
rabbis of Palestine attempted to foster the spread of tannaitic
Judaism. With the exception of two restrictions, the ban on
proselytism and the ban on Jews living in Jerusalem, Jewish life

CONTRACT FROM THE THIRD YEAR OF BAR KOKHBA. From the years
of the Bar Kokhba Revolt against Rome, 132–135 C.E., numerous
contracts survived in the caves of the Judean Desert. Above is part of
a Hebrew contract, found at Naḥal Ḥever, from Bar Kokhba's third
year, dividing land which had been leased jointly. In the first line the
letter preserves the name Simeon ben Kosiba (called here "Prince of
Israel"), the actual name of Bar Kokhba who was given the name "son
of a star" (Bar Kokhba) based on the messianic interpretation of Num.
24:17. *Courtesy of the Shrine of the Book of the Israel Museum.*

in this period was virtually unfettered. The latter restriction seems to have been often compromised. Under the Severan dynasty (193–225 C.E.) Jewish fortunes improved with the granting of a variety of legal privileges culminating in full Roman citizenship for Jews. The enjoyment of these privileges and the peace which Jewry enjoyed in the Roman Empire were interrupted only by the invasions by the barbarians in the West and the instability and economic decline they caused throughout the empire, and by the Parthian incursions against Roman territories in the East.

The latter years of Roman rule, in the aftermath of the Bar Kokhba Revolt and on the verge of the Christianization of the empire, were extremely fertile ones for the development of Judaism. It was in this period that tannaitic Judaism came to its final stages, and that the work of gathering its intellectual heritage, the Mishnah, into a redacted collection began. All the suffering and the fervent yearnings for redemption had culminated not in a messianic state, but in a collection of traditions which set forth the dreams and aspirations for the perfect holiness that state was to engender. As prayer had replaced sacrifice, Torah, in the form of the Mishnah, had now replaced messianism. A different kind of redemption was now at hand.

SUMMARY

The Roman period in Palestine brought a series of disappointments for the Jews. Two attempts to throw off the yoke of Roman rule and to return the nation to independent statehood were doomed to failure by Rome's superior military might. The first revolt, that of 66–73 C.E., was seriously undermined by the inability of the various groups of rebels to stand together. To some extent, these differences may have reflected the still unresolved conflicts of Second Temple times. At the same time, the failure of both revolts led to further advances in rabbinic influence. The necessary conditions were created for the profound development of the religious tradition that was eventually enshrined in the great corpus of rabbinic literature.

10
Mishnah: The New Scripture

The period beginning with the destruction (or rather, with the restoration in approximately 80 C.E.) saw a fundamental change in Jewish study and learning. This was the era in which the Mishnah was being compiled and in which many other tannaitic traditions were taking shape. The fundamental change was that the oral Torah gradually evolved into a fixed corpus of its own which eventually replaced the written Torah as the main object of Jewish study and guide for religious practice, at least for rabbinic Jews. This process may be seen as the culmination of the attempts of the tannaim (the teachers of the Mishnah) to make their traditions the way of the future. The redaction (collection and editing) of the Mishnah, and the subsequent tannaitic and amoraic compositions, ultimately made possible the expansion of Rabbinic Judaism to virtually all of the world's Jews in the early Middle Ages.

FROM PHARISEES TO RABBIS

Inherent in the later traditions, and indeed, in most modern scholarly treatments, is the assumption that the Pharisees bequeathed their traditions to the tannaim. The terms "Pharisees" and "tannaim" overlap chronologically. We speak of Pharisaic Judaism as emerging in the early Hasmonean period, around 150 B.C.E., and continuing up to the destruction of the Temple in 70 C.E., when it was succeeded by tannaitic Judaism. Yet the transition was not an immediate, sudden break. In order to understand how the development from Pharisees to tannaim took place, we must ask what typified the Pharisee and what typified the tanna. In what ways were they the same, and in what ways were they different?

The Pharisees were lay sages of the Torah who were only informally organized. Even before the days of the preeminent sages Hillel and Shammai, the Pharisees had made the transition from being a political force in the Hasmonean coalition to being a group of religious leaders, loosely joined together by the same interpretation of Judaism, who sought to teach their approach to the people at large. They did not see the collection, arrangement, or passing on of traditions as their function, nor were they an organized bureaucracy.

The tannaim, on the other hand, involved themselves in the systematic collection and transmission of traditions, and their efforts eventually culminated in the redaction of the Mishnah. (The very name *tanna* is Aramaic for a memorizer and reciter of traditions.) The tannaim belonged to schools (sometimes called academies) that were more formalized than those of the earlier Pharisees, and they sought to expand and to organize them.

A final, fundamental difference has to do with the concept of an oral law. Pharisaism traced its nonbiblical legal and exegetical traditions to the "tradition of the fathers" or "unwritten laws." Yet nowhere do we find the Pharisees asserting that these traditions came from Sinai. The tannaim, as we will soon see, asserted that their extrabiblical traditions, many of them inherited from the Pharisees, were part of the oral law, a second Torah given by God to Moses at Sinai along with the written law.

The evolution from the era of the Pharisees to that of the tannaim, like the later transition from tannaim to amoraim (the teachers of the Talmud [Gemara], ca. 200–500 C.E.), required time to allow for the necessary innovations as well as for organic development. Various external causes helped to foster the change. The desire to gather traditions and standardize Judaism was brought about by the Great Revolt of 66–73 C.E. and by the notion that the defeat was partly the result of the sectarian strife that had plagued the Jewish people in the years leading up to the revolt and even during the war. The tendency toward more organized schools replacing the informal circles of Pharisaic times was encouraged to some extent by the new status which the tannaitic academy was granted by the Roman overlords. The rise of a bureaucracy and the role of tannaim as judges throughout the land resulted from the new political situation. Finally, the desire to collect and preserve traditions is always strengthened in periods after wars and catastrophes, a pattern which can be observed repeatedly in the ancient Near East.

WRITTEN AND ORAL TORAH

One of the basic premises on which the tradition of the tannaim was based was the concept of the two Torahs, oral and written, which, the rabbis believed, had been given by God to Moses on Sinai. According to the rabbinic view, the two Torahs were complementary. The oral Torah provided the interpretations and explanations which made possible the application of the written Torah as a way of life. Therefore, the two Torahs were of equal status and authority with one another. Further, the accuracy of the transmission of the teachings of both Torahs was seen to depend not only on the correctness of the contents, but also upon the mode of transmission. The tannaim make clear that to be considered authentic, a tradition must be transmitted in the same way it was given at Sinai. Therefore, the written Torah had to be taught from a scroll, and the oral law had to be recited orally by a tanna.

The history of the oral law concept is complex. Its earliest attestation is found in Josephus. He asserts that the Pharisees possessed ancient traditions which they had inherited from past generations. These traditions, combined with ancient customary law as well as with the emerging midrashic exegesis which was developing in the Second Temple period, provided the basic content of what the rabbis later called the oral law. At some point between the late first century B.C.E. and the first century C.E., the notion began to be expressed that the oral law, along with the written, had been given at Sinai. This development has been explained by some modern scholars as the result of a

THE TANNAIM
(all dates are C.E.)

First Generation, ca. 10–90 C.E.

School of Hillel
School of Shammai
Akaviah ben Mahalalel
Gamaliel I

Simeon ben Gamaliel I
Yoḥanan ben Zakkai
Ḥanina ben Dosa
Eliezer ben Jacob I
Neḥuniah ben Ha-Kana

Second Generation, ca. 90–130 C.E.

Gamaliel II
Eliezer ben Hyrcanus
Joshua ben Ḥananiah
Eleazar ben Zadok I
Ishmael
Akiva ben Joseph
Eleazar ben Azariah

Ṭarfon
Yose the Galilean
Ḥananiah ben Teradion
Judah ben Batyra
Ben Azzai
Ben Zoma

Third Generation, ca. 120–140 C.E.

Meir
Simeon ben Yoḥai
Yose ben Ḥalafta
Judah ben Ilai
Eliezer ben Jacob II
Yoḥanan Ha-Sandlar

Nehemiah
Eleazar ben Shammua
Simeon ben Gamaliel II
Eliezer ben Yose
Joshua ben Qarḥa
Eleazar ben Zadok II

Fourth Generation, ca. 140–200 C.E.

Judah the Prince
Symmachus
Eleazar ben Simeon
Yose ben Judah

Ishmael ben Yose
Simeon ben Eleazar
Nathan
Eleazar Ha-Kappar

Fifth Generation, ca. 200–225

Gamaliel III
Ḥiyya the Elder
Bar Kappara

Simeon ben Ḥalafta
Levi bar Sisi
Huna

desire on the part of the Yavnean rabbinic authorities to solidify their authority by claiming divine origin for their own traditions. Actually, however, such ideas were developing naturally as the various approaches to Judaism in the Second Temple period strove to provide the written law with an appropriate supplement to make it possible for the Torah to serve as a genuine way of life in the Greco-Roman period. In Pharisaic-Rabbinic Judaism, this was accomplished by the oral law.

This idea allowed Pharisaic Judaism, and, later, the rabbinic tradition, to develop organically. It provided the basis for the assertion of continuity in Talmudic Judaism, an assertion maintained even in the face of numerous adaptations and adjustments, for in the view of the rabbis there had been no changes—all later developments had already been commanded as part of the Sinaitic revelation.

Talmudic tradition has always assumed that the notion that two Torahs were given on Sinai went all the way back in time. Modern scholars have come to question this assumption. In any case, firm evidence shows that the concept was fully developed by the aftermath of the revolt. By that time, appeals to the Sinaitic origin of laws were made, although the notion of a dual Torah and dual revelation was not nearly as evident as one might expect. Clearly, then, the idea was developing in Pharisaic times, and the unwritten laws of the fathers were an earlier stage in its development. The concept became more important in the period leading up to the destruction. In the difficult years after the revolt, when the support of the people at large (the *'am ha-'areṣ*) was so important, the rabbis, in order to guarantee the authority of their teachings, occasionally appealed to the divine origin and nature of the oral law. It was only in amoraic times, however, that the full midrashic basis for these ideas was worked out, with the rabbis asserting that the oral Torah and its authority were mentioned in the written law. In this case, though, the transition cannot be understood as the result of external political influences. It resulted from an organic trend in Judaism which developed in a manner consistent with the needs of the times. Indeed, this is the manner of most developments and changes in Judaism, the unique contribution of the Pharisaic heritage.

THE TANNAITIC ACADEMIES

In order to understand how this transition took place, and
how the tannaitic corpus developed, some explanation of the
history and function of the tannaitic academies is necessary. Yet
we must caution that the term "academies" may be anachronistic. It conjures up an image of institutions in which there is an
academic bureaucracy, a system of funding, and physical premises of some kind, but we cannot be sure that the tannaim always
worked under such ideal conditions. Although the patriarchate
sponsored the high court (Sanhedrin), it is not totally certain
how the academies were organized and who funded them. It is
also not clear whether they had specific premises. They may
have met in synagogues or other facilities. At the same time, it
should be noted that tannaitic sources mention houses of study
along with the synagogues. This tends to support the claim that
specific buildings and more organized institutions existed in the
mishnaic period. Among the duties of the patriarch (*nasi'*) was
the maintenance of the academies; and he designated an *'av bet
din*, "head of the court," to lead them. The power of the two
officials was not constant, however, and there is occasional
evidence of disagreement and even strife between them.

A generational scheme has traditionally been used since the
Middle Ages to classify the tannaim and trace their history. The
actual tannaim were preceded by a series of Pharisaic sages
known as pairs (Hebrew *zugot*), one of whom, in each instance,
is reported to have served as patriarch (*nasi'*), and the other as
head of the court (*'av bet din*), during the Hasmonean and
Herodian periods. These culminate in Hillel and Shammai, said
to be the last pair.

The last of the *zugot* were followed by the first generation of
tannaim, consisting of the Houses of Hillel and Shammai, the
two major schools, which were made up of the followers of these
two great sages. The figures of the first generation were prominent immediately before and after the Great Revolt, and among
the most notable were Rabban Gamaliel I, mentioned in the
New Testament, Simeon ben Gamaliel I, who probably died in
the revolt, and Rabban Yoḥanan ben Zakkai, credited with
organizing the academy at Yavneh after the destruction of
Jerusalem.

The second generation functioned after the revolt, from about 90 to 130 C.E., at Yavneh. Among these sages were Rabban Gamaliel II, who led the academy at Yavneh after Yoḥanan ben Zakkai, Rabbi Eliezer ben Hyrcanus, and the slightly younger Rabbi Akiva and Rabbi Ishmael. The second generation took the lead in reconstituting Jewish life in Palestine and in gathering together the traditions of their pre–70 C.E. Pharisaic and tannaitic forebears.

The third generation spanned the Bar Kokhba period and its aftermath, functioning from about 130 to 160 C.E. They were primarily the students of Rabbis Akiva and Ishmael of the previous generation. Prominent before the Bar Kokhba Revolt were Rabbi Meir, Rabbi Simeon ben Yoḥai, and Rabbi Judah ben Ilai. It is probable that Rabbi Meir began the editing of the Mishnah based on subject divisions he had learned from Rabbi Akiva. The leading rabbinic figure in the restoration of Jewish life after the Bar Kokhba Revolt was Rabban Simeon ben Gamaliel II, the patriarch. These scholars functioned primarily at Usha, in the Galilee, to which the patriarchal court had moved after the Bar Kokhba Revolt of 132–135 C.E.

The fourth generation covered the period of from about 160 to 200 C.E. This was the generation of Rabbi Judah the Prince (Hebrew *nasi'* = prince, i.e. patriarch), the majestic patriarch who edited the Mishnah. His court was at Beth Shearim in the Galilee, and among his contemporaries were Rabbi Eleazar ben Rabbi Simeon (ben Yoḥai), Rabbi Simeon ben Eleazar, and Rabbi Nathan.

The members of the fifth generation, from about 200 to 225 C.E., are said to be semi-tannaim, as they were primarily younger contemporaries of Rabbi Judah the Prince, who continued their work after the Mishnah was redacted. Among them were Rabban Gamaliel III, the son of Rabbi Judah the Prince and himself also a patriarch, Rabbi Ḥiyya the Elder, and Bar Kappara. By this time, the center of the patriarchate and the court had shifted to the Galilean city of Sepphoris, the economic and social climate of which made it an ideal home for the sages of the Sanhedrin.

While the system of generations provides a useful chronological framework for the development of tannaitic Judaism, it does not adequately portray the great diversity of the tannaitic teachers, the complex, interlocking student-master relationships, or the geographic diversity. Yet these are the very factors which made for the richness of the tannaitic legacy. Generational schemes are ultimately based on a linear view of history, an approach considered normative in the Middle Ages, but outmoded in modern times. Modern scholarship is only now in the process of building up a more complete picture that will take these other factors into account, and it is certain to enrich greatly our understanding of this period and its literature.

MIDRASH AND MISHNAH

There were two forms of study in the tannaitic period, respectively termed mishnah and midrash. There is a long-standing and important debate about which method of study came first. Mishnah is the study of abstract, apodictic principles of law (apodictic laws are unconditional legal prescriptions unaccompanied by reasons or biblical sources) which only later were organized into collections according to either literary form, attribution (the name of the sage reported to have said it), or subject. Ultimately, the method of organization by subject became most prominent and led to the organization of the text known as the Mishnah. Some remnants of earlier systems of organization are still visible in the Mishnah, however. In the mishnaic method, scholars are assumed to have stated their legal principles and the decisions of their predecessors without making reference to their scriptural or traditional basis or explaining, in most cases, the reasons behind them.

The midrashic method is a technique of scriptural exposition. It concentrated primarily on the Torah, which was the supreme authority for the midrashic method and was studied as the basic text. Scholars and students explained how specific laws derived from biblical verses or words and how the laws were to be applied.

Can we determine which of these methods actually came first? There is evidence from the very end of the biblical period, i.e., the Persian period (Ezra, Nehemiah, and Chronicles), that midrashic exegesis for legal purposes (*midrash halakhah*) was

CATACOMBS OF BETH SHEARIM. In the second century C.E. the patriarchal family and many aristocratic families from Palestine and the
Diaspora were buried in the catacombs of Beth Shearim, south-east of
Haifa. Among those buried there were Rabbi Judah the Prince and
members of his court. Photo A shows the entrance to the burial place
of the patriarchal family. Inside the catacombs (photo B) were found
numerous sarcophagi decorated with Greco-Roman motifs and inscriptions in Hebrew, Aramaic and Greek. *Courtesy of the Institute of
Archaeology of the Hebrew University.*

already becoming popular and being used for arriving at legal decisions. Non-rabbinic sources, including material from the Qumran sect and some other groups, give evidence that scriptural interpretation was used as the basis for law in the Second Temple period. Finally, while it is possible to suggest a logical progression from the midrashic method to the mishnaic, no sufficient explanation can be offered for how the reverse would have occurred. For all these reasons, the view that originally the study of the Bible was the primary method and then, secondarily, the method of mishnaic, apodictic formulation developed, is most likely to be historically correct.

The history of these methods of study may be traced as follows. After the close of the biblical period, the midrashic approach found in the later biblical books was taken over by the Pharisees. Other Second Temple groups used similar methods of biblical exegesis, as we know from the Dead Sea Scrolls. As the midrashic approach developed in Pharisaic circles, the amount of material supplementary to the Bible itself became greater and greater until at some point the laws themselves were formulated independently and concisely. These mishnah-like, apodictic laws began to be studied as a separate subject side by side with midrashim as the tradition developed. By the time Pharisaism gave way to tannaitic Judaism, the two were coexistent, and the tannaim practiced both methods.

Both methods of study were utilized in the tannaitic academies, and, hence, the materials which emerged from the academies all bear a common mark, that of accretion over a long period of time. Each generation of scholars began with the work of its predecessors and augmented and modified it. The amalgamation of the old tradition with the new was then passed down, so that constant development was taking place. Further, as the generations continued this chain, midrashic and mishnaic materials intermixed so that one influenced the other, and each sometimes quoted the other. Later mishnaic formulations emerged from continued study of the Bible, and even in the Mishnah one finds midrashic expansion.

Often, instead of the original pattern in which the midrashic method yielded laws or at least legal statements, entire midrashic sections of our texts are sometimes built retrospectively on mishnaic selections. With time, each corpus was filled out by the other, until they began to conform to a common, consistent tradition. By the close of the redaction of the tannaitic texts, the midrashic and mishnaic collections were, therefore, largely in agreement. Whereas mishnaic tradition was eventually distilled and redacted by the end of the second century C.E. by Rabbi Judah the Prince, the results of midrashic inquiry were not collected until much later, in fifth-century Palestine.

HALAKHAH AND AGGADAH

In tannaitic literature, two terms are employed which signified two aspects of the emerging tradition, halakhah and aggadah. The word *halakhah* was used to denote Jewish law as it was understood and determined by the tannaim and later by the amoraim. This term has been explained in two ways. Many have seen it as emerging from the root *hlk*, "to go," metaphorically suggesting the concept "a way of life." Another view derives the word *halakhah* from an ancient Mesopotamian tax on land called *ilku* in Akkadian, and *halakh* in biblical Aramaic.

In contrast, the second category, aggadah, known also as haggadah (a term later used to denote the Passover Seder text) is that part of rabbinic teaching not considered obligatory. Aggadah, derived from the verb *higgid* (from the root *ngd*), meaning "to tell," consists of interpretations, stories, and legends, all of which are designed to attract followers to Rabbinic Judaism and to explicate its teachings and principles. Since in many areas the aggadah provides differing positions on the same issues, no one position can be obligatory. Originally, this was also the case with halakhah, but a long process of decision-making eventually resulted in a normative set of laws by the Middle Ages. The practical aspects of the need to determine the authoritative ruling led more and more toward standardization. Such a process never occurred in regard to the non-legal aspects of rabbinic tradition, the aggadah. Hence, aggadah continued to demonstrate greater variety than did halakhah.

These two aspects of talmudic tradition demonstrate the creative tension in Rabbinic Judaism between the fixed and the flexible. The fixed body of law and practice is offset by the more open and nonobligatory teachings regarding which the rabbinic Jew is free to disagree. This characteristic is an important principle in the later development of traditional Judaism, since it allowed the eventual standardization of most of the halakhic norms while leaving open to debate the theological underpinnings, all within certain limits which emerged from the rabbinic consensus at the end of the talmudic period.

THE REDACTION OF THE MISHNAH

Scholars have long debated the exact nature and history of the process that led to the redaction, arrangement, and selection of the Mishnah, the first major document to emerge from and to represent the tannaitic tradition. The Mishnah was the only major text to be redacted in the tannaitic period, although other texts, edited afterwards in the amoraic period (200–500 C.E.), depended heavily on tannaitic materials. The Mishnah became the formative document in the shaping of Talmudic Judaism. The redaction of the Mishnah by Rabbi Judah the Prince (ca. 200 C.E.) represented the end of a process, although the extent of his contribution should not be minimized.

Most modern scholars agree that the Mishnah originated in discrete statements, some attached to specific named authorities. Only a small part of the mishnaic material is attributed to the period before the Roman conquest of Palestine in 63 B.C.E. Between then and the period leading up to the Great Revolt of 66–73 C.E. are attributed materials relating to Hillel and Shammai and to the Houses of Hillel and Shammai, the schools of tannaim consisting of the students of these two preeminent sages. Yet it must be recognized that the material preserved in the earliest strata of tannaitic literature was originally in forms different from those in which the material is preserved from the post-destruction period.

THE PERIODIZATION OF THE ORAL LAW

ca. 150 B.C.E.–ca. 70 C.E.	Pharisees
ca. 50 B.C.E.–ca. 200 C.E.	Tannaim (note overlap)
ca. 200 C.E.–ca. 500 C.E.	Amoraim
ca. 500 C.E.–ca. 700 C.E.	Savoraim (Babylonia only)

With the destruction of the Temple and the shifting of the activity of the tannaim to Yavneh, Usha, Beth Shearim, and Sepphoris, profound changes occurred in the manner by which tannaitic material was transmitted. A process began of bringing together divergent views on issues into disputes and shaping the statements so as to reflect the divergence of opinion. Further, mnemonic formulations became more common, as students and teachers were expected to be familiar with an increasingly large body of oral material.

It is difficult to determine at what point in the history of the mishnaic material the process of redaction began. By redaction, we mean the bringing together of diverse materials into blocks of material, assembled from disparate sources by a compiler. Among the earliest principles for the assembling of such materials, usually no larger than a chapter of the present Mishnah, were either the recurrence of a general formulary, such as "there is no difference between X and Y except Z," or attribution to a particular sage. There is evidence in the existing Mishnah text of earlier arrangements of small corpora of material which were ordered in this manner, rather than according to the dominant system of subject classification.

ORDERS AND TRACTATES OF THE MISHNAH, TOSEFTA, AND TALMUDS

Zera'im	*Agricultural Laws*
Berakhot	Benedictions
Pe'ah	Gleanings of the Field
Demai	Doubtfully Tithed Produce
Kilayim	Forbidden Mixtures
Shevi'it	Sabbatical Year
Terumot	Priestly Portions
Ma'aserot	Tithes for Levites and the Poor
Ma'aser Sheni	Tithe to Be Eaten in Jerusalem
Ḥallah	Dough Offering
Orlah	Fruit of Young Trees
Bikkurim	First Fruits
Mo'ed	*Holy Occasions, Festivals*
Shabbat	Sabbath
Eruvin	Extension of Sabbath Limits

Pesaḥim	Passover
Sheqalim	Half-Shekel Offering
Yoma	Day of Atonement
Sukkah	Festival of Sukkot
Beṣah	Festival Laws
Rosh Ha-Shanah	New Year
Ta'anit	Fast-Days
Megillah	Purim and Tora Reading
Mo'ed Qaṭan	Intermediate Days of Festivals
Ḥagigah	Festival Sacrifices

Nashim	*Women, Marriage Law*
Yevamot	Levirate Marriage
Ketubot	Marriage Contracts
Nedarim	Vows
Nazir	Nazirites
Soṭah	Suspected Adulteress
Giṭṭin	Divorce
Qiddushin	Marriage

Neziqin	*Damages and Civil Law*
Bava Qamma	Damages
Bava Meṣia	Civil Law
Bava Batra	Property Law
Sanhedrin	Courts and Penalties
Makkot	Flagellation
Shevu'ot	Oaths
Eduyot	Legal Traditions
Avodah Zarah	Idolatry
Avot	Ethics of the Fathers
Horayot	Erroneous Court Decisions

Qodashim	*Sacrifices*
Zevaḥim	Animal Offerings
Menaḥot	Meal Offerings
Ḥullin	Slaughter of Food Animals
Bekhorot	Firstborn Animals
Arakhin	Vows of Valuation
Temurah	Substitution of Offerings
Keritot	Penalty of Excision
Me'ilah	Misappropriation of Offerings

Tamid	Daily Sacrifices
Middot	Dimensions of the Temple
Kinim	Bird Offerings

Ṭahorot	*Purification Rituals*
Kelim	Impurity of Vessels
Ohalot	Impurity Through Overshadowing
Negaʻim	Skin Diseases
Parah	Red Heifer
Ṭahorot	Ritual Purification
Miqvaʼot	Ritual Baths
Niddah	Menstrual Impurity
Makhshirim	Liquids Rendering Food Susceptible to Impurity
Zavim	Bodily Fluxes
Ṭevul Yom	Ritual Impurity Between Immersion and Sunset
Yadayim	Impurity of the Hands
Uqṣin	Impurity of Parts of Plants

Sometime after the destruction, the approach of organizing the materials by subject became prominent. This opened the way to the development of large-scale "essays" on topics of law. Later tradition and many modern scholars ascribe the basic subject classification into orders (Hebrew *sedarim*) and tractates (*massekhtot*) to Rabbi Akiva, who flourished at the Yavneh academy around 80–132 C.E. Whether he was responsible for this concept is impossible to determine with precision. Yet the large number of highly developed treatises which remain embedded in, or which even constitute, mishnaic tractates from the period between the Great Revolt (66–73 C.E.) and the Bar Kokhba Revolt (132–135 C.E.) proves that this approach, at least on the level of individual tractates, was evolving in his day. It was left for those who came after Rabbi Akiva at the academy at Usha to bring many tractates to a well-developed state.

After the Bar Kokhba Revolt, the process continued with renewed vigor. Attempts were made to gather together traditions, as often happens after a tragedy of great proportions. Thus, many more tractates began to move toward completion while halakhic concepts developed over the years served as the basis for new organizational and redactional approaches. By the time Rabbi Judah the Prince began his work of final redaction,

he had most probably inherited many almost completed tractates and a basic system of classification by orders. He completed the compilation of the individual tractates and placed
them in the appropriate orders.

Rabbi Judah the Prince, known often as "Rabbi" in the
Mishnah, the rabbi par excellence, did not seek to create an
authoritative code of law. Had he, we would have to judge his
work a failure. After all, the amoraim, the teachers of the
Talmud (Gemara), set aside or modified so many of his rulings.
He provided variant rulings on many subjects, explaining that
his purpose was to keep options open for later courts of greater
authority and wisdom. He intended to create a curriculum for
the study of Jewish law. Yet he sought to point out which rulings
he favored by providing information on majority and minority
status of rulings, and by indicating the greater or lesser authority of individual tradents (transmitters of tradition) and decisors
whose statements he included. He even placed materials in his
text anonymously, though he was well aware of the tradents, in
order to indicate that the ruling was (in his view) to be followed.
These views, by and large, he reproduced anonymously, or with
the label "the opinion of the sages," where there was an individual who dissented.

The material was organized into six orders: Zera'im (Agricultural Laws), Mo'ed (Holy Occasions, Festivals), Nashim (Women,
Marriage Law), Neziqin (Damages and Civil Law), Qodashim
(Sacrifices), and Tahorot (Purification Rituals). Each order comprised several tractates. Today, these tractates are arranged
roughly in size order within each order, at least in Mishnah
texts. The same order was later used for the Tosefta, and for
the Babylonian and Palestinian Talmuds. Within the six orders
there are a total of sixty-three tractates.

Zera'im begins with a discussion of prayers and benedictions
(anomalous in this order) and then deals with produce given as
charity to the poor, tithing, priestly dues, Sabbatical years, and
first fruits. Mo'ed deals with the Sabbath and festivals, as well
as fast-days and other special occasions. In most tractates
emphasis is clearly on the aspects of Temple ritual associated
with the holiday. Nashim discusses marriage, divorce, adultery,
and vows. Neziqin prescribes the composition of the court and

MISHNAH FRAGMENT FROM THE CAIRO GENIZAH. The Ben Ezra Synagogue in Fustat, Old Cairo, served as a depository for old Hebrew manuscripts throughout the Middle Ages. When these texts began to come to light around the turn of the century, they led to profound developments in the study of Jewish literature and history. Among them were fragments of early manuscripts of the Mishnah. Above is an example of such a manuscript of Tractate Yevamot. *Courtesy of the Library of the Jewish Theological Seminary of America.*

then deals with criminal sanctions, damage law, idolatry, and incorrect rulings by the courts. The tractate Avot (known as Pirqe Avot, or Ethics of the Fathers) comes near the close of this order. It includes ethical teachings aimed at the rabbinic class. Qodashim deals with animal sacrifices, meal offerings, ritual slaughter, violations of sancta, daily sacrifice, and the structure of the Temple precincts. Ṭahorot discusses laws of purification pertaining to vessels for food, the impurity of the dead, the skin diseases described in Leviticus, menstrual and other impurities, and the construction of ritual baths for purification.

If there is anything to be learned from this survey it is that the Mishnah reflects the full variety of the Torah's laws, and that it is firmly anchored in a Temple-centered reality in which priests, sacrifices, and purity remain as important as Sabbath and festivals, civil law, marriage, and family. This does not mean that the Mishnah was created in the days of the Temple. Rather, it was edited in an atmosphere in which the restoration of a Temple-centered reality was still a living hope, and in which the conception of sanctity still flowed from that reality, even in its absence.

We have already noted that the tannaim believed the oral law to have been revealed to Moses by God at Sinai, alongside the written law. This should have required that the oral law be transmitted orally, and, indeed, so it was in the tannaitic period. At the same time, evidence indicates that individual tannaim kept notebooks in which they listed certain oral traditions. There was a debate throughout the medieval period on the question of when the Mishnah was written down. Some believed that Rabbi Judah the Prince himself had recorded the Mishnah in writing, while others believed that it had been written down in Babylonia at the end of the talmudic period, when the threat of an Islamic invasion led to fears that the oral traditions might be lost. The problem is best solved by realizing that the oral law concept required that the publication of the Mishnah, its teaching, and its exegesis all be carried on in oral form. For this reason, formal study in amoraic circles was based on oral tradition. While individual amoraim had written texts of various parts of the Mishnah, the formal transition to the use of a written Mishnah as an object of teaching, study, and exegesis took place only at the end of the amoraic period or later. Rabbi Judah the Prince, however, promulgated his Mishnah in oral form. To the rabbis, what God had given orally had to be transmitted orally, and so it was with the Mishnah, the consummate summary of the oral law.

OTHER TANNAITIC TEXTS

The corpus of materials assembled in the Mishnah did not exhaust the oral traditions of the tannaitic period. Other traditions were intentionally excluded by Rabbi Judah the Prince, and some were simply not known to him. At the same time, the "tannaitic" tradition continued to develop in early amoraic times, so that materials continued to be collected and even transformed as they were handed down and taught. These teachings eventually were collected in a number of different collections.

Tosefta

Tosefta, meaning literally "the addition," is a collection of *baraitot*, "external traditions," which are not found in the Mishnah but are attributed to tannaim. This collection is designed to serve as a supplement to and commentary on the Mishnah, following its arrangement of orders and tractates, and even, for the most part, the sequence of the chapters. Only a few tractates of the Mishnah have no parallel in the Tosefta, which represents the earliest sustained exegesis of the Mishnah as the canonical collection of oral law.

The material in the Tosefta relates to that in the Mishnah in a variety of ways. Some passages are exact parallels, or even quotations, of material in the Mishnah. Others are restatements of the very same views in different form or using different terminology. Many statements in the Tosefta are actually supplements to the Mishnah and cannot be understood independently at all. Often, Tosefta passages contain traditions which provide material germane to the subject matter under discussion in the Mishnah but which are in no way directly parallel. Finally, there is material in the Tosefta which is at best tangentially related to the corresponding sections of the Mishnah.

Although talmudic tradition attributes the redaction of a Tosefta to students of Rabbi Judah the Prince, it is certain that the Tosefta that has come down to us was not redacted so soon after the completion of the Mishnah. Careful comparison of *baraitot* in the Tosefta and the Talmuds of Babylonia and Palestine indicates that the Tosefta was most probably not redacted until the end of the fourth century C.E. or later. This explains why it was not available in its present form to the amoraim.

The dating of the individual traditions in the Tosefta is a matter of greater complexity. We have already noted that "tannaitic" activity continued into the amoraic period, and this is in evidence in the continued development and redaction of Tosefta traditions. At the same time, for many statements, careful comparison of Tosefta material with mishnaic material shows us that the Tosefta versions are earlier than those in the Mishnah. This is sometimes the case where the Tosefta preserves a tradition with an attribution and the Mishnah does not. In many cases, this is because the redactor of the Mishnah removed the attribution to present the statement as halakhah, whereas the Tosefta preserved the original version. Elsewhere, divergent opinions were reformulated as disputes in the Mishnah, whereas the original formulations, as separate opinions, are preserved in the Tosefta.

On the other hand, there are clearly many passages in which the reverse process has occurred. In such instances statements from the tannaitic period have been reworked in order to serve as interpretations of the Mishnah or have been used as the basis for entirely new, post-mishnaic formulations, designed to explain the Mishnah. Where such views assume rulings not determined until the redaction of the Mishnah, they are evidence of the continuation of tannaitic activity beyond the redaction of the Mishnah into the amoraic period.

Thus, the relationship of the Tosefta to the Mishnah is a complex one, and, in fact, different situations prevail in regard to different tractates. In general, however, we can say that the Tosefta, as the earliest commentary on the Mishnah, preserves evidence of tannaitic material not included in the Mishnah, on the one hand, and, on the other, of materials which evolved after the redaction of the Mishnah and are clearly dependent on a redacted Mishnah similar to the text in our possession today.

Tannaitic Midrashim

Dating to the same period as the Tosefta are the so-called "tannaitic" Midrashim. These midrashic expositions of Scripture were in reality redacted in the amoraic period, probably at the end of the fourth century and the beginning of the fifth, in Palestine. At this time, the same tendencies which led the redactors of the Tosefta to collect their material, namely, a desire to preserve the heritage of the tannaitic period and a need to assert that the authority of the mishnaic rulings was subject to challenge, also led those who collected the Midrashim to bring them to final form. Because they preserve much more halakhic material than do the later expositional Midrashim from the amoraic period and early Middle Ages, these Midrashim are also called halakhic Midrashim. This designation has the advantage of avoiding the anachronistic term "tannaitic" (up to 200 C.E.) for texts clearly redacted in the amoraic period (ca. 200–500 C.E.), but it has the disadvantage of veiling the fact that some of these texts are primarily aggadic. Scholarly convention has, therefore, chosen to use the term "tannaitic Midrashim," while remaining aware of its limitations.

The midrashic method of teaching had been in use since the time of Ezra and Nehemiah. It lost prominence to some degree in the tannaitic period as the mishnaic, apodictic method of teaching became more popular. The redaction of the Mishnah and the establishment of its authority was for the Midrashim a

TANNAITIC (HALAKHIC) MIDRASHIM

	Type A (Ishmael School)	Type B (Akiban School)
Exodus	Mekhilta of Rabbi Ishmael	Mekhilta of Rabbi Simeon ben Yoḥai
Leviticus		Sifra
Numbers	Sifre on Numbers	Sifre Zuṭa
Deuteronomy	Midrash Tannaim	Sifre on Deuteronomy

two-edged sword. On the one hand, it established for the rest of Jewish history the superior status of the apodictic law and in this way eclipsed, to some extent, the study of midrashic interpretation. On the other hand, the very existence of an apodictic code made it necessary for the code itself, its authority, and its regulations to be justified in light of the commandments of the Torah.

Put otherwise, the existence of this digest of oral law led to a renewed need to demonstrate the nexus of the oral and written laws. There was now a need to show that the two were in reality one, and this indeed was the main agenda of the tannaitic Midrashim. Thus they present much of the same halakhic material that is found in the Mishnah and Tosefta, but arranged in the order of the Torah. Whenever possible, the Midrashim seek to tie each particular halakhah directly to its scriptural basis, or to what the redactors argue is its scriptural basis.

The tannaitic Midrashim comprise five texts of central importance and a number of smaller texts which will not be detailed here. The major texts are the *Mekhilta of Rabbi Ishmael* and the *Mekhilta of Rabbi Simeon ben Yoḥai* to Exodus, the *Sifra* to Leviticus, the *Sifre to Numbers* and the *Sifre to Deuteronomy*. These titles themselves need to be explained. *Mekhilta* is an elusive term for a set of hermeneutical (exegetical) rules, or a body of tradition. *Sifra* means "the book," as Leviticus was, in priestly circles, the central book of the curriculum of study. *Sifre*, meaning "the books," is most probably an abbreviation for "the rest of the books of the house of study," a designation for the Midrashim on Numbers and Deuteronomy (meaning those other than Leviticus and Exodus, which are interpreted in the *Sifra* and *Mekhilta* texts, respectively).

These books are sometimes classified into schools, some said to stem from the school of Rabbi Akiva and some from that of Rabbi Ishmael. This theory claims that the literary products of each school, as they are now preserved, exhibit characteristic exegetical and redactional traits. Assigned to the school of Rabbi Ishmael are the *Mekhilta of Rabbi Ishmael*, the *Sifre to Numbers*, and some other texts. To the school of Rabbi Akiva are attributed the *Mekhilta of Rabbi Simeon ben Yoḥai*, *Sifra*, *Sifre Zuṭa* (to Numbers), and *Sifre to Deuteronomy*. This distinction has often been called into question, however, and its usefulness is extremely limited. In fact, despite the parallels that have been cited, the two groups of texts do not evidence uniform redactional traits, to say the least.

The form of these works may hark back to the techniques of scriptural study practiced in the tannaitic academies. The Torah, as well as relevant laws, some aggadic homilies, and a variety of related topics were discussed together. It was this method which provided the form for the post-tannaitic redactors of these materials. Yet here again, as is the case in the Tosefta, we are confronted with a mix of material. Some is clearly of tannaitic origin but not preserved in the other corpora. Other materials are constructed out of a continuation of "tannaitic" activity and tradition by later scholars in the amoraic period. Only careful literary and textual analysis allows the separation of the literary strata in these works. In fact, the *Sifra* adheres most closely to the Mishnah, and its neatly set out redaction is based heavily on the Mishnah. Yet even here much earlier material has been incorporated, including preredactional versions of mishnaic material. *Sifre to Deuteronomy* is somewhat less heavily mishnaic than *Sifra* but is still strongly influenced by the redacted mishnaic tradition. Much more earlier material is found in the two *Mekhilta* texts and in the *Sifre to Numbers*, which in general are looser agglomerations of material collected over a much longer period of time.

These Midrashim were intended to convey certain specific messages by those who labored to redact them. Essentially, in varying degrees, these texts argue strongly for the unity of the written and oral laws. In an age when mishnaic, apodictic law had become supreme, these texts sought to remind those who studied them of the inseparable link between the two Torahs, the oral and the written. Therefore, they derive many of the laws found in the Mishnah from Scripture, claiming biblical exegesis as their basis. At the same time, in many cases, these texts preserve the logical and exegetical argumentation which was indeed the source for the determination of the halakhah by the tannaim. In texts like the *Sifra* and *Sifre to Deuteronomy*, in which the Bible is followed closely, the point is made over and over that there is nothing superfluous in Scripture, and that each feature of the text, each apparent duplication, is designed to reveal the will of God. On the other hand, the *Mekhilta* texts tend to move much further away from these limited purposes, collecting many aggadot and often dealing with side issues. Nevertheless, the basic notion that Scripture and tradition are intimately linked is carried through all these works.

Many of the traditions included in the Tosefta and the tannaitic Midrashim found their way, in parallel versions, into the Palestinian and Babylonian Talmuds. Such traditions are termed *baraitot* ("external traditions"). While the process by which they were incorporated in amoraic collections will be taken up later, it should be noted that the versions of the traditions found there are often different from those in the collections surveyed here. This confirms the view that these collections were not available to the rabbis of the Talmuds in their present, edited form. Rather, the Talmuds drew their versions of the traditions from the same unedited and unredacted sources as did the so-called tannaitic Midrashim and the Tosefta. To a great extent medieval Judaism inherited a similar situation. For the tannaitic Midrashim were destined to be stepchildren in the family of rabbinic texts. Their contents were to be known largely from parallels in the Babylonian Talmud.

SUMMARY

The development of the tannaitic corpus of learning and its eventual redaction in the Mishnah, the Tosefta, and the "tannaitic" Midrashim, placed Rabbinic Judaism on a firm literary grounding. These texts, orally formulated and orally transmitted and taught, set forth the basic principles of the oral law and argued for the integrity of the Torah, written and oral. These documents served as the basis for the later development of Judaism and, in the case of the Mishnah, set the agenda for all future study of Jewish law. With the close of the tannaitic period, and the production of its main classic, the Mishnah, we can genuinely speak of the coming of age of Rabbinic Judaism. It was left for the amoraim to interpret this document, redact its sister tannaitic texts, and adapt this Judaism to the new historical circumstances of the Byzantine period in Palestine and the Sassanian period in Babylonia.

11
Formative Judaism Comes of Age

It is usual to speak of the passage of Rabbinic Judaism from the tannaitic to the amoraic period as if it had taken place in a historical vacuum, with some purely internal mechanism leading to the changes in the method and content of learning, as well as in the level of adherence to and popularity of the rabbinic movement. In fact, this was not the case. Very specific developments in the Greco-Roman Diaspora, Palestine, and Babylonia contributed to an atmosphere which nurtured the development of amoraic Judaism. These developments, themselves presaging the onset of the medieval period, helped to propel formative Judaism to the consensus that eventually enabled it to withstand the challenges of the Middle Ages.

DECLINE OF HELLENISTIC JUDAISM

From the third century B.C.E. a Greco-Roman, Hellenistic Judaism had existed alongside the Hebrew-speaking Judaism of Palestine. This Greek-speaking Judaism had come to terms with Greek literary forms and philosophies, had translated the Bible into Greek in several versions, and had in many ways synthesized the culture of Israel with that of Hellas. Its success lay in its having resisted isolationism, assimilation, and extreme Hellenization.

Testifying to the strength of Hellenistic Judaism was its ability to attract widespread attention among pagans. The existence of semi-proselytes and God-fearers (non-Jews drawn to the synagogue and Jewish practice) shows that Hellenistic Jewry's way of life was attractive to non-Jews who were searching for a replacement for the now waning Greek and Roman cults.

By the mid-second century C.E., however, Hellenistic Judaism had begun to decline. This was due in part to the losses, both human and material, suffered as a result of the Jewish uprising in many parts of the Diaspora in the years 115–117 C.E. While messianic fervor was certainly at the heart of this uprising, as it was in the two Palestinian revolts, the Diaspora insurrection was also a testimony to the steadily weakening position of the Jews in the Greco-Roman world, where they were often becoming economic or political scapegoats.

The decline might have set in without the uprising, however, for it may well be that the thin tightrope of Hellenistic Judaism could not have been walked for too many generations. Theoretically it may have seemed possible to partake of the Hellenistic world and remain a loyal Jew, but the challenges to such loyalty, and more so to traditional piety, were often too great to resist. Over the generations, the children and grandchildren of those who first entered into the Hellenistic environment acquired Greek educations, began to participate in commercial and cultural activities with their non-Jewish neighbors, and eventually intermarried with them. Thus assimilation took a heavy toll.

A final factor of great significance was the rise of gentile Christianity. The earliest Christians were Jews who believed that the messiah had come in the person of Jesus. By the last quarter of the first century, the Christian community had acceded to the demands of Peter and Paul that gentiles be permitted to join the new movement without formally converting to Judaism, a process which involved circumcision for males, and immersion in a ritual bath and acceptance of the commandments for all. (By this time the Temple was no longer standing, so the required sacrifice could not be offered.) Under Paul's influence, Christianity turned more and more toward the gentiles, that is, the Greco-Roman pagans of the Hellenistic world. As this process quickened in the second century C.E., gentile Christianity absorbed many of the semi-proselytes or potential semi-proselytes who had attached themselves to the Hellenistic Jewish communities—people who were attracted by the theological notions and ethical teachings of Judaism but were unwilling to undergo conversion. At the same time, the new movement undoubtedly absorbed some Hellenized Jews. Further, just as Christianity was becoming more popular, Judaism was beginning to abandon its Hellenistic manifestation, partly because of the gradual Hebraizing of the Greek-speaking synagogue, a process abetted by the many exiles from Palestine who fled to the Diaspora after the two unsuccessful revolts. As a result, the Greek Bible translations fell into disuse among Jews.

Thus, the rise of Christianity indirectly helped to bring about the decline of Hellenistic Jewry. In the early Middle Ages, when we again meet organized Jewish communities in the lands of the Hellenistic Diaspora—Asia Minor, Greece itself, Bulgaria (Macedonia), Italy, the Greek islands, and North Africa—these communities are praying in Hebrew and reading from Hebrew Torah scrolls. To be sure, some of their members were descended from the earlier Hellenized Jews. More importantly, the heritage of Hellas would no longer be synthesized with Judaism except as mediated by the Islamic tradition. Hellenistic Judaism did not pass on its traditions directly. Indeed, it was Christianity which preserved the books of the apocrypha and pseudepigrapha, the Greek translations of the Bible, and even the works of Philo and Josephus. The Jews would not rediscover these books until the Middle Ages and the Renaissance.

UNDER BYZANTINE CHRISTIANITY

Until the Arab conquest of the Near East (634–638 C.E.), the centers of Jewish creativity were Palestine and Babylonia. After the suppression of the Bar Kokhba Revolt of 132–135 C.E., the Palestinian Jewish community had recovered quickly. Institutions of self-rule, the patriarchate and the Sanhedrin, as well as local courts and other officials, had soon been reorganized with the toleration and eventually the support of the Romans. Indeed, the period from the end of the Bar Kokhba Revolt to the end of the patriarchate of Rabbi Judah the Prince, around 220 C.E., was one of prosperity, peace, and development in the sphere of rabbinic intellectual endeavor. It culminated in the redaction of the Mishnah, completed shortly before the death of Rabbi Judah the Prince. With this achievement the tannaitic era

Synagogues (1st-6th cent. C.E.)　　Byzantine Palestine (4th-6th cent.)

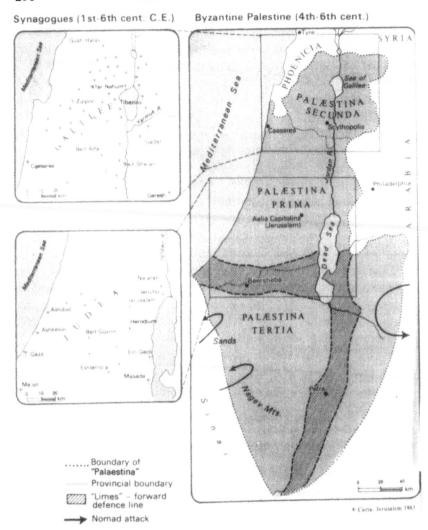

.... Boundary of
"Palaestina"
.... Provincial boundary
▨ "Limes" – forward
defence line
➤ Nomad attack

came to a close, as the amoraim, or "interpreters," struggled,
over the ensuing three centuries, to interpret, expound, and
even modify this document.

The history of Palestinian Jewry in the amoraic period, then,
began on a good note with the golden age of Judah the Prince
and his friendship with the high-ranking Roman whom rabbinic
literature refers to as "Antoninus" (either the emperor Marcus
Aurelius or some local official) carrying over into the days of his
immediate successors. The renewed prosperity which most of

THE PATRIARCHAL HOUSE
(all dates are approximate)

20 B.C.E.–20 C.E.	Hillel
20–50	Gamaliel I
70	Simeon ben Gamaliel I (death)
96–115	Gamaliel II
140–170	Simeon ben Gamaliel II
170–220	Rabbi Judah the Prince
220–230	Gamaliel III
230–270	Judah Nesiah II
270–290	Gamaliel IV
290–320	Judah III
320–365	Hillel II
365–385	Gamaliel V
385–400	Judah IV
400–425	Gamaliel VI (death)

the Jews of Palestine enjoyed resulted also from the continuation of the administrative system that had been instituted after the Great Revolt of 66–73 C.E. At that time Palestine had been detached from Syria and reorganized as a province in its own right, ruled by Roman officials of higher rank than the procurators and thus better able to understand the Jews and the special problems that the governance of Palestine entailed. The province retained this status and the concomitant better quality of government after the Bar Kokhba Revolt.

Judaism and its practices again became legal in the empire, and from 212 C.E. Jews were considered full Roman citizens. The patriarchate and the Sanhedrin were officially recognized, and Jews controlled those municipalities in the Galilee which were primarily Jewish. Jews still had to pay a special capitation tax, were officially forbidden to enter Jerusalem, and were enjoined from circumcising, i.e., converting, gentiles. With this legislative basis, a modus vivendi between the once rebellious Jews and the implacable Roman Empire had finally been achieved. Jewish agriculture and a limited spectrum of industry and commerce flourished.

In the second half of the third century, in response to the deepening economic crisis in the Roman Empire, Palestine was

BYZANTINE EMPERORS
(partial list, all dates are C.E.)

306–337	Constantine I
337–361	Constantius II
361–363	Julian the Apostate
379–395	Theodosius I
408–450	Theodosius II
527–565	Justinian I

plagued by inflation, devaluation of currency (especially between 230 and 260 C.E.), and increased taxation. Many farmers moved to the cities. With time, deep class divisions again appeared, a development which resulted in widespread disaffection between the people and the patriarchate. The patriarchs increasingly allied themselves with the rich, while the sages were allied more and more with the poorer classes.

Judah the Prince was succeeded by Gamaliel III (died ca. 230). He in turn was succeeded by Judah Nesiah (the Prince) II, who died around 270. From 260 to 273 C.E. Palestine was under the rule of the former Roman client state of Tadmor (Palmyra, an oasis in central Syria), a change that the Jews at first saw as a hopeful sign but that quickly turned out to be meaningless. Palestine and its Jews could not escape the general decline that had set in throughout the Roman Empire. While Christianization gave the empire a new lease on life, it soon presented the Jews of Palestine and the rest of the empire with new and even greater challenges.

Gamaliel IV served as patriarch from about 270 until his death around 290. Judah III succeeded him and died in 320. The patriarch Hillel II reigned from 320 to 365. Up to his time, the Jewish calendar had been based on the actual observation of the phases of the moon. He is said to have made public the mathematical rules for the calculation of the Jewish calendar due to his fear that the deteriorating Palestinian Jewish community would no longer be able to coordinate the calendar for world Jewry. In 324 C.E. Constantine the Great became ruler of the entire Roman Empire. Now for the first time, in both Palestine and the Diaspora, the Jews faced a Christian emperor. All the progress in legal status which the Jews had experienced in the

MOSAIC FROM ḤAMAT TIBERIAS. This portion of the floor of the synagogue of Ḥamat Tiberias dates from ca. 300–325 C.E. Crossing it can be seen a wall from a later stratum from the 5th century. This Galilean synagogue displays mosaics of the type common in Jewish and Christian houses of worship in the Land of Israel in this period. In the middle is the sun, depicted in the style of the Greek god Helios (Apollo). He is surrounded by the months represented by the familiar figures of the Zodiac. The figures in the corners are the four seasons. *Courtesy of the Institute of Archaeology of the Hebrew University.*

third century soon evaporated. They found themselves ruled by adherents of a religion that claimed it had supplanted the old Israel and accused them of deicide. Moreover, Christians considered the Land of Israel as holy, a view now shared by the Roman government. In consequence, the Jews of Palestine, already a minority in their own land, soon faced the process of its Christianization. But during the reign of Constantine this was only beginning, and its full ramifications were as yet unclear.

By 350 C.E. Constantius II (337–361 C.E.) had asserted control over his father's entire realm with the help (from 351) of Gallus, who administered the East. It was in this period that anti-Jewish legislation was first enacted. Jews were to be isolated from Christians, and penalties for converting gentiles were strengthened. The decisions of the church councils of Elvira (306) and later of Laodicea (431) became the law of the land. Jews were to be maintained in a lowly position in keeping with their having rejected the messiahship of Jesus. Their status, according to Christian teaching, was to bear witness to their replacement as the people of God by the Christians.

In the third and fourth centuries, Palestinian Jews now found themselves intermittently persecuted in their own land. As Christian intellectual life flourished there, Jews were increasingly compelled to enter into disputations and arguments with Christians. At the same time, life became harder and harder as the oppressive anti-Semitic measures combined with excessive taxation. It was not long before these pressures led some Jews, as had happened twice before, to rebel against their Roman overlords.

From 350 to 351 C.E. the Romans faced a variety of rebellions in the West, as well as continued pressure from Shapur II, the Sassanian king of Persia. In 351 many Jews rose in revolt against Gallus, the vice-emperor of the East under Constantius II. Like their brethren in the earlier revolts, they must have expected political and financial help from their contacts among the Jews of Babylonia and perhaps also from Shapur II. Although the revolt spread through the main cities of the Galilee, and, as excavations now show, into the Jewish communities of the Golan Heights as well, many rabbinic leaders and certain members of the upper classes do not seem to have participated. The Romans quickly put the revolt down, destroying many villages. Surprisingly, they did not exact vengeance on the population or carry out deportations, as they had after the previous revolts. A military government under the general Ursicinus ruled Palestine for the next ten years. In 354 Gallus was executed. It may be that the lenient treatment of the Jews after the revolt resulted from Roman recognition that mistreating them had precipitated the uprising. After the dust settled, the local Jewish authorities soon made peace with the new Roman administration and succeeded in reestablishing themselves. At the same time, however, the abortive rebellion further accelerated the economic decline of the Jewish population and its urbanization.

Between 355 and 360 C.E. Julian (Gallus's brother), known as the Apostate, gradually asserted power over the empire, becoming emperor in 361. Unlike his Christian predecessors, he wanted to reverse the Christianization of the empire. Encouraging the rebuilding of pagan temples and the revival of Hellenistic culture and religion, he saw all the non-Christian elements of the empire as his allies, and this naturally included the Jews. He also saw the Jews as necessary allies, for obvious geographical reasons, in his planned attack on Persia. Jews throughout the empire benefited from Julian's proclamation of religious freedom and rescission of the anti-Semitic laws enacted by his predecessors. He even corresponded with the patriarch, Hillel II.

Most notable was Julian's intention, announced in 362 C.E., to restore Jerusalem to the Jews and to rebuild the Temple and reinstitute its sacrificial worship. By doing so he intended to strengthen his ties with the Jews and disprove the Christian claim that they were living testimony to the folly of rejecting Jesus. Although the project must have excited many Jews both in Palestine and outside, the patriarchal house was hesitant, mindful of the dangers inherent in Julian's proposal. After all, Christians still remained very powerful in the empire.

In 363 C.E., when Julian attacked Persia, work on the Temple had already begun. Materials were being gathered, and the area was being prepared for building. Then a sudden fire swept

JEWS UNDER LATE ROMAN AND BYZANTINE RULE

ca. 220	Death of Rabbi Judah the Prince
212	Jews made citizens of empire
ca. 236	Sanhedrin at Tiberias
260–273	Palmyran rule over Palestine
324	Christianity official religion of the Roman Empire
351	Jewish revolt against Gallus
362	Julian the Apostate's attempt to rebuilt the Temple
363–364	Christian attacks on Palestinian Jews
382, 392, 404	Anti-Semitic legislation
395	Separation of eastern and western empires
425–429	Elimination of the patriarchate
476	Fall of western empire
484 and 529	Samaritan revolts
601–614	Persian rule
614–617	Jewish rule in Jerusalem
622–629	Byzantine Empire reasserts control of Palestine
638	Arab conquest of Palestine

through the area, injuring workmen, and the project was stopped. The Christians took this as a sign of divine intervention, although many historians have suspected them of having set the fire. In any case, the patriarchate was soon proven correct, for Julian was killed on the eastern front and replaced by a Christian emperor. The anti-Semitic restrictions were now reinstituted, and would remain in effect throughout our period, but the large-scale persecution that might well have befallen Palestinian Jewry under the circumstances was averted by the cautious approach of its leaders.

For a time it appeared that the Jews might benefit from the internal struggles in the Christian church and Roman Empire, but it soon became clear that they would again be crushed from all sides. In 363–64 C.E. the Jews of Palestine were subjected to Christian attacks designed to eliminate Jewish settlements from the south of the country. Although the attacks soon abated, the growth of Christianity in Palestine left the Jews under constant anti-Semitic pressure. In 365, with the death of Hillel II, Gamaliel V became patriarch, ruling until 385. The emperor Theodotius I (reigned from 379 C.E.) and his successors were fervent Christians who intensified anti-Jewish legislation as the government fell more and more under the influence of the church. By this time Judah IV was patriarch, serving from 385 to 400. He was succeeded by Gamaliel VI, who served until the abolition of the patriarchate in 425. The separation of the eastern empire from the western in 395 C.E. hastened the process of Christianization, since the church of the eastern portion speedily secured the increased support of the imperial government. All the while the Jews and the Hellenistic pagans were in the same boat. By the fifth century, Hellenistic paganism had virtually disappeared, leaving the Jews the sole target of the Byzantine Empire, as the Christianized eastern empire is generally termed.

A series of anti-Semitic laws was promulgated in 383, 392, and 404 C.E., prohibiting Jews from converting gentiles and from holding public office. A law enacted in 415 required Jews and Christians to use only the imperial courts for cases between them. Synagogues were destroyed with clerical encouragement, and laws were passed forbidding the construction of new synagogues or the repair of old ones.

The Christianization of Palestine was manifest in the building of churches and monasteries, the presence of large numbers of monks, and the coming of many Christian pilgrims. In the fifth century Christians finally became the majority of the country's

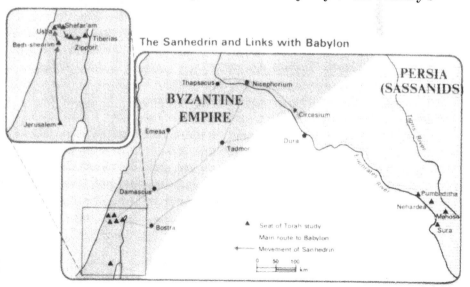

The Sanhedrin and Links with Babylon

PERSIA (SASSANIDS)

BYZANTINE EMPIRE

Shefar'am · Usha · Tiberias · Beth-shearim · Zippori
Jerusalem
Thapsacus · Nicephorium
Emesa · Circesium
Tadmor · Dura
Damascus
Bostra
Pumbeditha
Neharde
Mahosa
Sura

▲ Seat of Torah study
Main route to Babylon
◄—— Movement of Sanhedrin

0   50   100
|——————|
km

© Carta, Jerusalem 1983

population, a factor that must have been a cause of the Samaritan revolts of 484 and 529 C.E. The failure of the two revolts contributed greatly to the limited size of the Samaritan community in medieval and modern times. The Samaritans simply lacked the demographic, economic, and political resources necessary to effect a recovery.

Under the difficult conditions of Byzantine Christian rule, the rabbis of Palestine felt pressured to redact the various texts of tannaitic and Palestinian amoraic Judaism. The Tosefta and the tannaitic Midrashim, as well as the earliest of the amoraic midrashic collections, took on their final form, and the Palestinian Talmud was hastily redacted. These texts are an enduring monument to the ability of Judaism to flourish even under the adverse conditions of an anti-Semitic environment.

Considering the circumstances described in this chapter, it is remarkable that the patriarchate managed to continue for so long as the recognized central authority over the Jews of the empire. Yet in due course the general decline in the status of the Jews in the third and fourth centuries C.E. caught up with it. Between 399 and 404, because of internal dissension between the eastern and western halves of the Roman Empire, the patriarchate was forbidden to collect money in the West. Yet this was only a minor setback. In 415 the patriarch Gamaliel VI was accused of building synagogues, circumcising Christian slaves, and rendering judgments in cases involving Jews and Christians. These were violations of the anti-Semitic measures mentioned earlier, but the patriarch probably claimed that he was exercising ancestral rights granted in the time of the undivided Roman Empire and still legally valid. Nonetheless, the eastern emperor deprived the patriarch of the honorary title of praetor which had been traditionally associated with his office since its establishment and ordered that Jews free Christian slaves and demolish the synagogues which had been built. This set off a process which led, by 425 C.E. (or perhaps 429), to the complete elimination of the patriarchate. When the patriarch Gamaliel VI died in that year, and the empire did not confirm a successor, Jewish self-government in Palestine finally came to its official end.

The years 451–527 C.E. saw the Christians engaged in internal struggles over religious matters and their political repercussions (or perhaps we should say, in political struggles expressed through religious conflicts). During this period, because the Christians were distracted by these matters, Palestine's Jews suffered much less interference in their affairs. The economy improved and many synagogues with beautiful mosaics were built in the Galilee. Synagogues and houses of study were constructed in the Golan as well. The laws prohibiting the building of synagogues and Jews from holding public office were largely ignored. Jews even returned to Jerusalem. They constituted some ten percent of the population of Palestine. New institutions revolving around the rabbinic academies replaced the defunct patriarchate.

With the accession of Justinian in 527 C.E., things took a turn for the worse. Under the influence of the church, Judaism was again persecuted. New laws denied Judaism any official sanction. Jews were forbidden to hold office, even including serving on local councils in predominantly Jewish areas; Jews were also forbidden to own Christian slaves and were not accepted as witnesses against Christians, and various other proscriptions were enacted as well. These regulations all resulted from the Christian doctrine that the Jews should be kept in a lowly position as witnesses to the truth of Christianity. Under Justinian, persecution of Jews was now legal. Indeed, this may have led Jews to join in the Samaritan revolt of 529 C.E. From the sixth and early seventh centuries we begin to hear, in the Diaspora and even in Jerusalem, of Jews being forcibly converted to Christianity on the threat of death.

It is not difficult to see why the Jews hoped for deliverance at the hands of the Persians or why they aided the Persians when they invaded Palestine in 601–614 C.E. Yet the Jews were quickly disappointed when the conquerors, after permitting them to rule Jerusalem for a short time, turned against them. Finally, the Byzantine Empire, in campaigns between 622 and 629 C.E., retook Palestine from the Persians. Now, the Byzantine Christians slaughtered Jews throughout Palestine in revenge for their having sided with the Persians. From this point on the Jews became a minor factor in Palestine. When the Arabs conquered Palestine in 638 C.E., they found only a small Jewish community.

BY THE RIVERS OF BABYLON

The Jewish dispersion in Mesopotamia dates from the Assyrian conquest of the kingdom of Israel in 722 B.C.E. The mass deportations which followed brought Jews to the region of northern Mesopotamia. When the Babylonians conquered the kingdom of Judah and deported many of its people to Babylonia in central Mesopotamia in 597 and 586 B.C.E., the new exiles linked up with their brethren, and the Mesopotamian Jewish community began its climb to eventual ascendancy. It is most likely that the exiles from Israel moved south into Babylonia where the new exiles from Judah had been settled.

When the Achaemenid Persians under Cyrus the Great conquered Mesopotamia in the sixth century B.C.E. and allowed the Jews to return to their homeland, only a small percentage took advantage of the invitation, and thus the Babylonian Jewish community continued to grow. In 331 B.C.E. Babylonia was conquered by Alexander the Great. When it passed to the Seleucids on his death in 323, the Jews were granted a renewal of the privileges and freedoms proclaimed by Cyrus and some even served in the Seleucid armies. Yet the Jews of Mesopotamia must have been affected by the Hellenization policy pursued by the Seleucids in an effort to strengthen their hold on the land. They were certainly affected financially by the shift of the Seleucid Empire's commercial center from Babylon to the newly founded city of Seleucia on the Tigris River. Their fortunes must have declined further during the Maccabean uprising of 168–164 B.C.E. and the ensuing period of tension during which the Hasmonean dynasty established itself.

From 171 B.C.E., the Parthians, an Iranian people, under the Arsacid dynasty, began to pressure the Seleucids in Mesopotamia. Under Mithradates II, they conquered the area in 120 B.C.E. The Jews were treated well by the Parthians, who also maintained good relations with the Hasmoneans. The Parthians attempted to influence events in Palestine by supporting Antigonus in his bid for the high priesthood in 40–39 B.C.E., but Herod soon regained control.

The limited sources at our disposal tell us about the exploits of a few distinguished Babylonian Jews who played a role in the

THE BABYLONIAN DIASPORA

331 B.C.E.	Babylon conquered by Alexander the Great
323	Seleucid rule
120	Parthian control—Mithradates II
ca. 40	Conversion of royal house of Adiabene
20–35 C.E.	Jewish principality in Babylonia
114–117	Trajan invades Parthian Empire
170–210	Huna I (first known exilarch)
226	Arsacid dynasty falls to Sassanians
224–241	Ardashir I
242–272	Shapur I
259	Nehardea Academy moves to Pumbeditha
262–263	Palmyran invasion
272–292	Short-term monarchs
293–301	Narseh
309–379	Shapur II
363	Invasion of Julian the Apostate
397–417	Yezdegerd I
420–438	Bahram V
438–457	Yezdegerd II
455	Persecution of Jews
459–486	Firuz
468–474	Synagogues destroyed, Torah study banned
ca. 470	Execution of exilarch Huna V
488–531	Kovad I
520	Execution of exilarch Mar Zutra II
531–578	Chosroes
579–580	Hormizd IV
590–628	Chosroes Parwez
634	Arab conquest of Mesopotamia

Parthian nobility and dressed and behaved like members of this class. Little is known about the common people, however. From 20 to 35 B.C.E. there was a short-lived Jewish principality in Babylonia. Some Jews made pilgrimages to Jerusalem, though, and the royal family of Adiabene converted to Judaism in about 40 C.E. and then offered sacrifices at the Jerusalem Temple.

During the Great Revolt of 66–73 C.E. and the Bar Kokhba Revolt of 132–35 C.E., some Jews in Babylonia gave financial support to the rebel forces, and a few went to Palestine to fight the Romans. When Trajan invaded the Parthian Empire in 114–

SYNAGOGUE OF DURA EUROPOS. At Dura, on the banks of the Euphrates in Syria, are located the ruins of a synagogue which was completed
in 244/5 C.E. according to an Aramaic inscription. The interior of the
synagogue was covered with murals which depict biblical scenes.
These are in a provincial Late Roman style, and include depictions of
human forms. The paintings are in large part based on aggadic
traditions, some of which are previously unknown but many of which
have parallels in rabbinic literature. This panel shows Moses being
taken from the river by Pharoah's daughter, holding the Torah, and
anointing Joshua, as well as Ark of the Covenant. From C. H. Krael-
ing, *The Synagogue, The Excavations at Dura-Europos*, VIII, i (New
York: Ktav, 1979), plate XIX, *Courtesy of the Institute of Archaeology
of the Hebrew University.*

THE EXILARCHS
(all dates are C.E.)

170–210	Huna I
210–240	Mar Ukba I
240–260	Huna II
260–270	Nathan I
270–313	Nehemiah
313–337	Mar Ukba II
337–350	Huna III
350–370	Abba
370–400	Nathan II
400–415	Kahana I
415–442	Huna IV
442–455	Mar Zuṭra I
455–465	Kahana II
465–470	Huna V
484–508	Huna VI
508–520	Mar Zuṭra II
?–560	Aḥunai
560–580	Ḥofnai
580–590	Ḥaninai
?–670	Bustenai

117 C.E., the Jews joined in the resistance against him at the very same time that their brethren in the Greco-Roman dispersion were engaged in the Diaspora Revolt. Both Palestinian and Babylonian Jews are reported to have been active in the silk trade, which was, no doubt, interrupted by these disturbances.

Pre-70 C.E. Pharisaism had little impact, if any, in Babylonia, and only two Pharisaic sages are known to have lived there, at Nisibis and Nehardea. After the Bar Kokhba Revolt several Pharisaic rabbinic sages fled to Babylonia, where they established centers that trained Babylonian tannaim. A mechanism for centralized rule over Babylonian Jewry had certainly come into being by the mid-second century C.E., yet the title resh galuta (exilarch) first appears only for Huna I (170–210 C.E.). In Parthian times, the sons of the exilarchs were sent to study in the Land of Israel. At the same time, the exilarchs sought to staff their courts with Palestinian-trained scholars who would not be dependent on local Jewish noblemen.

The Arsacid dynasty of the Parthians fell in 226 C.E. to the Sassanians. This dynasty sought to rule more directly, through an extensive bureaucracy, and, having originated as a priestly family, was dedicated to the cult of Ohrmazd, Anahita, and other divinities. Its governmental policies were intended to advance the Mazdean religion, a form of Zoroastrianism. Thus the reign of Ardashir I (224–241 C.E.) was a difficult period for all other religious groups, including the Jews. This period saw a temporary suspension of Jewish self-government. There are also some reports of anti-Semitic decrees. All this changed with the ascent of Shapur I in 242 C.E. He granted tolerance and freedom to all religious groups. By pacifying his own citizens, he hoped to strengthen his empire for war against Rome in the west. In any case, he was hailed enthusiastically by the Jewish community of Babylonia.

In 262–263 C.E. the Palmyran king invaded Babylonia, destroying some Jewish settlements, but Shapur I quickly restored order. It is probable that during his reign arrangements regarding the exilarchate and Jewish self-government were renegotiated and that a modus vivendi was reached between Jewish needs and the administrative system of the Sassanian Empire.

A series of short-term monarchs ruled from 272 to 292 C.E. This was a period of religious persecution for all non-Mazdeans. Yet Jews apppear to have been treated better than Manichaeans (a Persian religious cult) and Christians. The persecutions came to an end under Narseh (293–301 C.E.). Although some minor persecutions may have taken place early in the reign of Shapur II (309–79 C.E.), while he was still a child, we hear of no such disturbances for the remainder of his reign. Yet this was a period in which Christians were persecuted. When Julian the Apostate invaded Babylonia in 363, a number of Jewish communities were attacked by his armies. Some Jews, who supported Julian because of his plan to rebuild the Temple in Jerusalem, were massacred by the Persians.

Little is known about the reigns of Yezdegerd I (397–417) and Bahram V (420–38). Yezdegerd II (438–57) renewed the persecution of the Jews. He was followed by his son Firuz (459–86), who further intensified the persecutions. In his reign Jews are reported to have been massacred and their children given to

Mazdeans. The exilarch Huna V was killed by the king. From 468 to 474 synagogues were destroyed, and Torah study was prohibited. Jews were again persecuted in the reign of Kovad I (488–531 C.E.), who had adopted the doctrines of Mazdak (founder of Mazdakism, a Zoroastrian offshoot, around the end of the fifth century) regarding community of property and women, which, of course, they rejected.

In 520 the exilarch Mar Zuṭra II was killed after establishing a short-lived independent Jewish principality at Maḥoza. Much less is known of the period leading up to the Arab conquest. Jews fared well under Chosroes (531–78) but were persecuted again under Hormizd IV (579–80). Calm again prevailed under Chosroes Parwez (590–628). When the Arabs conquered Mesopotamia in 634 C.E. they were well received by the Jews and a completely new chapter in Jewish history was opened.

It is against this background that the efforts of the amoraim of Babylonia must be seen. Despite the constant ups and downs of political and economic conditions, the rabbis labored on to study, collect, and redact amoraic traditions. When the Babylonian Talmud finally emerged from this process, it is no wonder that this great classic reflected in many ways the strange ambivalence of Jewish life in Babylonia. Here Jews could be a stable and respected part of society one day and a persecuted enemy the next. Yet no matter what, the study of the Torah continued and flourished.

SUMMARY

The Jews of Palestine and Babylonia felt the impact of major developments in world history. In Palestine, the gradual Christianization of the Roman Empire and the resulting decline in Jewish fortunes eventually led to the elimination of Jewish self-government and to the premature end of amoraic activity. Babylonian Jewry enjoyed a long and distinguished history. It was certainly one of ups and downs, alternating freedom and persecution. But religious and scholarly creativity continued unabated throughout, as can be seen from the internal history of the Babylonian Talmud. It is to the collective literary heritage of these two great Jewish communities that we now turn.

12
The Sea of the Talmud

During the fluctuations of Jewish fortunes in Palestine and Babylonia, a loosely organized group of scholars, known collectively as the amoraim ("explainers" of the Mishnah) continued to expound and develop the rabbinic tradition. From about 200 to 425 in Palestine and around 200 to 500 in Babylonia, they were busy discussing and analyzing the Mishnah, as well as *baraitot* (tannaitic traditions not included in the Mishnah) and midrashic traditions, in a process which ultimately led to a series of redacted documents, the Babylonian Talmud, the Palestinian (Jerusalem) Talmud, and the amoraic, exegetical Midrashim.

Before analyzing this process, a word of definition is in order. It is common practice to speak of the Talmud as consisting of two parts, the Mishnah and the Gemara, the discursive amoraic interpretation of the Mishnah. Indeed, if one purchases a volume of the Talmud, whether the Babylonian or the Palestinian, whether in the original language or in translation, it will include Gemara as well as the Mishnah. Yet in fact, this use of the word Gemara is very recent. Medieval Christian censors replaced the earlier term, "Talmud," which had become objectionable to them, with "Gemara," and only later did the term "Talmud" begin to designate the combination of Mishnah and Gemara.

AMORAIC SCHOOLS

The two Talmuds, the Palestinian and the Babylonian, emerged after centuries of debate, study, and clarification. In each country, groups of amoraim labored to understand and develop the traditions they had received from their tannaitic forebears. Even the most cursory examination of the Talmuds will show that individual scholars did not work alone. Senior scholars taught more junior scholars who eventually became colleagues. The senior colleagues usually possessed *reshut*, the authority to adjudicate legal cases, which was the Babylonian equivalent of the Palestinian *semikhah*, rabbinic ordination. Indeed, amoraim served the Jewish community as teachers and judges and gave guidance on matters of Jewish practice and faith. Scholars were often connected by shared discipleship, but many of them studied with more than one master, beginning with one teacher and on his death becoming the student of another.

THE AMORAIM
(all dates are C.E.)

1st Generation, ca. 220–260

Palestine	Babylonia
Ḥama bar Bisa	Shela
Ḥanina (bar Ḥama)	Abba bar Abba (father of Samuel)
Yannai ("the Elder")	Zeira the Elder
Judah bar Pedaiah	Karna
Oshaya Rabbah	Mar Ukba I
Judah Nesiah II	Samuel bar Abba (Yarḥinaah)
Joshua ben Levi	Rab (Abba Arikha)
Zabdai ben Levi	Rabbah bar Ḥana
Jonathan ben Eleazar	Assi

2nd Generation, ca. 260–290

Palestine	Babylonia
Kahana	Mar Ukba II
Yoḥanan bar Nappaḥa	Huna
Simeon ben Lakish	Judah bar Ezekiel
Ḥilfa	Adda bar Ahavah
Isaac ben Eleazar	Rabbah bar Avuha
Alexandri	Matnah
Simlai	Jeremiah bar Abba

Ḥiyya bar Joseph
Yose ben Ḥanina
Measha
Mani I
Tanḥum bar Ḥanilai

3rd Generation, ca. 290–320

Palestine	Babylonia
Samuel bar Naḥman	Huna bar Ḥiyya
Isaac Nappaḥa	Ḥisda
Eleazar ben Pedat	Ulla bar Ishmael
Abbahu	Hamnuna
Ammi (ben Nathan)	Sheshet
Assi	Rabbah bar Huna
Judah Nesiah III	Naḥman bar Jacob
Ḥiyya II bar Abba	Rami bar Abba
Simeon bar Abba	Rabbah bar bar Ḥana
Zeira	Rabbah bar Naḥmani
Samuel bar Isaac	Joseph bar Ḥiyya
Hela	
Abba bar Memel	
Abba bar Kahana	
Ḥanina bar Pappai	
Aḥa bar Ḥanina	
Tanḥum bar Ḥiyya	

4th Generation, ca. 320–350

Palestine	Babylonia
Jeremiah	Aḥa bar Jacob
Ḥelbo	Rabbah bar Shela
Aḥa of Lydda	Abba bar Ulla
Abin I	Rami bar Ḥama
Ḥanan of Sepphoris	Idi bar Abin
Yudan	Abaye
Huna bar Abin	Rava
Judah bar Simon	Adda II bar Ahavah
Joshua bar Nehemiah	Naḥman bar Isaac
Ḥanina ben Abbahu	
Ahavah ben Zeira	
Pinḥas bar Ḥama	
Dimi	
Aibu	

5th Generation, ca. 350–400

Palestine	Babylonia
Yonah	Papa bar Ḥanan
Yose bar Zavda (Zevida)	Bivai bar Abaye
Judah Hanasi IV	Ḥama of Nehardea
Berekhiah Ha-Kohen	Dimi of Nehardea
Yose bar Abin	

At a minimum, then, it is certain that circles of teachers and students, which, for convenience, we will call schools, existed among the amoraim. These schools met often, perhaps daily, and had an inner hierarchy. When the master died they often dissolved, with the students going to other masters, unless a senior student had attained enough status and learning to carry on as the master. In such cases, some disciples would remain with the new master. Many of the halakhic and aggadic interpretations found in the Talmuds stem from such circles or schools. These teachings sometimes gained prominence in both Babylonia and Palestine because they were carried from circle to circle as students moved and masters interacted. This interaction and communication was responsible for some of the many parallel passages in the Talmuds and other rabbinic texts, although in the greatest number of cases redactional activity was the cause.

The existence of actual institutions, academies, in amoraic times is difficult to confirm. More than likely, there were no formal institutions in Babylonia, where central institutions of learning did not develop because the exilarch's political authority was separate from the religious authority of the rabbis. On the other hand, in Palestine, the patriarchal academy, located for most of the amoraic period at Sepphoris or Tiberias, served as the center of much of the amoraic activity. In Babylonia, individual teachers occasionally had enough authority for their schools to function as de facto central academies, but the circles around them appear to have made no attempt to so constitute themselves as to automatically continue into the next generation. This is what distinguishes these schools from full-fledged academies.

It must be stressed that the students of these masters were often quite mature in their own scholarship. Many of the face-to-face discussions recorded in the Talmuds took place in such circles before the scholars in question became independent masters. Some modern scholars have suggested that there were no face-to-face discussions, maintaining that the ones recorded in the Talmud were virtually all constructed by its editors. That such debates did really occur, however, can be demonstrated by comparing their form with that of other disputes in which the redactors of the Talmuds artificially constructed arguments out of independent statements by individual amoraim. The artificial debates can usually be detected by examining the literary style of the text. In Palestine, however, much more of the activity can be safely assigned to the central academies at Tiberias, Sepphoris, and Caesarea and to other formalized institutions. It was only later, in the gaonic period, after the redaction of the Talmuds, that central institutions developed in Babylonia, to some extent under the influence of the Islamic academies located there.

FROM AMORAIC INTERPRETATION TO TALMUDIC TEXTS

The Talmuds (Gemaras) are complicated texts, originally constructed orally as part of the study sessions of the amoraim. These study sessions were organized around the formal curriculum provided by the mishnaic tractates. Different tractates were selected for detailed study in Palestine and Babylonia, and there were different emphases even within the various Palestinian and Babylonian schools. While the complex process whereby the oral records (or better, fragments) of these discussions and debates have come down to us precludes making definitive judgments about the discussion, it is certain that the mishnaic tractates served as their basis. Only occasionally do the amoraim base their discussions on a *baraita* (tannaitic tradition outside the Mishnah) or on a mishnaic passage which has been quoted incidentally. For the most part, the Mishnah endows the Talmuds with their organizational framework.

The Mishnah was studied orally in amoraic times. A memorizer (known in amoraic times as a *tanna*, a teacher of the Mishnah and *baraitot*) recited aloud the text to be studied. Discussion and analysis of the text then ensued, followed by comparison and contrast with other tannaitic traditions, including Mishnah and *baraita* material. This in turn led to various digressions, and to the comments and glosses of various amoraim to the tannaitic texts under discussion. Some digressions were rather extensive, and sometimes they included an aggadic analysis of related (or even unrelated) biblical material. The freewheeling character of many of the recorded discussions, which often range beyond the specific topic at hand, is one of the important indicators that they actually took place and were not invented by the compilers.

Typically, an amoraic discussion of a mishnah began by citing a contradiction from another mishnah or a *baraita* and then proceeded to resolve it. Indeed, in origin, the main activity of "Talmud" was the resolution of contradictions in tannaitic materials. It is in this sense that tannaitic sources (and one difficult passage in the Dead Sea Scrolls) can speak of "Talmud" even before the redaction of the Mishnah and its acceptance as the curriculum for the study of the rabbinic tradition. The resolution of a contradiction between the Mishnah and a *baraita* often serves as the jumping-off point for more extensive discussion of the details of the law on the specific topic.

Inquiry into the scriptural source (or proof-text) for a particular rule is another important aspect of amoraic analysis. The Mishnah, virtually devoid of biblical proof-texts, had separated the law from its biblical origins. The amoraim and the later redactors of the halakhic Midrashim (the so-called tannaitic Midrashim) sought to reintegrate law and Scripture, so as to demonstrate that the written and oral laws constituted one unified revelation of God.

Had the process stopped there, the structure of the Talmuds would have been much simpler, but the process described here continued over generations, even centuries. This led to the gradual development of what are called *sugyot*, talmudic discussions, or essays, as it were, on specific topics. As discussions were passed down, generation after generation, from one circle of scholars to another, they were augmented with comments and glosses. This process continued in both Babylonia and Palestine into the fifth century. At this point, the development of the Palestinian Talmud was virtually arrested by the anti-

Semitic legislation and the difficult economic and social situation faced by the Jews of Palestine under the sway of the Byzantine Empire.

In Babylonia, however, the developing Talmud underwent an additional process. It was at this time that the anonymous discussions, the *setam*, which weave together and interrelate all the earlier material, were intertwined in the text. In this way a more prolix and more easily understandable Talmud was achieved. This, indeed, was one of the several factors leading to the greater popularity and authority of the Babylonian Talmud in subsequent centuries. The redactors who inserted these anonymous links and glosses also added some of the more extensive digressions, and provided the formulary introductions which allow us to identify Mishnah, *baraita*, and the statements of individual amoraim. In essence, up through the early fifth century, the vast majority of the statements preserved in the Talmuds have attributions, i.e., the statement is cited in the name of a particular rabbi. Thereafter, the bulk of the material is anonymous, serving to fill in gaps and make the whole a unified, sensible creation. There is only a limited amount of anonymous material in the Palestinian Talmud because its amoraim ceased to be active in the fifth century. In Babylonia, however, where the activity of creating the Talmud was able to continue, the anonymous redactors did their work and then were followed by the *savoraim*, "interpreters", who added the final touches, including the occasional halakhic rulings ("the law is according to . . .") and certain philological explanations. Their work continued up to the seventh century.

While we know that some of the amoraim kept written notes, the formal activity of the amoraim, like that of their tannaitic predecessors, was conducted orally. There is little information about the writing down of the two Talmuds—so little, in fact, that it is impossible to speculate confidently about the process. The best we can say is only that written manuscripts of the Babylonian and Palestinian Talmuds are first mentioned after the Islamic conquest (634 C.E.), and that the dissemination of manuscripts continued through the Middle Ages until the invention of printing.

THE PALESTINIAN TALMUD

Although it is popularly known as the Jerusalem Talmud (Talmud Yerushalmi), a more accurate name for this text is either "Palestinian Talmud" or "Talmud of the Land of Israel." Indeed, for most of the amoraic age, under both Rome and Byzantium, Jews were prohibited from living in the holy city, and the centers of Jewish population had shifted northwards, in the aftermath of the two revolts, to the Galilee and Golan regions. The Palestinian Talmud emerged primarily from the activity of the sages of Tiberias and Sepphoris, with some input, perhaps entire tractates, from sages of the "south" (Lydda, modern Lod) and the coastal plain, most notably Caesarea.

In these centers, the output of which included the exegetical Midrashim as well as the Palestinian Talmud, the activity of studying and transmitting the traditions of the tannaim occupied rabbis and their students from about 200 C.E. until the early fifth century. From that point on, because of anti-Semitism and economic difficulties, as well as abolition of the patriarchate, Jewish scholarship in Palestine played a secondary role.

In form, the Palestinian Talmud is arranged, essentially, as a commentary on the Mishnah. The Mishnah text which serves as its basis diverges in some ways from that used in the Babylonian Talmud. Exactly why this is the case is difficult to determine, and several theories have been advanced. More than likely the divergences resulted from the process of oral transmission and do not constitute evidence for separate recensions of the Mishnah, as has been suggested by some.

By far the greater part of the Palestinian Talmud emerged in the north, but the redaction of several tractates seems to have occurred in Caesarea, where the material was hurriedly and incompletely redacted. All told the Palestinian Talmud includes only thirty-nine of the sixty-three tractates of the Mishnah— the orders of Zera'im, Mo'ed, Nashim, and Neziqin, plus the first part of tractate Niddah of the order Ṭahorot. In view of the difficult circumstances under which it was compiled, it is unlikely that it ever included any other Mishnah tractates. The supposed Palestinian text of the order Qodashim, published only in 1905, has proven inauthentic.

REHOV INSCRIPTION. This mosaic inscription was found on a synagogue floor at Reḥav, 7 km. south of Beth Shean. The inscription, dating most probably to the 5th century C.E., is a series of laws pertaining to the tithing of agricultural produce and the areas of the Land of Israel in which these laws applied. It was fixed into the floor of the synagogue, most probably because the applicability of these laws had to be emphasized in areas adjacent to the borders. The inscription closely parallels various rabbinic sources and may be considered the earliest written evidence of rabbinic texts. *Courtesy of the Israel Antiquities Authority.*

The distribution of material in the Palestinian Talmud is often said to accord well with its provenance. Thus, since the agricultural laws were still observed in Palestine, it has extensive Gemara for tractates pertaining to agriculture, whereas such material is not found in the Babylonian Talmud. That the no longer relevant purity laws of most of Ṭahorot should be absent in both Talmuds is understandable. Tractate Niddah is an exception, since it deals with menstrual impurity and married life, an area of Jewish law which remained operative even after the destruction of the Second Temple. Yet it is difficult to explain the presence of the sacrificial law of the order Qodashim in the Babylonian Talmud and its absence in the Palestinian.

For the most part, the Palestinian Talmud was produced at the academy at Tiberias, which was under the patronage of the patriarchs. While the earlier patriarchs had been scholars, their successors were primarily political leaders and administrative officials. As the role of the patriarchs in the academies and the study of the oral Torah lessened, the heads of the Tiberias academy, beginning with Rabbi Yoḥanan, became extremely powerful and important in the development of the Palestinian tradition. The Palestinian Talmud bears Rabbi Yoḥanan's mark, and that of his student and colleague Resh Lakish, on virtually every page.

Other prominent Palestinian amoraim included Ḥanina bar Ḥama at Sepphoris, Oshaya Rabbah at Caesarea, and Joshua ben Levi at Lydda (ca. 220–260 C.E.). An important contemporary of Yoḥanan and Resh Lakish (both of whom flourished ca. 250–290 C.E.) was Eleazar ben Pedat of Tiberias. Ammi bar Nathan and Assi at Tiberias, Abbahu at Caesarea (or, according to some, at Qatsrin in the Golan) followed them (ca. 290–320 C.E.). Rabbi Yonah and Rabbi Yose then led the Tiberias academy (ca. 320–350 C.E.). The Palestinian amoraic chain of tradition came to an end not long afterwards, after the careers of Mana and Yose bar Abin (ca. 350–375 C.E.). Scholars in Caesarea, in the middle of the fourth century, brought to completion the initial tractates of Neziqin, Bava Qamma, Bava Meṣia, and Bava Batra. Since these tractates have a different literary and linguistic form from that of the rest of the Palestinian Talmud, and feature a somewhat different group of scholars, most mod-

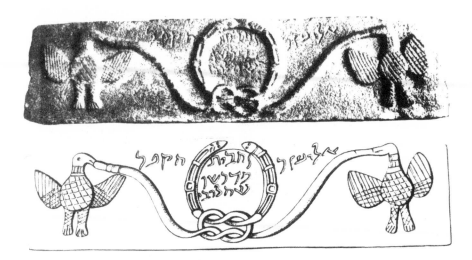

LINTEL OF HOUSE OF STUDY. This lintel from a *bet midrash* (house of study) was found at Dabbura in the Golan Heights. During the Byzantine period, the Golan was dotted with Jewish villages and synagogues. It reads "This is the House of Rabbi Eleazar Ha-Kappar." This late second century tanna is known from many quotations in rabbinic literature. The inscription indicates either that this was indeed his house of study, or that it was named for him. *Courtesy of the Institute of Archaeology of the Hebrew University and Dr. Dan Urman.*

ern scholars have maintained that they were redacted separately. The rest of the Palestinian Talmud was somewhat hastily redacted out of developing *sugyot* in the fifth century, completed soon after the dismantling of the patriarchate. This final redaction took place at Tiberias. Because the Palestinian Talmud was completed during the period in which the named amoraim flourished, it lacks the last layer of anonymous material (*setam*) that occurs in the Babylonian Talmud. This is one of the main reasons for the difficulties encountered in studying the Palestinian Talmud.

The character of the Palestinian Talmud has often been misunderstood. At first glance it seems to be simply a collection of *baraitot*, amoraic dicta, and aggadot, arranged with no internal logic. However, the Palestinian Talmud does indeed develop logical arguments in its discussions and is organized to indicate this logic. It lacks the connecting terminology that was added to the Babylonian Talmud during the last stages in its history because no comparable stage took place in Palestine.

THE BABYLONIAN TALMUD

The Babylonian Talmud was produced by circles of Babylonian amoraim who were led in each generation by masters whose schools constituted the center of amoraic activity. Although there was some tannaitic activity there, Babylonia did not become a center of talmudic study until the time of Rav and Samuel in the first half of the third century.

The most important centers of amoraic activity were Nehardea, Sura, Pumbedita, Mahoza, Naresh, and Mata Mehasya. The amora Samuel functioned at Nehardea, and his colleague Rav is said to have founded the center at Sura. After Samuel's death in 259 C.E., Nehardea was destroyed by Palmyrene marauders. After Rav's death, the dominant figure at Sura was Rav Huna (d. 297). (The title "rav," the Babylonian Jewish equivalent of rabbi, indicated that the holder had been empowered to render legal decisions.) Rav Huna was associated with several younger scholars, Rav Judah, Rav Hisda, Rav Sheshet, and Rav Nahman bar Jacob (d. 320). Rav Judah was said to have founded a circle of scholars at Pumbedita. Rabba bar Nahmani (d. 320) and Rav

BABYLONIAN TALMUD, VILNA EDITION. In modern times, the standard edition of the Babylonian Talmud is that printed in Vilna (presently called Vilnius), Lithuania between 1880–86 (20 folio-sized volumes) and which has been reprinted numerous times. Included in this edition, besides the Mishnah and the Babylonian Gemara, are the commentaries of Rashi (1040–1105), the Tosafists (12th–14th centuries), and numerous marginal references and other commentaries. In the back of each volume are additional commentaries, as well as the codes of Isaac Alfasi (1013–1103) and Asher ben Yeḥiel (ca. 1250–1327). Also included is the Tosefta. Shown here is the first page of tractate Berakhot dealing with blessings and prayers.

Joseph (d. 323) were both active in Pumbedita. Abaye carried on his school there (from 323 to 338). Rava served there from 338 to 352, and afterwards relocated to Mahoza. Historians see the Mahoza school as a continuation of that of Pumbedita. In any case, the importance of the Mahoza circle was greatly diminished by Rava's death in 352. Papa founded a circle at Naresh which he headed until 371, and Rav Nahman bar Isaac then took over at Pumbedita. The next generation of scholars included Rav Ashi, the preeminent figure of the age, in Mata Mehasya, near Sura. At the same time Amemar was active in Nehardea, and Rav Zevid, Rav Dimi, and Mar Zutra were the leading sages at Pumbedita. Amoraic activity continued thereafter for only one final generation, with Meremar, Rav Idi bar Abin, and Mar bar Rav Ashi in Sura. These scholars, as already mentioned, most probably did not head formal academies, but rather schools or circles of disciples organized along informal lines. From a variety of talmudic sources it is clear that the leading amoraim and their disciples also played a role in the public life of Babylonian Jewry, as homilists, judges, and teachers, seeking to spread the Judaism of the rabbinic tradition to the Babylonian Jewish masses, a goal in which they ultimately succeeded.

The Babylonian Talmud, like its Palestinian counterpart, is not complete for the entire Mishnah. For the order Zera'im there is only Berakhot. Virtually all of the orders Mo'ed, Nashim, Neziqin, and Qodashim are covered. Of Tahorot, only tractate Niddah is found. A variety of explanations is possible. Most likely, this distribution reflects the curriculum of study in Babylonia, in which agricultural laws did not apply and most of the purification rituals were no longer practiced. Sacrifice was studied to some degree, since study of its laws served as a substitute for its performance. Another view holds that all aspects of Jewish law were studied but the redactor of the Babylonian Talmud chose to include only those which were still applicable. Finally, it may be that more material existed but that some was lost to the vicissitudes of oral transmission and then of written preservation.

Various attempts have been made to sketch and compare the basic characteristics of the two Talmuds. Many of the comparisons have turned out to be exaggerated and overdrawn. At the same time, it is true that the Babylonian Talmud, because of the longer period of amoraic activity in Babylonia, abounds in detailed logical debates, whereas material of this kind is less often found in the Palestinian Talmud. The claim that the Babylonian Talmud makes less use of tannaitic tradition cannot be substantiated. Since it contains much amoraic material of Palestinian provenance (and vice versa), attempts to look for Babylonian (or Palestinian) social and economic conditions in the amoraic traditions cannot be based on the collections in their complete form. Such studies must be grounded rather on the provenance and dating of individual statements and traditions.

One definite difference between the Talmuds, however, is the use of different dialects of Aramaic. Since ancient times the Aramaic language had been divided into western and eastern dialects. The Jews of Palestine used the Galilean form of the western one, close in many ways to the Imperial Aramaic of biblical times, while those of Babylonia used the eastern, which was similar to Syriac and Mandaic. Not surprisingly, the two Talmuds reflect this pattern. Further, while they have many linguistic features in common, they often employ different technical terminology.

Medieval opinion held that the Babylonian Talmud had been redacted by Ravina I (d. ca. 420) and Rav Ashi (d. 427), who were among the last of the amoraim. While it is reasonable to credit their generation with having collected and edited the tannaitic and amoraic materials that had come down to them, often in the form of *sugyot*, the final redaction must have postdated these sages. In all probability the redactional process extended well into the sixth century. The final redactors, who left their mark in the anonymous (*setam*) layer of the Babylonian Talmud, wove together the traditions they had received with the anonymous discussions, the *shaqla' we-ṭarya'* ("give and take"), and added the many formulary expressions that designate the various types of material which make up the Babylonian Gemara.

THE EXEGETICAL AND HOMILETICAL MIDRASHIM

While it is certainly true that the great collections of so-called halakhic or tannaitic Midrashim were redacted mainly in the amoraic period, the content of these texts reflects the traditions and ideas of the tannaitic period. In amoraic times, a different type of aggadic Midrash, termed exegetical and homiletical, was developed. Whereas the Midrashim of tannaitic times were primarily a product of the schoolhouse, those of amoraic times originated in the homilies of the synagogue, rapidly emerging in this period as the central institution of Jewish life. The exegetical Midrashim were a Palestinian product, as reflected in their Galilean Aramaic dialect (like that of the Aramaic portions of the Palestinian Talmud), and the constant allusions and attributions to Palestinian rabbis, many of whom are not known from the Talmuds.

The earliest of these Midrashim, those actually dating to the amoraic period, were edited in the fifth and sixth centuries. The exegetical type are arranged in scriptural order and, usually, proceed in a sustained manner verse by verse through the biblical book they treat. They include Genesis Rabbah, Lamentations Rabbah, Esther Rabbah I (i.e., the first part), Song of Songs Rabbah, and Ruth Rabbah. (Rabbah means, "the Great," signifying the primacy of these Midrashim over other such collections.) The homiletical type of Midrash, made up of topi-

AMORAIC MIDRASHIM
(dates of compilation are all C.E.)

400–500	Genesis Rabbah
	Leviticus Rabbah
	Lamentations Rabbah
	Esther Rabbah, pt. I
500–640	Pesiqta De-Rav Kahana
	Song of Songs Rabbah
	Ruth Rabbah
640–900	Ecclesiastes Rabbah
	Deuteronomy Rabbah
	Pirqe Rabbi Eliezer
	Tanna De-Ve Eliyahu
775–900	Tanḥuma Midrashim
	Exodus Rabbah, pt. II
	Numbers Rabbah, pt. II
	Pesiqta Rabbati

cally organized discourses, includes Leviticus Rabbah and Pesiqta de-Rav Kahana. The former provides comments on the
first verse of each section of the Torah according to the triennial
order of reading (a cycle by which the Torah is apportioned for
public reading in the synagogue over three years). In the Pesiqta
de-Rav Kahana homilies are provided for holidays and special
occasions.

The amoraic Midrashim typically include a literary form
known as the proem. A proem is an introduction to the midrashic exposition of a verse, usually the first verse of a specific
Torah portion. It begins by citing a verse from elsewhere and
then proceeds through a chain of interpretations until it arrives
at the very first verse of the Torah reading, which it then
identifies as echoing the notions derived in the previous exegesis. This rhetorical technique was a favorite one in the homiletical discourses given in the synagogues of Byzantine Palestine on
Sabbath afternoons. As the midrashic collections were edited,
proems were often invented to fill out the needs of the redactor
where none had actually existed in the received tradition, thus
giving rise to their ubiquity.

The redaction of the remaining "Rabbah" Midrashim—Exodus, Leviticus, Numbers, Deuteronomy, Ecclesiastes Rabbah,
and Esther Rabbah II (i.e., the second part) as well as the texts
of the Tanhuma type—belongs to a later period, beyond the
scope of this book. Yet these works also preserve material from
the amoraic period which can be dated with some accuracy by
careful literary and historical analysis. These later aggadic
compilations were more influenced by apocryphal, pseudepigraphal, apocalyptic, and mystical elements than those produced in
amoraic Palestine, and also diverged from them in literary form
and linguistic character. Indeed, Babylonian Jewry had a hand
in the later collections, and similar texts were still being redacted in Europe through the twelfth century.

JEWISH LITURGY

We cannot leave the discussion of the great literary heritage
of Talmudic Judaism without discussing the development of
Jewish liturgy and the eventual emergence of canonized prayer

collections. Ultimately, it was the contribution of the rabbis that provided the raw material for the early medieval attempt to collect the prayers into texts which we call prayer books (*Siddurim* and *Maḥzorim*).

Tannaitic and amoraic scholars made essential contributions to the development of Jewish liturgy, although it would be naive and simplistic to claim a controlling role for them. Jewish liturgy has its earliest roots in the individual prayers of the biblical period. We cannot know for sure whether prayer had a regular place in the Temple's sacrificial ritual, but it is quite certain that individuals sometimes recited prayers while bringing sacrifices, and it is also true that in both Temples the levitical choir chanted psalms as an accompaniment to the sacrifices. Nonetheless, the prayers of individuals and the psalms of the choir did not constitute a fixed communal ritual or what we would describe as an organized worship service.

The Second Temple period offers the first evidence of fixed liturgical prayers. During this period the Jewish people was gradually turning toward prayer, and it was slowly becoming institutionalized even in the Temple. Indeed, various passages in the apocrypha, pseudepigrapha, and, especially, the Dead Sea Scrolls testify to the growth of fixed patterns of daily, Sabbath, and festival prayer among at least some Jews. As a result, when the Temple was destroyed in 70 C.E., and the sacrificial ritual ceased, Judaism was prepared to make the transition to prayer.

The destruction afforded the rabbis a unique opportunity to develop a liturgical system. Soon after the destruction, the tannaim at Yavneh began to standardize ritual practice. They began by fixing a definite list of benedictions for the Amidah prayer and, as well, by setting the times for prayer. The Amidah (literally "standing" prayer), also known as the Eighteen Benedictions, is the central part of every service, according to rabbinic practice. Further developments, regarding the recitation of the Shema ("Hear, O Israel," Deut. 6:5, etc.), the Grace after Meals, and other benedictions, took place over the first two centuries C.E. Nonetheless, tannaitic sources preserve few actual liturgical texts because prayer remained so fluid in this formative period. It was during the amoraic period that the liturgy began taking on a more fixed nature.

No fixed prayer collections are known to have existed in talmudic times. Although there was a basic sequence of obligatory prayers, the text of the liturgy had not yet been standardized, but different versions of the various prayers were available and some of these had attained written form in private notes.

The liturgy was standardized much less quickly in Babylonia than in Palestine, where the patriarchate and the centralized academies made the process easier. The Jewish masses, especially in Babylonia, were sometimes not very receptive to the new liturgy being introduced by the sages. It took a long time to win their acceptance, and sometimes the rabbis had to fight against popular custom and superstition. In due course, however, forms of worship and liturgical texts became more and more standardized throughout the amoraic period.

Meanwhile, highly significant developments were taking place in Palestine. Alongside the statutory prayers instituted in tannaitic times, the tradition of *piyyuṭ* (liturgical poetry) developed. Based in large part on midrashic teachings, this poetry sought to expand the traditional prayers for various occasions. The composers of *piyyuṭim* (liturgical poems) followed a long-standing pattern of literary and poetic expansion of existing material. The new poetry, alongside the increasingly standardized prayer service, served as the model for the great liturgical collections of the gaonic period, which set the pattern for all future Jewish worship.

SUMMARY

The amoraic period bequeathed a rich literary heritage when the Palestinian and Babylonian Talmuds, the Midrashim, and the various liturgical texts were eventually committed to writing. It is in the amoraic materials that much of the application of tannaitic tradition was explained and amplified. Yet the amoraim made their own unique contribution to Judaism by beginning the exegesis of the oral law, recovering ancient traditions on mysticism and messianism, and formulating the basis of the Jewish liturgy. The products of their scholarship provided the greatest literary models for Jewish intellectual striving, and opened a new world to the Jewish people, that of the Talmud. The collections of traditions which the amoraim created would serve as the basis for Jewish life, thought, and scholarship for the next millennium and a half. Countless generations of Jews would dedicate their lives to learning to navigate the sea of the Talmud.

13
The Life of Torah

The Mishnah brought to fruition a long period in the development of halakhah (rabbinic law). There was now a comprehen-
sive document spelling out the nature of the life of Torah as
understood by the rabbis. The Mishnah explained how the
existence of the Jew in this world was to be sanctified. In the
aftermath of the destruction of the Temple, the Mishnah and
the associated tannaitic traditions provided guidance on how the
close relationship of Israel to its God, secured in earlier days
through sacrifice and Temple, was now to be achieved by other
means.

Many aspects of Jewish life, however, had still not been
completely clarified and had to be elucidated further in the
Palestinian and Babylonian Talmuds. This chapter will set out
but a small part of the system of halakhah as it unfolded in
tannaitic and amoraic sources, providing a glimpse of how
rabbinic Judaism sought to sanctify the life of each and every
Jew. Although, on balance, tannaitic literature devoted a large
proportion of its discussions to laws of agriculture, sacrifice,
ritual purity, and other matters no longer practiced after the
destruction of the Temple, we will concentrate here on the
remaining elements, which constituted the piety of the rabbis
and their followers in Late Antiquity. First, though, we will
briefly outline the message of rabbinic aggadah, for it is in the
aggadah that the beliefs at the foundation of rabbinic piety were
expounded.

THE WORLD OF THE AGGADAH

Rabbinic tradition, in both its tannaitic and amoraic stages, preserved the contributions of some two thousand named authorities and countless others over a period of almost a millennium. For this reason, and because the systematic organization of theological tenets was itself totally foreign to the rabbis of the Talmud, whose beliefs can only be extrapolated from their various exegetical and legal traditions, any attempt to speak of the theology or religion of the rabbis is futile. All we can do is to survey some of the ideas that eventually constituted the consensus that emerged when the rabbinic period drew to a close with the Islamization of the Near East. In the last stages of the editing and redaction of the Talmuds and in the later aggadic literature, there emerged a general view on certain issues that are prominently dealt with in the aggadic materials. While we cannot expect all rabbis (let alone all Jews) to have subscribed to every one of these ideas, they can be described, nonetheless, as the common aggadic heritage of most rabbinic Jews at the end of the talmudic period and as the basis for the later development of medieval Jewish philosophy and mysticism.

Basic to Rabbinic Judaism was the belief that the world was created by one God who had existed from eternity and will exist forever. This God is omnipotent and omniscient. He created the world by fiat and remains master of its affairs. He desires only that His creatures observe His Torah, the instrument by which He reveals the divine will to His people. To the rabbis, the Torah was the instruction that God revealed to Moses at Sinai in both the written law and the oral law. The former is preserved in the Hebrew Bible, the latter is expounded in rabbinic teachings. Together, and in creative tension, these two corpora form the basis of Judaism. Following the way of the Torah ensures God's people entrance to and reward in the world-to-come. Non-Jews may also gain this reward, by observing a few commandments, the Noachide laws, a sort of rabbinic equivalent of natural law to which all humanity is subject. The option of proselytism, conversion to Judaism, is open to the sincere non-Jew who wishes to identify fully with the Jewish people and adopt its way of life.

BINDING OF ISAAC FROM BETH ALPHA. The mosaic floor of the synagogue at Beth Alpha near Beth Shean, laid in ca. 518–27 C.E. (the building is a somewhat earlier), included a panel detailing the binding of Isaac. This motif is central to the Rosh Ha-Shanah liturgy since midrashic tradition teaches that the binding of Isaac took place on Rosh Ha-Shanah, and the ram's horn (shofar) is blown on this holiday. To the left, Abraham's two servants wait with the donkey while in the center the ram, which is ultimately sacrificed, is caught up in the thicket. Abraham, holding Isaac and the knife, prepares to sacrifice his son on the altar where a fire is already burning. *Photo by Steven Fine.*

The halakhah seeks to sanctify the Jew's entire life and his relations both with God and his fellow man. In it and through it one achieves perfection in both ritual matters and ethical and moral concerns. In fact, for Judaism, there is no distinction between these spheres: ritual, ethical, and moral matters are all presented as one all-encompassing and indivisible entity. All guidance comes from the halakhah, which seeks to sanctify even the most mundane of human activities with a view to infusing the divine into the life of mortals.

The study and teaching of the law is itself seen as a religious value. Through it, one not only learns how to fulfill the divine will, but also participates in the ongoing handing down of the tradition. The student of the Torah becomes a link in the unbroken chain which connects the Jewish people to the revelation at Sinai.

The observance or nonobservance of the commandments (mitzvot) leads people either to reward or to punishment, both in this life and the next. Although sometimes the righteous appear to suffer in this world, reward is stored up for them in the next. Similarly, although the wicked appear to prosper in this life, their success is only illusory. In the next life they will receive their just punishment.

Yet the issue of reward and punishment extends well beyond the individual. The community of Israel seeks to achieve a collective reward, the messianic era. At some time in the future, it is believed, a series of events will transform the world and the people of Israel, and a period of perfection will be ushered in. This era will begin with a series of cataclysmic events, but ultimately peace will prevail. At the end of days, the people of Israel will be free of foreign domination and will be ruled in its own land by a Davidic king, a messiah who is but a mortal elevated to special wisdom, power, and responsibility. When the messianic era dawns, the nations of the world will finally recognize the truthfulness of the God of Israel, and this, in turn, will lead to the universal participation of all peoples in the messianic age. All will obey the will of God and worship at His mountain. The Temple will be rebuilt in Jerusalem, and the final resurrection will bring all who lived righteously to the experience of eternal bliss.

THE DAILY LIFE OF THE JEW

The rabbis sought to sanctify all of man's actions, even the most mundane. Accordingly, it was expected that such matters as personal hygiene and dress would come under the halakhah as well as matters usually understood as "religious" in the modern sense. Jews were expected to begin their day by washing their hands, a practice that was meant to purify them from any impurities they might have contracted during sleep. Clothing was to be modest, especially in the case of women. Certain clothing and haircuts were excluded because of their pagan associations.

Men were expected to have the biblically mandated fringes (tsitsit) on their garments, as reminders of the obligation to observe the commandments. The fringes included the sky-blue fringe coiled around the others, the dye for which ceased to be available after talmudic times. Throughout the tannaitic and amoraic periods, such garments were part of the normal garb of Jews. It was only later that they evolved into specific ritual or prayer garments, such as the modern ṭallit (prayer shawl).

The tefillin (phylacteries), leather boxes bound with thongs to the arm and head, contained parchments inscribed with biblical passages interpreted by the rabbis as dealing with the requirement of wearing tefillin (Exod. 13:1–10, 11–16; Deut. 6:4–9, 11:13–21). The tefillin were put on in accord with the rabbinic interpretation of the very same passages and were intended to symbolize the notion that a man's actions and thoughts should all be harnessed to do the will of his Creator. Despite certain theoretical debates, the amoraim saw the fringed garments and phylacteries as the garb of men, not women. The tefillin were originally worn by the pious all day, but in rabbinic times were evolving into prayer accoutrements for male Jews. Phylacteries have been found among the Dead Sea Scrolls.

By tannaitic times there had evolved a series of benedictions to be recited while getting up and dressing in the morning. They were intended to thank God for providing for the day-to-day needs of His creatures. (Much later, in the Middle Ages, these benedictions were grouped together and placed at the start of the morning service.)

TEFILLIN (PHYLACTERIES) FROM QUMRAN. This head Tefillin (phylactery) was found intact in the Qumran caves. It has been dated to the first half of the first century C.E. The view on the right is actual size. A large number of such Tefillin, or parts of Tefillin, have been found in the caves. Inside are biblical texts. One type includes the very same texts as required by Talmudic law; another has some additional texts. Tefillin were certainly a part of the life of various groups of Second Temple period Jews and continued to be worn, at least for morning prayer, in the Rabbinic period. *Courtesy of the Shrine of the Book of the Israel Museum.*

The Jew was to pray three times daily. In tannaitic tradition the Shema (Deut. 6:4–9, 11:13–21, Num. 15:37–41) and the benedictions surrounding it were to be recited both morning and night, but they were still not integrally connected with the Amidah (the Eighteen Benedictions), recited morning, after-noon, and night. The morning and afternoon Amidah prayers were considered to be required, since they were recited at the same time as the two daily sacrifices and, after the destruction, came to be regarded as replacements for them. The tannaim debated whether the evening Amidah was obligatory or not. By the end of the amoraic period, both in Palestine and Babylonia, the Shema unit (the Shema and its benedictions) was associated with the Amidah unit, so that the system of daily prayer consisted of services based on the Shema and its benedictions followed by the Amidah in the morning, the Amidah alone in the afternoon, and the sequence of Shema with benedictions and Amidah again in the evening. In amoraic times, the morning benedictions had already been expanded to include the blessings on the Torah and a variety of other passages, and the prelimi-nary psalms had been fixed at the beginning of the morning service.

The obligation to recite the entire Amidah was only in the process of being fixed in tannaitic times. Some tannaim believed that abbreviated texts might be recited instead. The decision to require all eighteen benedictions was made only in the amoraic

PRAYER SERVICES

	Daily	Sabbaths, Festivals and New Moons	Yom Kippur (Day of Atonement)
Shaḥarit	X	X	X
Musaf (Additional)		X	X
Minḥah (Afternoon)	X	X	X
Ne'ilah (Twilight)			X
Ma'ariv (Evening)	X	X	X

period. Moreover, at Yavneh, soon after the destruction of the Temple, an imprecation against heretics, including the Jewish Christians (Birkat Ha-Minim), was inserted into the Amidah. It was intended to exclude them from leading the services, since no one would recite a prayer against himself. Other adjustments to the text were still occurring in the tannaitic period, but the order and contents of the benedictions were certainly fixed by the end of the tannaitic era.

It was in the amoraic period that the supplicatory prayers (Taḥanun) recited after the Amidah at the morning and afternoon services were introduced. Torah readings, however, were central to the service by tannaitic times, taking place on Mondays and Thursdays, the market days when people assembled in the towns, and on Sabbath mornings and afternoons, as well as on holidays and special occasions.

The tannaim outlined a detailed set of benedictions to be recited before and after eating (a full meal had to begin with the eating of bread). The benedictions after eating were in accord with the Torah's command, "You shall eat, be satisfied and bless the Lord your God" (Deut. 8:10), but the rabbis required benedictions before partaking of food as well. They reasoned that man owed a debt of gratitude to the Creator which had to be discharged before eating; one had to praise God and acknowledge His gift of sustenance to be entitled to partake. The text of the Grace after Meals from the rabbinic period has not come down to us, but evidence indicates that the basic structure known from later texts was already in effect in tannaitic times. Most rabbis took the view that while the specific obligations of daily worship applied only to men, reciting the benedictions on food was equally incumbent on women, since they too benefited from God's bounty.

In rabbinic times, although women took a substantial role in economic life, their primary responsibility was that of mother and wife. For this reason, the tannaim distanced women from a small number of commandments which had specific time requirements, such as prayer at fixed times, hearing the shofar on Rosh Ha-Shanah, and dwelling in the sukkah. Amoraic sources maintain that these commandments may be performed by women but are not obligatory for them. Over time, it became

SYNAGOGUE AT BARAM. The Galilee in the fourth through sixth centuries was dotted with synagogues. The synagogue at Baram in the Upper Galilee is the best preserved. The entrance faced south, the direction of Jerusalem. Worshippers entered and then turned toward the entrance to pray. The building was constructed in the Byzantine period. A nearby synagogue contained the inscription: "May there be peace in this place and in all the places of Israel. . . ." *Photo by Steven Fine.*

customary for women to perform most of these commandments. When the values and customs of the era in which the Talmud developed are taken into account, and especially when the surrounding societies are compared, Rabbinic Judaism is certainly seen to have accorded an elevated and respectful status to women. The differing roles assigned by halakhah to men and women had their basis in a view which saw male and female as complementary, not competitive, aspects of humanity. In the same way, rabbinic aggadah depicted God in both male and female terms.

The system of prayers and benedictions was meant to give sanctity to the life of the Jew, but rituals were by no means the totality of Rabbinic Judaism. Also required, and often stressed in tannaitic sources, was equal attention to the commandments pertaining to relations between man and his fellow man. These were enshrined in the many commercial, civil, and criminal laws as well as in the mishnaic tractate Avot, known in English as Ethics of the Fathers, in reality a guide for the rabbis on the conduct becoming their station and role as judges. Aspects of modesty in behavior, respect for one's parents, spouse, and other people, and similar topics are treated in great detail by tannaim and amoraim, both in halakhic and aggadic contexts. The Jew was to live a holy life each and every minute of the day, "walking humbly" with God (Micah 6:8), and loving and respecting others.

SANCTUARIES IN TIME

The Jewish calendar utilized the ancient Babylonian system of employing lunar months within a solar year. The eleven-day difference between the lunar and solar years was dealt with by intercalating an extra month (Adar II) at the end of the winter, approximately every three years. In Second Temple and rabbinic times, a complex system of empirical observation was employed to synchronize the calendar with actual lunar changes. While certain sectarian groups in Second Temple times, among them the Boethusians and the Dead Sea sect, used a calendar based on solar months, this innovation never gained substantial ground. Tannaitic Jews regarded the luni-solar calendar as di-

vinely ordained and as the ancient calendar of biblical Israel.
Moreover, the sectarian calendars in our sources were not as
astronomically accurate.

Besides the need for a system of intercalation, it was also
necessary to fix the exact day of the new moon each month.
Both of these functions involved a detailed procedure of lunar
observation undertaken in tannaitic times by a court of the
patriarchal house. Thus, although the Sabbath was considered
to occur on the very day on which God had desisted from labor
during creation, the seventh day, and hence its sanctity had
been fixed by God, the festivals and other Jewish holidays were
regarded as controlled by the people of Israel through their
system of courts. Rabbinic Judaism, therefore, recognized two
kinds of holy occasions, those determined by God and those
determined by His people. In other words, it was possible, in
the rabbinic view, for God to sanctify time, an act built into the
very order of creation, but it was the privilege of His people to
be able to do the same in regard to the festivals. In this way, as
in so many others, man becomes God's partner in the creation
and perfection of the world.

As long as there was a Temple in Jerusalem, with sacrificial
worship and the accompanying rituals, the Jewish people had a
sanctuary in space that allowed them to commune with God.
Tannaitic Judaism, as part of its adjustment to the destruction
of the Temple, placed ever greater emphasis on other sanctuaries. While this was certainly a factor in the rise of the synagogue
in amoraic times, the Sabbath and festivals had already, in the
tannaitic period, begun to replace the Temple and its sacrifices
as the sancta of Israel, becoming, as it were, sanctuaries in
time.

The Sabbath

In the tannaitic sources, the main issue regarding the Sabbath
was the conditions under which one who accidentally violated
the Sabbath was obligated to bring a sacrifice of expiation. This
question determined the content of the largest part of the
tractate Sabbath in the Mishnah. Indirectly, we learn from this
tractate that the tannaim understood as prohibited on the
Sabbath a wide range of creative labors that were said to have

been performed in the building of the Tabernacle, the portable shrine, in the desert. Since the Tabernacle was God's sanctuary, the labors outlined in the biblical accounts of its construction must have been the most important of creative labors. Since they were designated *melakhah*, "creative labor," and *melakhah* is prohibited on the Sabbath by the Torah, they must be the ones that pentateuchal law intended to prohibit. By abstaining from creative labors on the Sabbath one imitated the Creator, who, according to Genesis (2:1–3), had rested in this way after bringing the world into being.

The positive aspects of Sabbath observance, such as the Sabbath meals, the reading of the Torah, the special prayers of sanctification (Kiddush) and the concluding ceremony (Havdalah), both of which are mentioned prominently in tannaitic sources, and the requirements of rejoicing and dedicating the day to spiritual pursuits, were elaborated in amoraic sources. By the close of the talmudic period, these aspects were thoroughly spelled out in a series of laws designed to ensure that the positive character of the Sabbath would not be lost in light of its restrictions. Observed as the rabbis intended, the Sabbath provided a sanctuary in time from everyday work activities and created an atmosphere of sanctity in home and family.

Festivals and Other Occasions

Along with the Sabbath, several other days were set apart by biblical legislation as occasions for special sacrificial offerings. As such, they had special significance in First and Second Temple times. In tannaitic times, after the destruction they were adapted to the new situation that had become the norm and were given a more important place in the home and synagogue.

First and foremost, by tannaitic times, were Rosh Ha-Shanah (the New Year) and Yom Kippur (the Day of Atonement). In the absence of Temple and sacrifices, the High Holy Days and the period between them, the Days of Penitence, became a period of repentance, atonement, and forgiveness. The ceremonies and prayers for these days expressed Rabbinic Judaism's belief in free will and the human being's ability to change his or her life. The emphasis on God as king and sovereign on Rosh Ha-Shanah

THE JEWISH FESTIVALS IN TALMUDIC TIMES
(Dates in parentheses refer to the additional days celebrated
only outside of the Land of Israel)

Month	Festival
Tishre 1–2	Rosh Ha-Shanah
3	Fast of Gedaliah
10	Yom Kippur
15–21	Sukkot
21(–22)	Shemini Atzeret (Simḥat Torah)
Ḥeshvan	—
Kislev 25–Tevet 2	Hanukkah
Tevet 10	Fast of the Tenth of Tevet
Shevaṭ 15	Tu-Bi-Shevaṭ
Adar 13	Fast of Esther
14	Purim
15	"Shushan" Purim
Nisan 15–21(22)	Passover
Iyyar	—
Sivan 6(–7)	Shavuot
Tammuz 17	Fast of Seventeenth of Tammuz
Av 9	Fast of Ninth of Av (Ṭish'ah Be-Av)
Elul	—

accented such concepts as God's remembrance of Israel and His use of the shofar to herald the Sinaitic revelation and, in the future, the coming of the messiah. Yom Kippur became a remembrance of the atonement service in the Temple, serving to replace the sacrifice described in Leviticus 16.

Of ancient origins are the three pilgrimage festivals, Passover, Shavuot (Pentecost), and Sukkot (Tabernacles). In biblical times, these agricultural turning points were given new significance as celebrations of the redemptive history of Israel. Now, in rabbinic times, this meaning was deepened and heightened. The week-long Passover, the festival of the barley harvest, became the focal point of the commemoration of the Exodus from Egypt. Originally, in the days of the Temple, the Passover Seder had been a sacrificial meal at which certain praises and a midrash were recited. After the destruction, the Seder became a central part of the home ritual. Shavuot, a wheat harvest festival, was defined by talmudic chronology as the day on which the Torah had been given at Mount Sinai, and so it became the celebration of God's covenant with Israel, an event which had followed closely on the heels of the liberation from Egyptian bondage.

Sukkot, a seven-day celebration likewise connected with the Exodus, took on increased significance as a fall festival at which the Jewish people asked for rain to nourish the crops of the coming year. The lulav (palm branch) and etrog (citron), carried in processions during this festival, while given many symbolic explanations, were understood to express the fervent hope for a rainy winter and to represent the bountiful crops and fertility of the land for which the Jew prayed at the onset of fall, the planting season for grains. The *sukkah* ("booth") in which the Jews were commanded to dwell for the duration of the festival represented the temporary dwellings of the Israelites on their way to the promised land but was also a reminder of the clouds of the Divine Glory which had protected them in the desert, and, hence, of the fragility of human existence. In the Temple a special water-drawing ceremony and willow procession expressed the agricultural aspect of the holiday. In amoraic times, these ceremonies were increasingly reenacted in the synagogue services. It was in the amoraic period that the last day of this festival, the ninth day in the Diaspora (where an extra day was added to avoid confusion regarding the exact date), began to take on significance as a festival celebrating the completion of the reading of the Torah according to the Babylonian custom, which read the entire Pentateuch in one year. Yet it was only in the Middle Ages that this day developed its full significance and became known as Simḥat Torah (Rejoicing in the Torah).

Two other holidays, Hanukkah and Purim, are of special importance because they were instituted to celebrate Jewish victories over anti-Semitism and religious oppression. Both of these holidays, because of their late origin, elicited some reservations before they were finally accepted as part of the Jewish calendar.

Purim, based on the story told in the Book of Esther, commemorates the Jewish victory over the courtier Haman and his supporters in the Persian Empire. While biblical scholars in modern times have doubted the story's historicity, talmudic tradition accepted it as fact. The rabbis saw the tale's humor and irony, but recognized the hand of God behind the story line. In accord with the commands given toward the end of the tale, they spun out detailed observances for the holiday—the reading of the Scroll of Esther morning and night, gifts of food and alms to be given the poor, special holiday additions to the service and the Grace after Meals, and a festive meal. Yet at the same time, there is tannaitic evidence that the book's canonicity was challenged and amoraic evidence that the obligatory character of the Purim observances was questioned. Ultimately, authoritative rabbinic opinion sided with the celebration of Purim. Yet the discomfort of some rabbinic Jews with a story of deliverance in which prayer and God are not explicitly mentioned can still be felt in our sources.

Hanukkah is a holiday commemorating the Hasmonean victory over the Seleucids in 168–164 B.C.E. The tannaim had little information about its origins and historical background, for I and II Maccabees were not known to rabbinic Jews. Nonetheless, the tannaim set down the regulations for the lighting of candles, and for additions to the service and the Grace after Meals. Once again there was some hesitancy about the commemoration, this time because the Maccabean priests had arrogated both the high priesthood and the kingship to themselves even though the two offices were supposed to be separate according to the Torah. It has been suggested that Rabbi Judah the Prince did not include a specific tractate for Hanukkah in the Mishnah because of resentment over this: he claimed to be a member of the Davidic house, which had effectively been displaced by the Hasmonean priest-kings.

Besides these joyous holidays, there was a series of sad occasions, fast-days, to commemorate destruction of the First and Second Temples. The most notable of these are the Seventeenth of Tamuz and the Ninth of Av. Both of these fast-days are mentioned by the prophet Zechariah (8:19) early in the Second Temple period, and originally they commemorated the first destruction. However, we can only gauge their significance from the period after the destruction of the Second Temple. Abstinence from food and drink, special prayers, and the reading of the Torah all served to highlight the tragic quality of the destruction. Although much of Talmudic Judaism developed in its aftermath, the rabbis regarded this break in the intimate contact between God and the world to have been the greatest disaster in Jewish history.

The various days surveyed here, both happy and sad, provided the rabbinic Jewish community in Palestine and Babylonia with an opportunity to remember and transmit its communal history and to forge its communal identity. Despite the many local differences in observance, as well as the historical development of the various holidays, the basic list of observances remained uniform from the mid-second century on. These days constituted the Jewish ritual calendar, the rhythm of the Jewish year.

THE SANCTIFIED TABLE

In Rabbinic Judaism, already by tannaitic times, the act of eating was to be sanctified. It has already been observed how a set of blessings served to inculcate the notion that physical sustenance was a gift from God for which man had eternally to acknowledge dependence and gratitude. Yet this otherwise physical function had another dimension, that of the laws of kosher food.

The laws of *kashrut* have their origins in biblical tradition. The division of the animal kingdom into pure and impure animals is enshrined both in the biblical narrative and in the laws of the Torah. The Bible prohibits the consumption of animals that have cloven hoofs and do not chew the cud, as well as a long list of birds of prey, most insects, fish without fins and scales, and shellfish of all kinds. In the rabbinic view, these creatures are proscribed as food because the behavior patterns that typify them are undesirable in various ways. Those who eat them in some symbolic sense internalize these patterns and take on the undesirable traits.

Biblical tradition spoke of two kinds of slaughter, sacrificial and non-sacral (often termed "profane"). Sacrificial slaughter had to take place in the Tabernacle or Temple and constituted a sacral act in the sense that the slaughter itself in some way bound man to God. Non-sacral slaughter was not a sanctified act and its significance was limited to rendering an animal so slaughtered permissible as food. The tannaim understood the Torah as requiring that an animal could be eaten only if it was slaughtered in the same way as a sacrifice.

In addition to the requirements that only permitted animals may be eaten and that they must be slaughtered properly, the Torah further specifies that the blood must not be consumed. Indeed, the method of slaughter required by talmudic halakhah is designed to facilitate the draining of the blood. For this law to be fulfilled, the meat must be properly cut, certain blood vessels must be removed, and the meat must be salted, washed, and drained of all blood. It is forbidden, even in the case of non-sacral slaughter, to eat the blood, as well as the parts of the entrails that were normally offered in sacrificial worship.

All the foregoing laws, with the exception of the details of ritual slaughter, were explicitly stated in the Torah. Much more difficult is the thrice-repeated requirement: "Thou shalt not boil a kid in its mother's milk" (Exod. 23:19, 34:26, Deut. 14:21). By tannaitic times, the interpretation of this commandment had given rise to the notion that meat and milk and foods containing them are to be kept totally separate. To accomplish this separation, distinct sets of utensils were to be used for meat and milk foods.

The separation of meat and milk must be understood as a law that seeks to maintain what was seen as the natural order of things. The Torah's conception of this order was violated by the mixing of milk, the giver of life and sustenance, with the meat of the very animal it had been intended to sustain. Hence they were to be kept separate. The extension of this law to a requirement that all milk and meat be separated can be understood in the same way; the forces of sustenance may not be mixed with those of death.

All these laws, together with the benedictions and rituals, the ritual handwashing before eating bread, and the agricultural tithes, had led, by amoraic times, to the idea that the table was a substitute for the sacrificial altar. This meant that, at every meal, each and every Jew stood at an altar before the Creator, offering his or her own sacrifice. These ideas contributed to stricter interpretations of the laws of diet and food, but they elevated the taking of physical sustenance to an act of great spiritual meaning for those who lived in accord with the teachings of the amoraim. Taken together with the laws of marriage and of ritual impurity, they affirmed that the Jew, in the talmudic vision, had to sanctify the everyday physical drives and harness them to the service of God. As distinct from Christianity, this approach to sanctification argued that man's physical needs and their satisfaction were inherently good, requiring for their fulfillment and sanctification only that the appropriate laws and regulations be observed.

MARRIAGE AND THE FAMILY

The Book of Genesis taught the rabbis the ideals of family life. It began by introducing monogamy as the ideal of the Garden of Eden and then accepted polygamy as a compromise, illustrating the difficulties entailed with examples from the lives of the patriarchs. The legal codes of the Torah provided for marriage and divorce and required the marriage bond as a prerequisite for sexual relations. The ancient customs of dowry and bride-price, as well as the procedures for entering into the marital union, were already changing in the fifth century B.C.E., as is known from the documents of the Jewish military colony at Elephantine. By the time of the tannaim, they had been turned into a set of provisions, contractual and financial, for securing the welfare of the wife and children in the event of the death of the husband or a divorce. These developments went hand in hand with other evidence of the rising status of women, an amelioration that clearly resulted from the influence of the biblical tradition, as can be seen when biblical laws regarding women and marriage are compared to their ancient Near Eastern counterparts.

By tannaitic times, marriage was entered into by a procedure which had to be formally witnessed. Women had to be provided with marriage contracts for their protection, and some tannaim regarded the provisions of such contracts as binding even when the document could not be produced or had not been executed. Marriage could be entered into either by the giving of a sum of money (usually in the form of a ring), the giving of a written declaration (distinct from the marriage contract), or consummating the marriage for the purpose of entering into a permanent bond.

Marriage was dissolved either by the death of one spouse or by divorce. Although the Torah specified that a divorce was to be initiated by the husband, the amoraim developed methods for bringing about a divorce at the wife's request under certain circumstances. Moreover, divorce was made easier in several ways in cases where ending the marriage was in the wife's interest. At the same time, the rabbis continued to take the view that women were always better off married than single, which certainly was so in the society in which they lived. While the amoraim ruled that divorce could take place for any reason, not only for adultery, they saw the failure of a marriage as a personal and even cosmic tragedy, for the marital relationship symbolized the covenant between God and Israel.

The ultimate purpose of marriage was to carry out the commandment to procreate. The tannaim disagreed about the limits of this commandment, but the amoraim decided in favor of the Hillelite view that two children, one boy and one girl, satisfied the requirement for the man. This commandment, curiously, was not seen as obligatory on women. Several halakhic and aggadic passages are designed to inculcate an approach to the raising of children and their training in the commandments. Many of the beautiful stories preserved in the aggadah may have been intended for children, a role these tales still play in contemporary Jewish life.

To the amoraim, the concept of marriage was one of completion. Through marriage each partner was to be fulfilled. Among the rabbis themselves, polygamy was virtually unknown. Indeed, the economic conditions of the times, including the process of urbanization, which was marked in this period, led increasingly toward monogamy.

Various talmudic and midrashic passages lead us to believe that the family unit was the basic context in which the continuity of Judaism was ensured. For example, the father is obligated to teach his son Torah; he can employ others to do this for him, but the responsibility remains his nonetheless. The mother was expected to teach her daughter about the laws of *kashrut* and the observance of family purity. Children could expect to grow up in close proximity to grandparents and other members of the extended family, and to maintain permanent and harmonious relationships with their brothers and sisters. The family was the center from which all other aspects of community and peoplehood emanated.

RITUAL PURITY AND IMPURITY

In biblical and Second Temple times the entire system of ritual purity and impurity, as outlined in the levitical codes of the Torah, was in effect. The system of ritual purity and impurity is based on the notion that certain bodily discharges, physical experiences, diseases, and animals can render one impure. Being impure means that one cannot approach the sancta, the Temple, and, in the case of menstruation, that one must abstain from sexual relations. The various purification rituals—quarantine, sprinkling, shaving, laundering of clothes, immersion in a ritual bath—can return the impure person to a state of ritual purity, and thus to full participation in family life and Temple worship.

By applying themselves to detailed study of the purity laws even after the destruction of the Temple, the tannaim indicated that in their view the observance of these laws would once again be the norm in the perfect society of the messianic future. Nonetheless, the destruction was followed by a gradual period of transition in which it became clear that virtually all of these laws had become inapplicable. Despite this, ritual purity remained in force in two major domains, the washing of the hands before eating bread (a rabbinic ordinance) and the observance of menstrual purification in marriage.

The Torah had required that a seven-day purification period, followed by immersion in a mikveh (ritual bath), take place after the onset of menstruation. Around the end of the tannaitic period or the beginning of the amoraic, because of the possibility of confusing menstruation with a flow of non-menstrual blood (which required a seven-day waiting period before immersion),

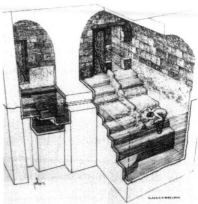

THE RITUAL BATH (MIKVEH). Jewish law requires bathing in a ritual bath to effect purification from certain impurities. After the destruction of the Temple the mikveh continued to be used primarily by married women as part of the monthly purification process. Photo A shows a Second Temple period mikveh from Qumran, used by the sectarians. B is a diagram of a mikveh which accords with the requirements of rabbinic law. Natural rain water is collected on the left and then led into the bath on the right, rendering the entirety fit for ritual use. *Photo A by Lawrence H. Schiffman, B courtesy of the Institute of Archaeology of the Hebrew University.*

it was decided that the counting of the seven days was to begin after the menstrual flow had ended.

This resulted in the system of ritual purification still followed in Judaism. It works as follows: From the onset of her menstrual period, the woman is impure for at least five days. Thereafter, when the flow stops, she begins to count seven days in which there is no flow. When those days are completed, on the night after the seventh day, she immerses and returns to having sexual relations with her husband. Although these laws are to be observed by the woman, the man violates a prohibition of the Torah if he has relations with his wife when she is ritually impure.

In Second Temple times, certain groups, such as the author(s) of the *Temple Scroll* from Qumran, sought to completely separate menstruating women from the community. Further, certain rabbinic works reflect a tendency to regard the menstrually impure woman as a source of impurity and even as an object of disgust. These approaches were clearly on the decline in the amoraic period and were preserved thereafter only in sectarian circles, including those which came together to form the Karaite movement in the early Middle Ages.

Women, then, became the guardians of the remnants of the vast system of purity which had existed in the days of the Temple. In amoraic times, as is clear from aggadic material, menstrual purity came to symbolize the notion that the family and home life had to aspire to the purity of the Temple. Indeed, the home itself, and specifically the marriage relationship, became another sanctuary which the Jews could carry with them and which would help to sustain them in the millennia ahead.

LIFE-CYCLE

Besides marriage and the attendant aspects of ritual purity, birth, puberty, and death were also dealt with in the halakhic system. From biblical times on the newborn Jewish boy was ushered into the Jewish people through the covenant of circumcision at the age of eight days. This rite distinguished the Jews in the Greco-Roman world, according to numerous pagan sources. Accordingly it was a requirement for conversion to

Judaism. The detailed laws regarding the performance of circumcision are spelled out in tannaitic and amoraic sources. They are designed to ensure the procedure's safety and its performance in accord with the legal requirements. Circumcision is a commandment which the father is obligated to perform for his son. By tannaitic times, specially trained personnel were performing the ritual, but this development may have taken place earlier. Circumcisions were accompanied by festive parties and special benedictions. In Seleucid and again in Roman times, when circumcision was briefly outlawed for anti-Semitic reasons, Jews risked their lives to fulfill this commandment.

Although Second Temple sources indicate that twenty was the age of majority among some groups, the tannaim selected the onset of puberty, which they took to be twelve years and a day for girls (bat mitzvah, literally "daughter of the commandment") and thirteen and a day for boys (bar mitzvah, "son of the commandment"), as the minimum age for the obligation to perform the commandments. From this point on the child was obligated to observe all the commandments. According to the tannaim, a small number of commandments were obligatory even for children, but the amoraim saw these as involving the parent's obligation to educate the child. (The celebrations associated with reaching the age of religious majority did not exist until much later.)

Tannaitic Judaism also sought to codify the various aspects of the end of life in this world. Although the Bible provides little direct legislation in this area, the tannaim were able to glean certain details, no doubt with the help of ancient customs. They required that the body be washed and buried within three days. There were two forms of burial. In one, the body was laid to rest in a hollowed-out niche where it remained for the first year. Thereafter, the bones were gathered and reinterred in an ossuary. This procedure gave rise to the celebration of the anniversary of the passing of close relatives. The second method was direct burial in an ossuary. From the Bible the rabbis learned of seven-day and thirty-day mourning periods. The tannaim ruled that a seven-day period of intense mourning and a thirty-day period of lesser mourning must be observed following the death of one's parent, sibling, or child. A full year of mourning was required for parents. Amoraic sources clarify many details of these rites, but their basis clearly rests in the tannaitic period. From the amoraim we learn that Jewish tradition regarded the human body as the repository of a God-given soul, and hence as possessing great sanctity. Over and over the rabbis speak of the burial of the dead and the comforting of the mourners as among the greatest of commandments.

STUDY IN THE SERVICE OF GOD

The history of virtually every aspect of halakhah discussed here conforms to a pattern. In the tannaitic period an adjustment to the absence of the Temple took place, and then, in amoraic times, the ritual or law was given significance as a replacement for the Temple. The most significant example of the transition from Temple to non-Temple Judaism is that of Torah study. For the rabbis, study replaced sacrifice as a form of worship alongside prayer.

The modes of study in tannaitic and amoraic times have already been sketched in an earlier chapter. Here we must reflect on the function of study. When the Temple ritual was still in effect, study was seen as a way of knowing God's commands and word. In this sense it was a cognitive experience, designed to open up the world of revelation to contemporary Israel, a pattern evidenced among the various groups of Second Commonwealth times. Once sacrifice and the other Temple-centered rituals were no longer possible, study gradually became an act of worship. In tannaitic times, Rabbinic Judaism concentrated on its own students and teachers. In the amoraic period, however, when it became a mass movement seeking to gain the adherence of all Jews, it steadily popularized the idea that Torah study was an act of worship, ultimately making it central to the whole of Jewish life.

THE MYSTIC WAY

While most rabbis and their followers pursued a life of piety based on the practices surveyed in this chapter, some began, in the tannaitic period, to involve themselves in mystical speculation regarding creation and the divine chariot vision of Ezekiel (chaps. 1 and 10). These speculations are referred to explicitly in both tannaitic and amoraic texts. From other literary sources, it seems that the scope of this movement widened greatly in amoraic times.

Actually, the same speculations are in evidence, in formative stages, in the literature of the Second Temple period, including some of the apocrypha, pseudepigrapha, and Dead Sea Scrolls. It may even be that these traditions entered tannaitic Judaism via the various sectarian groups, since there is no evidence for them in Pharisaic circles before 70 C.E.

Sometime in the amoraic period and continuing into the early Middle Ages, these speculative approaches gave rise to an experiential, practical mysticism in which the aim of the adept was to experience visions of the divine throne (Merkavah, literally "chariot"). This mysticism was later enshrined in a variety of textual collections known as *Hekhalot* literature. These documents, at least as now known, stem from the early Middle Ages and are beyond the scope of this volume, but they indicate that such speculations and groups of adepts devoted to them existed already in amoraic times, most likely in circles connected with the rabbis but somewhat separate. Adherents of Merkavah mysticism were probably influenced as well by the interest in angelology, demonology, magic, apocalypticism, and mysticism among the Babylonian amoraim, who were echoing the society in which they lived, both Jewish and non-Jewish. The wealth of ancient Mesopotamian materials relating to these topics demonstrates that traditions of this kind had long been part of life in Babylonia, from earliest times up through the Middle Ages.

SUMMARY

The rabbis of the tannaitic and amoraic periods spelled out the way of life which they saw as emerging from their exegesis of the Torah, as enshrined in the written and oral laws. The system of laws they created sought to vest every aspect of life with sanctity. The rabbis succeeded in bringing their version of Judaism to the masses of Palestinian and Babylonian Jews and thus set the pattern for the Judaism of the Middle Ages and the modern period. Their laws and customs became the trademark of the Jews as they traveled and settled throughout the expanding world. It was this way of life that preserved the Jews, providing the basis for their collective identity and their survival as a people.

14
Epilogue: The Hegemony of the Babylonian Talmud

The history of Judaism has been studied here over a span of some one thousand years. Its development has been examined from the last years of the biblical period up through the close of the Talmuds and the onset of the Middle Ages. We have seen how competing ideologies sought to shape the manner in which the religion, culture, and civilization of biblical Israel would function in the new world of Greco-Roman Late Antiquity, and how Rabbinic Judaism emerged from this crucible as the heritage which would carry forward the future of the Jewish people. It remains for us to explain the primacy of the Babylonian Talmud in medieval and modern Judaism.

Central to the subsequent history of Judaism is the process by which the Babylonian Talmud attained hegemony and authority as the preponderant source of Jewish legal rulings and the main object of study for Jewish scholars. There were two aspects to this process, first, the displacement of biblical tradition as the central authority in Judaism, and second, the ascendancy of the Babylonian tradition over the Palestinian.

The displacement of the Bible was a process long in the making. Fear of such a development led the tannaim to practice a system of oral teaching designed to highlight the greater authority of the written word. The rabbis went so far as to prohibit the writing down of the oral law. Yet as the oral tradition became so extensive and complex, and as individuals began to keep private written texts, the distinction between oral and written materials no longer held. More important, the ever-expanding, developing nature of the oral law attracted the best minds, leaving the written Torah to serve as a subject of elementary instruction, midrashic exegesis, and technical grammatical study by a select few. By the amoraic period, the rabbis were openly asserting the superiority of the oral law, and so it was natural that the Mishnah became the central teaching to be studied. When the amoraic commentary in the form of the Talmuds became available, this material became the new scripture of Judaism, and the authority of the Bible was now defined in terms of how it was interpreted in the rabbinic tradition. Scripture had been displaced by Talmud.

The second process by which the Babylonian tradition attained ascendancy was somewhat more complicated. The Hellenistic Diaspora had also provided an approach to Judaism in competition with that of the tannaim, which was based in the Land of Israel, but Hellenistic Judaism had lacked the necessary vitality, and had failed to survive the rise of Christianity and the Christianization of the Greco-Roman world. Babylonian Talmudic Judaism attained this vitality precisely because it was so strongly linked to that of Palestine and almost identical with it. Most of the differences between the two concerned detailed halakhic rulings or certain ideas prominent in Babylonian society that entered the Jewish tradition there.

The primacy of the Land of Israel should have been expected to have guaranteed first place for its Talmud. However, two factors militated against this development: first, the nature of the Palestinian Talmud, and second, the political history of Jewry under the Islamic caliphate in the seventh and eighth centuries.

The deteriorating political situation in Byzantine Palestine, and the accompanying anti-Semitism, brought the amoraic development of the Palestinian Talmud to an early end. Not only were the amoraim unable to complete their work, but the Talmud of the Land of Israel had to be compiled in haste. The contribution of the anonymous scholars who wove together the traditions in the Babylonian Talmud had no parallel in Palestine, either because of the difficult historical conditions or because the final redactors defined their role in quite different terms. In any event, the lack of this final interweaving element makes the Palestinian Talmud a more difficult text than the Babylonian.

From the standpoint of later Jewish tradition, there was another factor that enabled the Babylonian Talmud to attain dominance. Medieval Jewry in general adhered to the rule that the law follows the most recent authority. Since the Babylonian Talmud was redacted after the Palestinian, many medieval Jews believed, incorrectly we think, that the redactors of the Babylonian Talmud had the work of the Palestinian amoraim at their disposal and consciously selected or rejected its views. Accordingly, they concluded that the Babylonian Talmud had greater authority than the Palestinian.

It may simply be, however, that this halakhic argument is a post facto way of explaining what the forces of history had brought about on their own, namely, the ascendancy of the rabbinical authorities of Babylonia. This development dated from the Arab conquest in 634 C.E. and the establishment of the caliphate of Baghdad, which initially ruled virtually the entire Islamic world, including most of world Jewry, and continued to hold considerable sway even after the territorial fragmentation of Islam. As residents of the heartland of a powerful empire, the Jews of Babylonia enjoyed a high degree of prestige, prosperity, and influence compared to their fellow Jews in other countries. As a result, the foremost Babylonian rabbis, known as geonim, "eminences," soon became the de facto chief rabbis of world Jewry, wielding the authority of the state to enforce rabbinic law and spread the Babylonian Talmud, an effort facilitated by their use of the Islamic postal system and administrative apparatus. Together with the factors we have already discussed, this development led to the hegemony of the Babylonian Talmud, which thereafter was the Talmud par excellence and the basis of all later development in talmudic law and thought.

The ascendancy of the Babylonian Talmud as the final source of authority marks the transition from the close of Late Antiquity to the onset of the Middle Ages. Postbiblical Judaism had finally reached a consensus, expressed in forms which would retain their vitality in the dark days to come. It is the development of this consensus which this book has chronicled.

We have traced the history of Judaism from Temple to house

of study and synagogue, from Torah to Talmud, from priest to rabbi, from text to tradition. We have seen unity emerge out of great diversity to create a Judaism which then, as now, united past, present and future into a continuous tradition.

Nevertheless, this unity tolerated within itself the debate and dialectic of talmudic literature. This openness to debate allowed for the development of an interpretation of Judaism for each new generation. The adaptation of talmudic law and thought to later circumstances was the genius of the rabbis who studied and taught the Torah of Israel. It was the rabbis of the Talmud who ensured that its message would continue to resonate among the Jewish people until the present day.

Glossary

AGGADAH. That portion of rabbinic literature and tradition which consists of stories about biblical or rabbinic figures, ethical teachings or interpretations of Scripture which teach the principles of Jewish thought and theology. The aggadah includes also the reasons for the commandments, but not the law (halakhah) itself.

AMIDAH. Hebrew for "the standing (prayer)," the Eighteen Benedictions which constituted the core of the rabbinic daily prayer service.

AMORAIM. The teachers of the Talmud or Gemara (ca. 200–500 C.E.) whose main activity was interpreting the Mishnah and tannaitic traditions.

APOCALYPTIC. Pertaining to a genre of literature which divulges otherworldly secrets about the nature of God and the heavens and the end of days. Also used to describe the immediate messianism which is often part of these texts.

APOCRYPHA. The books found in the Septuagint Bible but not in the canon of the Hebrew Bible. More loosely, this term can refer to pseudo-biblical books composed in the Second Temple period.

ARCHISYNAGOGOS. Greek for "head of the synagogue," referring to an official of the Jewish community organization in the Hellenistic world.

ARCHON. Greek for "chief," a title for a Hellenistic Jewish communal leader.

BARAITA, plural BARAITOT. A tannaitic tradition not included in the Mishnah.

BET DIN HA-GADOL. Hebrew for "The Great Court," the high court of seventy-one judges called the Sanhedrin in talmudic sources.

BOETHUSIANS. A sect of Jews closely linked to the Sadducees in their ideology and interpretation of Jewish law.

CALIPHATE. The central government of the Islamic world under the authority of the Caliph.

CANON. The corpus of Holy Scriptures.

271

CANONIZATION. The process by which the contents of the Holy Scriptures, and specifically each of the sections the Hebrew Bible, were closed and determined to be authoritative.

CHRONICLER The author of the biblical Book of Chronicles.

CLERUCHY. A military colony in which the soldiers were given land to farm which they settled permanently.

COELE-SYRIA. The region between the Lebanon and Anti-Lebanon mountains, known today as the Bekaa Valley. At times this term designated the entirety of Palestine and Phoenicia (present-day Lebanon).

COLOPHON. A notation at the end of a book indicating its author, time of composition, or other bibliographic details.

DIADOCHI. Greek for "successors," used to describe the generals who divided up Alexander the Great's empire after his death and established the smaller political units of the Hellenistic world.

DIASPORA. Greek for "dispersion," referring to the Jewish population outside of the Land of Israel.

EPHEBEION. A Hellenistic educational institution for young men.

ESCHATOLOGY. Doctrines concerning the end of days or messianic era.

ESSENES. A sect of Jews distinguished by its withdrawal from the mainstream of society, its piety, and its ascetic ideals. Many scholars identify this group with the sect of the Dead Sea Scrolls.

ETHNARCH. Greek for "ruler of the people," a title bestowed by the Romans on the Hasmonean high priests and Herod's son Archelaus.

EXEGESIS. Interpretation, as in the interpretation of the Bible in the Midrash or of the Mishnah in the Talmud (Gemara).

EXILARCH. The political head of the Babylonian Jewish community in the talmudic period. The authority of this official was recognized by the Sassanian Babylonian government.

FALASHAS. The black Jews of Ethiopia whose Judaism preserves traditions from Second Temple literature.

FIRST TEMPLE. The Jerusalem Temple erected by Solomon ca. 961 B.C.E. which was destroyed by the Babylonians in 586 B.C.E.

FISCUS JUDAICUS. The capitation tax Jews were required to pay the Roman government after their defeat by the Romans in the Great Revolt of 66–73 C.E.

GAONIC. Pertaining to the geonim, the leaders of the rabbinic academies of Babylonia after the Moslem conquest in 634 C.E.

GEMARA. The interpretation of the Mishnah by the amoraim, known also as Talmud although the latter term sometimes designates both the Mishnah and the Gemara together.

GENIZAH. A storeroom for old Hebrew books no longer used for holy purposes. The famous Cairo *genizah* yielded up a treasure of manu-scripts of Second Temple and rabbinic texts.

GEROUSIA. Greek for "council of elders," a body which advised the high priestly rulers in the Hasmonean period.

GEROUSIARCH. Greek for "a leader of the council of elders," a designation for Jewish communal leaders in the Hellenistic Diaspora.

GYMNASIUM. A Hellenistic educational and cultural institution in which youths received academic and athletic training.

HALAKHAH. A Hebrew designation for Jewish law.

HANUKKAH. Hebrew for "dedication," referring to the Jewish holiday celebrating the Maccabean victory over the Seleucids and the rededication of the Jerusalem Temple.

HASIDIM. Hebrew for "pious ones," a loose group of pietists known from the Maccabean period through mishnaic times.

HASMONEAN. Pertaining to the dynasty of Maccabean descendents and the period of their rule (152–63 B.C.E.).

HELLENISM. The amalgamation of the Greek and native Near Eastern cultures which swept over the entire Near East in the wake of Alexander the Great's conquest.

HISTORIOGRAPHY. The writing of history. This term often denotes the study of how historians often approach their work with preconceptions or ulterior motives which color the manner in which they understand and, hence, write about the past.

JUBILEE. The last year in a cycle of fifty. The jubilee is preceded by seven units of seven years, each culminating in a sabbatical year.

IDUMEA. In Second Temple times this name referred to the region south of Judea occupied by Idumeans (Edomites) who migrated from Transjordan under pressure from the growing Nabatean Arab population.

KASHRUT. The laws and regulations concerning ritually fit ("kosher") food.

KATOIKIA. Greek for a community of residents in a foreign city with corporate status. This term is used to describe Diaspora Jewish communities.

LATE ANTIQUITY. The period between the rise of Alexander the Great (ca. 330 B.C.E.) and the Moslem conquest (ca. 638 C.E.).

MACCABEES. The family of Judah the Maccabee. This term is often used imprecisely to designate later members of the Hasmonean dynasty as well.

MAHZOR. The special Jewish prayerbook for festivals. Usually this term designates the liturgy for the High Holidays, Rosh Ha-Shanah and Yom Kippur.

MASORETIC TEXT. The traditional, received Hebrew text of the Bible which has been considered authoritative by Jews from tannaitic times until the present.

MESSIANISM. The belief that a messiah will come to bring redemption to the world in the end of days.

MIDRASH. A Hebrew term for the method of biblical interpretation which was current in rabbinic times and earlier. This term can also designate a collection of such interpretations produced by the rabbis.

MINIM. Jews with incorrect beliefs, often a designation in tannaitic literature for Jewish Christians.

MISHNAH. The great collection of tannaitic law edited by Rabbi Judah the Prince, ca. 200 C.E. This term can also designate a particular paragraph of this code.

MONOLATRY. A religious system in which only one god is worshipped although the existence of other gods is acknowledged.

PALEOGRAPHY. The study of the shapes of letters and their history, usually to facilitate the dating of inscriptions and manuscripts.

PATRIARCH. The political and religious leader of Palestinian Jewry in the Roman and Byzantine periods. His office was termed the "patriarchate."

PENTATEUCH. The first five books of the Hebrew Bible, also known as the Five Books of Moses or the Torah.

PESHER, plural PESHARIM. Commentaries on Hebrew biblical books authored by the members of the Qumran sect. These commentaries understand the biblical prophecies as being fulfilled in the time of the sect.

PHARISEES. That group of Jews in Second Temple times which became the dominant sect. Many Pharisaic traditions were in large part continued by the tannaim.

PIYYUT. Jewish liturgical poetry composed in the rabbinic period and in the early Middle Ages.

POLITEUMA. A Greek designation for a Jewish community in the Hellenistic Diaspora.

PRAETOR. A Roman official, originally of the civil government, but later of the military.

PREFECT. A Roman government official in the imperial administration; in Judea, later termed "procurator."

PROCURATOR. A Roman government official who ruled over Judea.

PROEM. The introduction to a section of exegetical Midrash. The proem begins with a seemingly irrelevant quotation from the Prophets or Writings and then works its way back to the verse which it seeks to interpret.

PROSELYTE. A non-Jew who formally converts to Judaism.

PROSEUCHE. Greek for "prayer room," meaning synagogue.

PSEUDEPIGRAPHA. Literally, books written in the Hellenistic age in the name of an ancient biblical figure. More generally, the term is used to designate much of the religious literature of the various groups within Second Temple Judaism.

PTOLEMIES. The rulers of Egypt and its empire in the Hellenistic era. This dynasty took its name from Ptolemy, the general of Alexander the Great who retained control of Egypt after Alexander's death.

PURIM. The Jewish holiday celebrating the deliverance of the Jews of the Persian empire from an anti-Semitic plot designed to bring about their extermination.

QUMRAN. A site on the western shore of Dead Sea. The Dead Sea Scrolls were uncovered in nearby caves. Qumran itself preserves the ruins of a building complex which served as the headquarters of the sect in the Second Temple period.

RABBI. Hebrew for "my master, my teacher," referring to the teachers and judges of the Jews of Palestine in the Roman and Byzantine periods. This term became the designation for the Jewish clergy in the Middle Ages.

RAV. Hebrew for "master, teacher." Technically this term designates the rabbis of Babylonia who were called Rav, not Rabbi. In the Middle Ages this became the standard Hebrew word for a rabbi.

REDACT, REDACTION. This verb and noun refer to the act of collecting, selecting and editing traditions.

RESHUT. The official sanction given to a Babylonian rabbi allowing him to function as a judge in monetary and religious cases.

REVELATION. The process by which God is believed to have revealed His will to the people of Israel and the world.

SABBATICAL. The designation for every seventh year in which the Bible commands the remission of debts and prescribes leaving the land fallow.

SACRIFICE. The offering to God of the produce of the field or the animals of the flock for purposes of commemoration of sacred occasions, expiation of transgressions, or thanking God.

SADDUCEES. A sect of Second Temple period Jews, primarily connected with the priestly aristocracy, which accepted only the authority of teachings based strictly on the Bible and its interpretation.

SAMARITANS. A mixed people inhabiting certain parts of the Land of Israel, descended from the original Northern Israelites who were not exiled in 722 B.C.E. and the tribes introduced into the area by the Assyrians.

SANHEDRIN. The highest court or council of the Jews in the last years of the Second Temple.

SATRAP. The head of a province in the Persian Empire.

SAVORAIM. The scholars who put the finishing touches on the Babylonian Talmud, adding explanations and legal decisions to the text they received.

SECOND COMMONWEALTH. The political organization of the Jewish people in the Land of Israel from the return from exile in the sixth century B.C.E. until the final dismantling of the Herodian dynasty in the first century C.E.

SECOND TEMPLE. The Jerusalem Temple which was in use from 520 B.C.E. until its destruction by the Romans in 70 C.E. This term can also designate the period in which this Temple stood.

SECT, SECTARIAN. These terms designate the various groups of Jews and their particular approaches to Judaism in Second Temple times. This usage does not imply that any one of the groups is to be considered a mainstream.

SELEUCIDS. The dynasty which ruled Syria in Hellenistic times, tracing itself back to Seleucus, one of the generals of Alexander the Great.

SEMIKHAH. Rabbinic ordination. In the talmudic period this term was used exclusively to refer to the ordination of the Palestinian rabbis.

SEPTUAGINT. The Greek translation of the Bible produced in Egypt in the Hellenistic period.

SETAM. Hebrew for "anonymous," referring to those portions of the tannaitic and amoraic texts which are not attributed to any specific rabbi.

SHAVUOT. The Jewish holiday which in biblical times was connected with the offering of the first fruits of the wheat harvest. Later, Shavuot came to commemorate the giving of the Torah at Sinai as well.

SHEMA. The Jewish prayer recited morning and night proclaiming acceptance of God's kingdom and His commandments. It consists of Deut. 6:4–9, Deut. 11:13–22, and Num. 15:37–41.

SIDDUR. The Jewish prayerbook, from a Hebrew root meaning "to arrange in order," hence, "order of prayers."

STOIC. Pertaining to a school of Greek philosophy which taught that men should be free of passion and of emotions such as joy or grief and submit to unalterable destiny.

STRATEGOS. Greek for a general, or a high official with both military and civil authority.

SUGYAH, plural SUGYOT. A unit of talmudic discussion which investigates a particular issue or theme, and proceeds logically through a series of questions and answers until it reaches its conclusion.

SUKKOT. The Jewish holiday of Tabernacles which is connected with the fall harvest and which also commemorates the exodus from Egypt and God's protection of the people of Israel during the period of their wandering in the desert.

SYNAGOGUE. A Jewish house of worship. In Hellenistic usage, this term can also refer to a Jewish community.

SYNHEDROI. Local district councils set up by the Romans after their conquest of Judea in 63 B.C.E.

SYNCRETISM. The grafting of diverse religious traditions onto one another. This process was manifested in the amalgamation of Judaism with the religion of the Canaanites and, later, with that of the Greco-Roman pagans.

ṬALLIT.. The prayer shawl worn by Jewish men in accord with Num. 15:37–41.

TALMUD. Technically, the Gemara, the amoraic discussions of the Mishnah. This term is sometimes used to refer to both Mishnah and Gemara together.

TANNAIM. The teachers of the Mishnah, Tosefta and halakhic Midrashim who flourished ca. 50 B.C.E.–200 C.E.

TEFILLIN. The phylacteries, black boxes with scriptural portions inside, which Jewish men are required by talmudic law to affix on their arms and heads during morning prayer.

TETRARCH. Originally, the ruler of a fourth of a larger area. This term later served as a Roman administrative title for a local ruler below a king or an ethnarch.

TOPARCHIES. A Greek term referring to geographically defined administrative districts which were subsections of the province in the Hellenistic and Roman administrative systems.

TORAH. The Five Books of Moses, the Pentateuch. Literally, the Hebrew word Torah means "instruction, teaching."

TOSEFTA. A collection of tannaitic traditions which were not included in the Mishnah. The Tosefta is the earliest commentary to the Mishnah and is organized in approximately the same manner.

TRADENT. A rabbi who passes on a tradition to others, often his students of the next generation.

TSITSIT. The ritual fringes attached to the Ṭallit to remind the wearer of the commandments of God.

WISDOM LITERATURE. A genre of literature known throughout the ancient Near East. It preaches common sense wisdom and values designed to result in a happier and more just life.

Bibliography for Further Reading

This is a selection of works in English which provide further information on many of the topics dealt with in this volume. They reflect a diversity of opinions on the issues raised here and represent only a small part of the material which served as the basis for this book. Translations of primary sources are not included in this bibliography. Full bibliographic details are given only for the first citation of a work. Collected studies are cited only under the name of the editor. For general reference, readers should consult the *Encyclopaedia Judaica*, 16 vols. (Jerusalem: Keter, 1971–72).

Chapter 1: Introduction

Cohen, S. J. D., *From the Maccabees to the Mishnah* (Philadelphia: Westminster, 1987), pp. 13–26.

Hachlili, R., *Ancient Jewish Art and Archaeology* (Leiden: E. J. Brill, 1988).

Kraft, R. A., and G. W. E. Nickelsburg, *Early Judaism and Its Interpreters* (Atlanta: Scholars Press, 1986).

Meyers, E. M., and J. F. Strange, *Archaeology, the Rabbis and Early Christianity* (London: SCM Press, 1981), pp. 19–30.

Neusner, J., *The Academic Study of Judaism* (Chico, Calif.: Scholars Press, 1982).

Safrai, S., and M. Stern, with D. Flusser and C. van Unnik, *The Jewish People in the First Century*. Compendium Rerum Iudaicarum ad Novum Testamentum I, vol. 1 (Philadelphia: Fortress, 1974), pp. 1–77.

Schürer, E., *A History of the Jewish People in the Age of Jesus*, ed. G. Vermes, F. Millar, with P. Vermes, M. Black, vol. 1 (Edinburgh: T. & T. Clark, 1973), pp. 17–122.

Smith, M., "Palestinian Judaism in the First Century," in *Israel: Its*

Role in Civilization, ed. M. Davis (New York: Harper, 1956), pp. 67–81.

Chapter 2: The Biblical Heritage

Bright, J., *A History of Israel* (London: SCM Press, 1972), pp. 47–339.

Crenshaw, J. L., ed., *Studies in Ancient Israelite Wisdom* (New York: Ktav, 1976).

Fishbane, M., *Biblical Interpretation in Ancient Israel* (Oxford: Clarendon Press, 1985).

Hayes, J. H. and J. M. Miller, eds., *Israelite and Judaean History* (London: SCM Press, 1977), pp. 70–476.

Heschel, A. J., *The Prophets* (Philadelphia: Jewish Publication Society, 1962).

Kaufmann, Y., *The Religion of Israel* (Chicago: University of Chicago Press, 1960).

Levine, B. A., *In the Presence of the Lord* (Leiden: E. J. Brill, 1974).

Lindblom, J., *Prophecy in Ancient Israel* (Oxford: Basil Blackwell, 1962), pp. 47–403.

Rad, G. von, *Wisdom in Israel* (London: SCM Press, 1972).

Shanks, H., ed., *Ancient Israel* (Englewood Cliffs, N.J.: Prentice-Hall and Biblical Archaeology Society, 1988), pp. 1–149.

Smith, M., *Palestinian Parties and Politics That Shaped the Old Testament* (New York: Columbia University Press, 1971).

Weinfeld, M., *Deuteronomy and the Deuteronomic School* (Oxford: Oxford University Press, 1972).

Chapter 3: Judaism in the Persian Period

Baron, S. W., *A Social and Religious History of the Jews*, vol. 1 (New York: Columbia University Press, 1952), pp. 102–64.

Bright, *A History of Israel*, pp. 341–403.

Coggins, R. J., *Samaritans and Jews: The Origins of Samaritanism Reconsidered* (Atlanta: John Knox, 1975).

Davies, W. D., and L. Finkelstein, eds., *The Cambridge History of Judaism*, vol. 1, *Introduction: The Persian Period* (Cambridge: Cambridge University Press), pp. 70–114, 130–278, 326–400.

Hayes and Miller, *Israelite and Judaean History*, pp. 489–538.

Kaufmann, Y., *A History of the Religion of Israel* (New York: Ktav, 1977).

Schürer, E., *A History of the Jewish People in the Age of Jesus*, ed. G. Vermes, F. Millar, and M. Black, with P. Vermes, vol. 2 (Edinburgh: T. & T. Clark, 1979), pp. 314–21.

Shanks, *Ancient Israel*, pp. 151–75.

Chapter 4: The Hellenistic Age

Bickerman, E. J., *The God of the Maccabees: Studies on the Meaning and the Origin of the Maccabean Revolt* (Leiden: E. J. Brill, 1979).

Cohen, *From the Maccabees to the Mishnah*, pp. 25–59, 174–213.

Hayes and Miller, *Israelite and Judaean History*, pp. 539–96.

Hengel, M., *Judaism and Hellenism*, 2 vols. (London: SCM Press, 1974).

Safrai, S., and M. Stern, with D. Flusser and W. C. van Unnik, *The Jewish People in the First Century*, Compendium Rerum Iudaicarum ad Novum Testamentum II, vol. 2 (Philadelphia: Fortress, 1976), pp. 561–630, 865–907.

Schürer, *A History of the Jewish People in the Age of Jesus*, vol. 1, pp. 137–73; vol. 2, pp. 237–313.

Shanks, *Ancient Israel*, pp. 177–94.

Tcherikover, V., *Hellenistic Civilization and the Jews*, trans. S. Applebaum (Philadelphia: Jewish Publication Society, 1959), pp. 1–234.

Chapter 5: Judaism in the Hellenistic Diaspora

Baron, *A Social and Religious History of the Jews*, vol. 1, pp. 165–212.

Collins, J. J., *Between Athens and Jerusalem: Jewish Identity in the Hellenistic Diaspora* (New York: Crossroad, 1983).

Gager, J., *Origins of Anti-Semitism: Attitudes Toward Judaism in Pagan and Christian Antiquity* (New York: Oxford University Press, 1983).

Neusner, J., *A History of the Jews in Babylonia*, vol. 1 (Leiden: E. J. Brill), 1965, pp. 1–67.

Safrai and Stern, *The Jewish People in the First Century*, vol. 1, pp. 117–215, 420–503; vol. 2, pp. 701–727.

Schürer, E., *A History of the Jewish People in the Age of Jesus*, ed. G. Vermes, F. Millar, and M. Goodman, with P. Vermes and M. Black, vol. 3, pts. 1–2 (Edinburgh: T. & T. Clark, 1986), pt. 1, pp. 1–176, 470–704, pt. 2, pp. 809–889.

Smallwood, E. M., *The Jews under Roman Rule* (Leiden: E. J. Brill, 1981), pp. 120–43, 201–225.

Stone, M. E., ed., *Jewish Writings of the Second Temple Period*, Compenium Rerum Iudaicarum ad Novum Testamentum II, vol. 2 (Fortress: Philadelphia, 1984), pp. 233–82.

Tcherikover, *Hellenistic Civilization and the Jews*, pp. 269–377.

Wolfson, H. A., *Philo*. 2 vols. (Cambridge: Harvard University Press, 1947).

Chapter 6: Sectarianism in the Second Commonwealth

Cohen, *From the Maccabees to the Mishnah*, pp. 60–173.

Finkelstein, L., *The Pharisees*, 2 vols. (Philadelphia: Jewish Publication Society, 1962).

Neusner, J., *From Politics to Piety: The Emergence of Pharisaic Judaism* (Englewood Cliffs: Prentice-Hall, 1973).

————, *The Rabbinic Traditions about the Pharisees before 70*, 3 vols. (Leiden: E. J. Brill, 1971).

Rabin, C., *Qumran Studies* (Oxford: Clarendon Press, 1957).

Schiffman, L. H., "Jewish Sectarianism in Second Temple Times," in *Great Schisms in Jewish History*, ed. R. Jospe and S. Wagner (New York: Center for Judaic Studies and Ktav, 1981), pp. 1–46.

Schürer, *A History of the Jewish People in the Age of Jesus*, vol. 1, pp. 174–242; vol. 2, pp. 381–414, 355–97.

Shanks, *Ancient Israel*, pp. 194–204.

Smallwood, *The Jews under Roman Rule*, pp. 21–43.

Stone, M. E., *Scriptures, Sects and Visions* (Philadelphia: Fortress, 1980).

Vaux, R. de, *Archaeology and the Dead Sea Scrolls* (Oxford: Oxford University Press, 1973).

Vermes, G., with P. Vermes, *Qumran in Perspective* (London: Collins, 1977).

Yadin, Y., *The Message of the Scrolls* (New York: Simon & Schuster, 1957).

Chapter 7: Apocrypha, Pseudepigrapha, and the Dead Sea Scrolls

Baumgarten, J. M., *Studies in Qumran Law* (Leiden: E. J. Brill, 1977).

Cross, F. M., *The Ancient Library of Qumran and Modern Biblical Studies* (Garden City, N.Y.: Doubleday, 1964).

Nickelsburg, G. W. E., *Jewish Literature between the Bible and the Mishnah* (Philadelphia: Fortress, 1981).

Schiffman, L. H., *The Eschatological Community of the Dead Sea Scrolls* (Atlanta: Society of Biblical Literature, 1989).

————, *Halakhah at Qumran* (Leiden: E. J. Brill, 1975).

————, *Sectarian Law in the Dead Sea Scrolls: Courts, Testimony and the Penal Code* (Chico, Calif.: Scholars Press, 1983).

Schürer, *A History of the Jews in the Age of Jesus*, vol. 3, pt. 1, pp. 177–469; pt. 2, pp. 705–808.

Stone, *Jewish Writings of the Second Temple Period*, pp. 33–156, 283–577.

Yadin, Y., *The Temple Scroll: The Hidden Law of the Dead Sea Sect* (London: Weidenfeld & Nicholson, 1985).

Chapter 8: The Jewish-Christian Schism

Avi-Yonah, M., and Z. Baras, eds. *The Herodian Period*, World History of the Jewish People, vol. 7 (Jerusalem: Massada, 1975), pp. 26–178.

Meyers and Strange, *Archaeology, the Rabbis and Early Christianity*, pp. 31–61, 125–39.

Parkes, J., *The Conflict of the Church and the Synagogue* (London: Soncino, 1934).

Safrai and Stern, *The Jewish People in the First Century*, vol. 1, pp. 216–376.

Sanders, E. P., *Paul and Palestinian Judaism* (Philadelphia: Fortress, 1977).

Schiffman, L. H., *Who Was a Jew? Rabbinic Perspectives on the Jewish Christian Schism* (Hoboken, N.J.: Ktav, 1985).

Schürer, *A History of the Jews in the Age of Jesus*, vol. 1, pp. 267–484.

Smallwood, *The Jews under Roman Rule*, pp. 44–119, 144–200, 256–92.

Chapter 9: Revolt and Restoration

Alon, G., *The Jews in Their Land*, trans. G. Levi, 2 vols. (Jerusalem: Magnes, 1980, 1984).

Avi-Yonah, M., *The Jews under Roman and Byzantine Rule* (Jerusalem: Magnes, 1984), pp. 15–88.

Avi-Yonah, M., and Z. Baras, *Society and Religion in the Second Temple Period*, World History of the Jewish People, vol. 8 (Jerusalem: Massada, 1977), pp. 263–94.

Baron, S., *A Social and Religious History of the Jews*, vol. 2 (New York: Columbia University Press, 1952), 89–214.

Cohen, S. J. D., *Josephus in Galilee and Rome: His Vita and Development as a Historian* (Leiden: E. J. Brill, 1979).

———. *From the Maccabees to the Mishnah*, pp. 214–31.

Neusner, J., *First Century Judaism in Crisis: Yohanan ben Zakkai and the Renaissance of Torah* (New York: Ktav, 1982).

Rhoads, D. M., *Israel in Revolution 6–74 C.E.* (Philadelphia: Fortress, 1976).

Schürer, *A History of the Jewish People in the Age of Jesus*, vol. 1, pp. 485–557.

Shanks, *Ancient Israel*, pp. 205–35.

Smallwood, *The Jews under Roman Rule*, pp. 293–506.

Stone, *Jewish Writings of the Second Temple*, pp. 185–232.

Yadin, Y., *Bar Kokhba: The Rediscovery of the Legendary Hero of the Last Jewish Revolt against Imperial Rome* (London: Weidenfeld & Nicholson, 1971).

———, *Masada: The Zealots' Last Stand* (London: Weidenfeld & Nicholson, 1968).

Chapter 10: Mishnah: The New Scripture

Neusner, J., *Ancient Israel After Catastrophe: The Religious World View of the Mishnah* (Charlottesville: University of Virginia Press, 1983).

———, *Judaism: The Evidence of the Mishnah* (Chicago: University of Chicago Press).

———, ed., *The Modern Study of the Mishnah* (Leiden: E. J. Brill, 1973).

Safrai, S., ed., *The Literature of the Sages*, Compendium Rerum Iudaicarum and Novum Testamentum II, vol. 3, first part (Philadelphia: Fortress, 1987), pp. 35–251, 283–302.

Schürer, *A History of the Jewish People in the Age of Jesus*, vol. 2, pp. 322–80.

Chapter 11: Formative Judaism Comes of Age

Avi-Yonah, *The Jews under Roman and Byzantine Rule*, pp. 89–278.

Neusner, J., *A History of the Jews in Babylonia*, 5 vols. (Leiden: E. J. Brill, 1965–70).

———, *There We Sat Down: Talmudic Judaism in the Making* (Nashville: Abingdon, 1972).

Smallwood, *The Jews under Roman Rule*, pp. 507–45.

Chapter 12: The Sea of the Talmud

Bokser, B. M., *Post-Mishnaic Judaism in Transition: Samuel on Berakhot and the Beginnings of Gemara* (Chico, Calif.: Scholars Press, 1980).

———, *Samuel's Commentary on the Mishnah: Its Nature, Forms and Content* (Leiden: E. J. Brill, 1975).

Ginzberg, L., "An Introduction to the Palestinian Talmud," in *On Jewish Law and Lore* (Philadelphia: Jewish Publication Society, 1955), pp. 3–57.

Halivni, D. W., *Midrash, Mishnah and Gemara* (Cambridge: Harvard University Press, 1986).

Mielziner, M., *Introduction to the Talmud* (New York: Bloch, 1968).

Neusner, J., *The Bavli and Its Sources: The Question of Tradition in Regard to Tractate Sukkah* (Atlanta: Scholars Press, 1987).

———, *Judaism and Scripture: The Evidence of Leviticus Rabbah* (Chicago: University of Chicago Press, 1986).

———, *Judaism in Society: The Evidence of the Yerushalmi* (Chicago: University of Chicago Press, 1983).

———, *Midrash in Context: Exegesis in Formative Judaism* (Philadelphia: Fortress, 1983).

———, ed., *The Formation of the Babylonian Talmud* (Leiden: E. J. Brill, 1970).

Safrai, *Literature of the Sages*, pp. 303–45.

Strack, H. L., *Introduction to the Talmud and Midrash* (Philadelphia: Jewish Publication Society, 1931).

Chapter 13: The Life of Torah

Baron, *A Social and Religious History of the Jews*, vol. 2, pp. 215–321.

Bokser, B. M., *The Origins of the Seder: The Passover Rite and Early Rabbinic Judaism* (Berkeley: University of California Press, 1984).

Heinemann, J., *Prayer in the Talmud: Forms and Patterns*, trans. R. Sarason (New York: Walter de Gruyter, 1977).

Levine, L., *Ancient Synagogues Revealed* (Jerusalem: Israel Exploration Society, 1981).

Meyers and Strange, *Archaeology, the Rabbis and Early Christianity*, pp. 92–124, 140–54.

Neusner, J., *The Way of Torah: An Introduction to Judaism* (Belmont, Calif.: Wadsworth, 1972).

Scholem, G., *Jewish Gnosticism, Merkavah Mysticism and Talmudic Tradition* (New York: Jewish Theological Seminary, 1965).

Schürer, *A History of the Jews in the Age of Jesus*, vol. 2, pp. 415–87.

Shanks, H., *Judaism in Stone: The Archaeology of Ancient Synagogues* (New York: Harper & Row, 1979).

Steinsalz, A., *The Essential Talmud*, trans. C. Galai (New York: Basic Books, 1976).

Urbach, E. E., *The Halakhah: Its Sources and Development* (Israel: Massada, 1986).

———, *The Sages: Their Concepts and Beliefs*, 2 vols. (Jerusalem: Magnes Press, 1965).

Chapter 14: Epilogue: The Hegemony of the Babylonian Talmud

Baron, S., *A Social and Religious History of the Jews*, vol. 3 (New York: Columbia University Press, 1957), pp. 75–119.

Goldin, J., "The Period of the Talmud (135 B.C.E.–1035 C.E.)," in *The Jews: Their History*, ed. L. Finkelstein (New York: Schocken, 1970), pp. 189–209.

Index

Aaron, 28, 67
Aaronide priests, 28, 54
Abaye, 234
Abbahu, 230
Abraham, 243
Abraham, Isaac, Jacob (the Patriarchs), 17–18, 23, 28, 95, 128, 258
Academies, 214, 224, 225, 234, 239; Talmudic, 225; tannaitic, 11, 171, 178, 179, 182–184, 186, 199
Actium, 144
Acts of the Apostles, 152
Adam, 51
Adiabene, 82, 216
Adultery, 194, 259
Aegeans, 34, 60
Aelia Capitolina, 172
Age of majority, 262, 263
Aggadah, 187, 188, 197, 199, 200, 217, 224, 226, 232, 236, 237, 241, 242, 250, 259, 262
Agriculture, 88, 114, 161, 206, 253, 254; laws of, 229, 230, 234, 241
Agrippa I, 148
Agrippa II, 158
Akiva, Rabbi, 183, 191; school of, 198, 199
Akkadian language, 187
Akko. *See* Ptolemais
Akra, 76, 77, 100
Alcimus, 78, 84, 168
Alexander (son of Herod), 146
Alexander Balas, 79
Alexander Janneus, 84, 100, 102, 106, 111
Alexander the Great, 34, 53, 57, 60, 62, 81, 216
Alexandria, 84, 91, 94, 95, 120, 126, 129; Jewish community, 122, 130
Alfasi, Isaac, 233
Allegory, 90, 96, 115
Altar, 29, 243
'Am ha-' areṣ, 104, 105, 145, 168, 181

Amemar, 234
Ammi bar Nathan, 230
Amoraic period, 11, 181, 188, 195–197, 199, 202, 204–220, 224, 225, 228, 236–238, 245, 248, 251, 254, 257, 259, 260, 262–265, 268
Amoraim, 10, 13, 177, 178, 187, 192, 195, 196, 200, 201, 205, 220–227, 230, 232, 234, 235, 238, 240, 241, 242, 248, 250, 252, 255, 258, 259, 262, 265, 268; Babylonian, 220, 232
Amos, 31
Ampitheaters, 144, 151
Amulet, 25
Anahita, cult of, 219
Angels, 18, 105, 110, 114, 117, 121, 126, 127, 128, 135, 265
Anonymous material, 227, 232, 235, 268; rulings, 192
Antigonus (brother of Aristobulus I), 100
Antigonus, 216
Antigonus II (Mattathias), the Hasmonean, 142
Antioch (name for Jerusalem), 73
Antioch (Syria), 72, 85
Antiochus III the Great, 65, 66, 70, 72, 73, 75–77, 85
Antiochus IV Epiphanes, 66, 70, 72–74, 76, 78, 103, 123, 173
Antiochus V Eupator, 78
Antiochus VII Sidetes, 75, 100
Antipas, 146
Antipater, son of Herod, 146
Antipater the Idumaean, 140
Anti-Semitism, 82, 87, 90, 91, 155, 170, 211, 213, 228, 254, 263, 268; legislation, 155, 156, 209, 211–214, 219, 227. *See also* Synagogues, legislation against; New Testament, anti-Semitism
Antonia Fortress. *See* Fortresses
Antoninus Pius, 175, 205